THE LIFE AND TIMES OF AN ECCENTRIC YORKSHIREMAN

AN AUTOBIOGRAPHY BY

JOHN A LEAVER

2QT Limited (Publishing)

First Edition Published 2013
2QT Limited (Publishing)
Burton In Kendal
Cumbria LA6 1NJ
www.2qt.co.uk

Cover Design by John A Leaver

Illustrations by Doug Lawrence

Printed in Great Britain

A CIP catalogue record for this book is available
from the British Library
ISBN 978-1-908098-92-4

ACKNOWLEDGEMENTS

Janice Ward for her support and for putting up with my obsession of writing this book for the past five years, and sadly other obsessions for quite a lot longer.

John Trenouth for a lot of the stories in this book as a fellow, dare I say eccentric, and for help in funding this publication by pointing out a few interesting skips.

Doug Lawrence who has illustrated quite a few of my little escapades over the years and some of which appear in this book.

Geraldine Keenan from 2QT Publishing for proof reading this book and making it readable

Thank you all.

INTRODUCTION

Well, you are about to delve into my life. The good, the bad, the adventurous, the eccentric, the spontaneous, the crazy and sensi... Yes, well I was about to say sensible but perhaps that needs another book that will disclose more of my sensitive, caring, artistic, and spiritual side of my life. But for now you will have to settle for the present book with the most appropriate advice I can put to it.

'PLEASE DON'T TRY MOST OF THIS AT HOME'

Having said that, as I look back over my life there are very few things I would actually change even if I could, and I have only mild reservations writing about certain of them.

My life, I feel, has been character building in an eccentric kind of way, and perhaps the younger generation could do with a shot of that. So my message to all those who sit in front of their computers, slouch in front of their TVs, text garbage to all and sundry, or constantly bombard their lugholes with Rap, it is to put your mobile phones away, get off your backsides and get a life.

Read on and I hope you enjoy.

CONTENTS

— 1 —

I WAS BORN AT A VERY EARLY AGE

YOU MUST ALL excuse me for the title of this first chapter. It was always in my mind to write an autobiography, even as a child, (perhaps a little premature) and I would consistently remind myself that that was how I was going to start when I heard a comedian say this on stage. But by now I'm afraid it's a rather poor play on words.

However it does bring me to the point of my early traits and failings. I'm rather stubborn! Although, I prefer the word tenacious. I think most people who have known me through my life would describe me as stubborn to a fault, and it is a Taurus trait which I appear to have fully embraced. Of course Taureans have other more positive traits like, kind, caring, reliable, unhurried, dependable. Of course I have all of these traits as well - in abundance!

The stubbornness even started in the womb as I refused to be born and my poor mother had to have a caesarean section to launch me into the world. At this point I cannot help quoting Macbeth, it's my Thespian side, 'Man not born of woman.' But on the up side I was born lucky, starting with being one of the first free babies born in the newly created NHS. It was at the beginning of May 1948, two months before the official birth of the NHS on the fifth of July, but I managed to be a freebie which was very fortunate as my parents weren't all that well off. A bit of a mystery that, as I have recently been told that even up to a few days before the official start date for the NHS women were still being charged for giving birth in hospital. But my mother was always adamant I was a freebie. Another bit of luck as far as I was concerned was that I was born an only one. 'They threw the mould away after me' as they say, probably something due to the caesarean operation my mum endured. This meant I didn't have to share my parents with a brother or sister. Some may say that was a disadvantage as it makes a child selfish, but not knowing any different, I was quite happy with the arrangement.

At the time of my birth at that particular hospital it appeared that circumcision was carried out as routine on newborn babies. My mother strongly objected to the practice as she thought it a barbaric and cruel thing to do and managed to stop them before they whisked me away and snipped me. Years later at school it was a game to go round asking your mates if they were Roundheads or Cavaliers. Not having had the cut I was proud to be a Cavalier.

Funnily enough I've developed into an anti-royalist mainly due to the antics of our Prince Charles, but I'm still a Cavalier way down. It reminds me of a joke I heard a while back which was, why can't Jews be Morris Dancers? Because you have to be a complete prick to be a Morris Dancer! (Only a joke, to all my friends who are Flag Crackers)

I definitely lean to the Buddhist theory that we are reincarnated time and time again until we experience certain lessons about life. For according to Buddhism we stand up in heaven and decide before we are born exactly what this life's lesson will be.

The main topic of discussion on that celestial cloud must have been on my continual stubbornness during previous lives, and how to modify the worst manifestations of this trait in the next. I can only believe this was conceived to be achieved by giving me a larger proportion of it than the lives before, and seeing how I cope with it. For instance I was born a Yorkshireman. That's about as stubborn as you can get. Then if that wasn't enough, I was born in May under the sign of Taurus, one of whose main traits, as I stated before, is being on the stubborn side. Then to cap it all I was born to parents, Estella and Lawrence, who passed on a fair truckload of genetic stubbornness. So all in all, it was the kill-or-cure tactics on that celestial plain which could be working here, although

I'm not sure it has yet, so it could well be back to that heavenly cloud for further reappraisal of my stubbornness, eventually.

My mother and dad met during the war in the Land Army. My father was almost a Geordie as he was born in small village called Eldon, just along from the town of Bishop Auckland, which has the notoriety of having Stan Laurel of Laurel and Hardy fame attend the local Grammar school there. Good grounding for his future as they are all a bit of a comic up there. Eldon was not exactly in Geordie land but near enough for dad to have a bit of a sing-song accent, which he mostly lost when he moved down to Yorkshire. As much as my dad adapted well to a more civilised accent, he still kept a few colloquialisms which I eventually adopted and would get some quizzical looks from my Yorkshire school friends.

Bishop Auckland and the surrounding villages were all involved in mining and almost everyone worked down the mine or was connected in its service industry. When my father left school he was taken down the mine with a view to becoming a miner. He wasn't a wimp but the dire working conditions and the claustrophobic environment did not appeal at all, as my dad was definitely the outdoors type and after just one day he immediately got a job on a local farm, and worked outdoors for the rest of his life. The little terraced house where my dad lived was overshadowed by a monstrous black slag heap, with two of the houses at the end of the row being demolished as they were slowly subsiding into a mine shaft below, so he would be constantly reminded how lucky he was to be a farmer and not a miner.

Having visited the street were he lived recently, I was amazed to see all the houses were still lived in with the dominating slag heap being partially removed, landscaped and grassed over.

One of the stories he told was that when he was a lad on the farm, one of his jobs was transporting hay with a horse and cart from field to barn. One day the farm-workers who were loading his cart thought they would overload his cart for a laugh. The horse was struggling and my dad was going really carefully so as not to lose his load of hay in the road. He was nearly home when he had to negotiate under a rather low railway bridge. Half way through, sure enough the cart became wedged on the roof of the bridge. It wasn't a busy road but there was soon a traffic jam and a local bobby arrived and was harassing my dad to shift his cart. Realising that inevitably the horse, cart and hay weren't going anywhere my father cut the ropes holding the load and dumped the lot in the middle of the tunnel. He then unharnessed the horse from the cart, mounted it, and rode off to the farm to round up the jokers who had overloaded the cart to go and get them to clear up the tunnel. Needless to say they suddenly lost their sense of humour.

The cart horses my dad was responsible for were huge but quite gentle, except for one who had a real mean streak. Its party trick was to grab unsuspecting carters, or, for that matter, anyone it took a dislike to who came close. It would grab them by the scruff of the neck with its teeth, lift them clean off their feet and then hurl them away. The horse wasn't too fussy either about distinguishing between clothes and flesh and could leave a very nasty wound.

I've recently found out that my dad's four brothers and family had a bit of a reputation for being local rogues. Nothing serious you understand, just a little entrepreneurial, on the edge of legality. As far as I know my father's only brush with the law concerned him and his brother. They both had identical motorbikes, even down to the registration plates, as a tax dodge. This was a constant vexation to the local bobby who knew what was going on but could never catch them together.

The whole family was, shall I say, a little eccentric. Not that there's anything wrong with eccentric, I'm personally called it regularly and treat it as a compliment.

My dad's mother had a monkey called Mona for a pet. Not one of your little, cuddly, cute ones. This beast was more akin to a large baboon. God knows where it came from but my granny was the only one who could handle it. She used to tie it up outside their little terraced house. It would sit on the outhouse roof and pinch people's hats as they walked past, and if they weren't wearing a hat, a hand full of hair would suffice.

What came as more of a shock was a revelation about my cousin, who I always thought of as my aunty as she was very 'auntish', if you know what I mean! Very nice and respectable, married, genteel, quiet, kind, and ladylike. The revelation came as we were looking through an old photo album. There appeared to be two sets of wedding pictures, with different grooms. Confronted subtly about this she confessed to being married before, a marriage that only lasted five weeks when she threw him out. She even pushed him over a wall when he started to pester her, broke his arm and received a criminal record for assault!

The revelations continued when she confessed to being a barmaid in a club. One night a couple of drunken sailors causing trouble tried to come in to the club as it was closing. My aunty ... no sorry cousin, told her boyfriend to keep out of the way and then proceeded to give them a good hiding, bundling them down the stairs and then threw them from the club. I was really impressed. It got even better when I asked where she developed her fighting skills. She proudly explained that when she was a young teenager there was a running bare-knuckle fight competition down her street, proper Queensbury rules and all. The reigning champion had his name painted on the wall of an outhouse at the bottom of the street and it was there that the boxing match took place on some waste ground. Not only was my cousin the only girl on the list of competitors she was at the top, as the champion! Going by the name of Basher Forbes. My cousin was always very high in my estimation but with these revelations she definitely went up at least another ten points.

My dad's sister, my real aunty, was also a little, dare I say, eccentric. When he moved down to Yorkshire he lodged with her, as she had a large house and she took in lodgers. One day he came home from work and asked the rest of the lodgers where his sister was. He got a very strange look and was informed that his sister was at the registry office getting married. 'Didn't you know?' She never did explain her reason for the secrecy. 'Ah thas nowt as queer as folks.'

My father's working on the land was what they called a protected occupation during the war and could not be conscripted and was even prevented from joining up. Although as he was given the job of a land army foreman in charge of a large portion of the Yorkshire Dales dealing with cantankerous, set-in-their-ways, Yorkshire Dales farmers and also had the job of managing quite a number of inexperienced land army girls, I think at times he wished he could join up.

My mother was one of his girls and my father was impressed by her capability to drive tractors, handle agricultural machinery, and work without supervision. In fact my father was so impressed he married her - well, that and love of course! My mother could even start the big, old tractors with the starting handle which some of the men could not achieve. It was not that she was muscular, it was all in the technique. The first thing you were taught when gripping the starting handle was to keep your thumb and fingers on the same side of the handle, this was essential for if and when the tractor backfired, as it was liable to do, your thumb would be painfully aligned with your arm but facing backward. If the backfire was particularly violent, it could, if you were unprepared, throw your hand into your face, usually breaking your nose. This actually happened to my mother while she was working for my father. Luckily he had his motorbike handy and run her to a hospital about twenty miles away. She riding on the pillion seat with a badly broken nose, clinging grimly on to my dad with one hand and a hanky pressed to her nose with the other.

My mother came from a little village called Oxenhope, where, after the war, they got married and ran a little general store. As far as I can make out they eloped to Gretna Green to marry, not because of her family objecting, it was just a romantic thing to do. My mother's family were mill owners until my mother's grandfather was disinherited because of his womanising, gambling, and drinking. In retrospect it might well have ruined my life being born into money! Although I would have liked to have had the opportunity to try it out.

My mother and father were very caring and free from many prejudices that were rife at the time and would help any one, regardless of their circumstances and consequently had a great number of friends. I gained a deeper respect for them from learning of one incident which happened before I was born.

My father was working in a field next door to a large prisoner of war camp at Skipton. As he was driving up and down in his tractor there was a German POW standing at the high fence watching him. Eventually my father stopped the tractor next to the fence, dismounted and went over to him and said hello! They exchanged names as the German prisoner could speak a little English. Next day my father went to the camp to see the army captain in charge. This was 1943 and the war was still in full swing, but the Skipton camp was for prisoners that didn't pose any threat or would not particularly want to escape. When my father had explained to the captain in charge of the camp that he was looking for someone to work on a farm and he had spoken to a prisoner named Josef, who was duly summonsed and stood before my father and the captain. Josef was very worried that he had broken some rule for speaking to my father through the fence, but he was soon reassured, and jumped at the chance to work outside the camp on a farm my father had chosen for him. I must explain that Josef was a very special case, as my father found out later. He was a German pilot with a conscience. As much as he was a patriotic German he hated the Nazis and was appalled at the atrocities that were being perpetrated in his own country and occupied lands.

As the war progressed he became even more disillusioned but because he was a superb pilot and loved flying, he was moved from reconnaissance which he could live with, to bombing missions. That was too much for Josef and he decided, with the rest of his crew, to get out. He was reputed to have dropped his bombs on his first bombing mission on the SS canteen. Talk about burning your bridges! He then flew his plane to Belgium where, despite surrendering, was treated very badly by the Belgians. But was rescued by a British officer and sent to England. He says he was kept at a camp near London and was spoken to by the one and only Winston Churchill who, when he heard his story, had him sent up to Yorkshire to an open camp. He obviously had no desire to return to Germany, till hopefully the war ended with the Nazis defeated.

When the captain at the camp told Josef he would have to return to the camp every night my father said it would be impossible for him to get from the camp to the farm he had chosen for him every morning to milk the cows at six am. He would be responsible for Josef while he stayed at the farm

So it was settled. Josef was installed at this farm in Cowling. My father had chosen well for they treated him as part of the family and he lived and worked there for a number of years. In fact the story goes that a neighbour of the farmer was invited for lunch but refused to sit at the same table as a 'bloody Gerry'. The neighbour was given the option in no uncertain terms by the farmer, 'Either tha sits down wi us all at table or tha eats artside on tha owen.'

Josef even spent a Christmas with my parents at the flat above the shop but went back to Germany before I was born. He would have loved to stay in England and would have been given citizenship but he was worried about his family back in Germany. We have kept in touch over the years and his family still visit from Germany and we have been over there to visit in Cologne many times.

One of my first memories must have been when I was taken on holiday as a baby. I was being put to bed in a makeshift cot, improvised from a pulled-out drawer, as my usual cot would not fit in our little car. The smell of mahogany, mothballs, and a hint of lavender always brings the memory back to me. They say that smell is the strongest nostalgia provoker there is, and it's certainly true for me. I also have a photographic memory triggered by the smell of wet vintage cars and hot oil. This was ingrained in me as a very small baby, when my parents drove down to

Dover from Yorkshire for holidays, in a rather dilapidated Austin Seven with a soft top that leaked like the proverbial sieve, and a top speed of thirty-five mile per hour down hill with a prevailing wind. I can't say for sure whether it was my first trip, although it must have been as I was only a few months old.

There were many trips down to the little town of Deal to stay with my father's brother who lived and worked there by the seaside. These were horrendous journeys undertaken in the late forties long before Motorways and even before the great A1 stretched unimpeded from London to Scotch Corner and beyond. They had huge bottlenecks like Doncaster, Grantham Peterborough, Stevenage and of course London to confront and this was long before the Blackwall Tunnel. There were still a few horse-drawn vehicles about to make my dad feel at home, but London was in particular a bit of a nightmare for a Yorkshire farmer. Undaunted he would drive our little Austin Seven with my mother cradling me in her arms, it could take as long as twelve to fourteen hours, assuming no breakdowns!

It was the time of saluting AA and RAC men on motorbikes and sidecar combinations. Not that they would have been any use with our frequent breakdowns as my parents could not afford the annual fee, and anyway my father was very resourceful and a bit of a mechanic. But they did salute, which amused my dad greatly as he was not a member but had come across two appropriate badges and bolted them on the front bumper for show.

CHAPTER ONE

It was much later when I could appreciate my father's driving skills both for cars and tractors, and of course my mother was also good as she was taught to drive as a land army girl. She never took a test as a licence was issued automatically if you drove in the land army, and in fact she was given a HGV licence of which she was very proud. Albeit, her driving was a little fast for my father's taste and he kept on threatening to put half a house brick under the accelerator pedal to slow her down when she took the wheel. At sixty-five my mother sent off for her driving licence to be renewed, and when it came back to her disgust DVLA had removed her HGV designation. She was so incensed she rang them up and had a long argument about her need to keep her ability to drive heavy good vehicles. But I'm afraid she lost that argument as she had some difficulty justifying driving wagons at sixty-five.

My father was quite a sedate driver but did have a thing about cyclists and people with caravans of whom he was rather derogatory, as he called them 'road lice' and 'weekend gypsies' respectively, or you could say disrespectfully. His only traffic fine in his entire life was one for dangerous driving which did have mitigating circumstances. It was for demolishing a railway crossing barrier which came down on top of the wagon he was driving at the time, but that is another story.

I have been told that I was quite a good baby for I didn't cry much, took food without throwing up, gurgled appropriately when tickled by friends and relatives, and was late to walk giving some respite for my parents from 'being into everything,' as my mother used to say. All this angelic behaviour of sleeping, gurgling, and taking to the breast then bottle without problems won my mother admiration from friends and relatives. Eventually I could even drink from a straw at the tender age of about two, which skill my mother was quick to display at any opportunity. The first time I entertained a collection of aunts, uncles, and cousins, with my straw sucking ability was in a roadside café on a day out to the seaside. I was presented with a large milk shake with two straws. After performing my demonstration of straw drinking for a while I decided to vary my act a little by blowing down the straws instead of the now boring sucking. The effect was spectacular, far surpassing the usual 'oohs' and 'ahhs' I usually received, although my mother did not seem all that pleased as she used napkins to mop up the colourful splatters of strawberry milk shake from the table and relatives. This was only to lull my parents into a feeling of false security for the real dramas to follow.

Anxiety was to stalk their later years of parenthood. Take the time at the tender age of two my mother placed me in my cot upstairs for my afternoon nap. The cot was under the window with the window open because it was a sunny, warm day. Going down stairs she then sat with a cup of tea in the back yard, where she could hear me if I cried. Picture my mother's horror ten minutes later to look up to a noise and see me perched on the window sill waving and cooing down at Mummy below. Big decision time, does she run up stairs and drag me back through the window hoping in the meantime I hadn't taken up flying lessons. Or hover under the window in the hope of catching me when and if I fell? Quite a dilemma that one. Probably luckily she chose the former because I remember being rather roughly dragged back through the window by my nappy, and crushed to my mother's ample bosoms, and smothered in kisses while being told off about the dangers of heights, which was rather lost on a two-year-old!

Another dilemma I put my mother through (although there were definitely others before and since that I never even realised) was at the age of seven when trying to carve my name in a piece of old lino. I was trying to imitate the older boys at school who were doing lino cut printing where you cut artistic chunks out of thick lino with a special tool, spread ink on it and make prints from it on paper or cloth. Not having the desired implement I ingeniously used an L shaped potato peeling knife which slipped and instead of finishing my artistic carvings, it became embedded into my right eye. After the initial shock of not feeling much pain and having my vision impaired by the handle of the knife I asked my mother who was baking in the kitchen next to where I was standing, 'Shall I pull it out, or leave it in?' I can still picture (albeit with one eye) the look of panic suddenly galvanising her face as she glanced over to me. I thought my question was very reasonable. If I pull it out I could imagine my eye shrivelling up as all the liquid squirted out or, even a worse scenario, would be that my eye would pop out impaled on the knife. Anyway, by this time it was beginning to sting a bit so I pulled the knife out anyway. Luckily neither scenario came to fruition although it felt marginally more comfortable, and now the decision of whether to leave it in was replaced by the simple act of bundling me into the car and rushing me off to the local Accident and Emergency.

After some months of walking around like Long John Silver, with a green eye patch (they did not have any black ones which was a little disappointing), and pulling my ankle up to my behind, and shouting, ‘Aha, Jim lad’, my eyesight did miraculously recover. Although to see reasonably well I need to wear glasses with a bottlebottom lens for the right eye.

I do get some amusement from the incident and the consequent inconvenience of glasses, by the fact that every time a new optician looks at the back of my eye with his little scope, the usual comment mumbled under his breath is ‘What the hell is that?’ as he spots the L-shaped scar on my retina. I tell them it is just my initial. That must make me pretty unique to have your initial tattooed on your retina, don't you think?

To add a bit of a mysterious twist to that story, recently I had a look at my medical records (a fascinating two inch thick bundle of notes) and close to the front was the episode documented by the doctor at the A&E. To my surprise my age was stated as three years old. What the hell was I doing making lino cuts at three? Where did I get the idea from? A TV didn't enter our house till the Coronation, (not as in street!) so I can't blame Blue Peter even if it was running then. I was at least another two to three years off school as I thought that was where I got the idea from.

My books were all about faeries and Janet and John so that wasn't the source. Weird or what?

Another medical anomaly is that I appear to have been born with some kind of heart defect, something to do with one of the valves. This produces a funny gurgle at the end of a beat. It doesn't seem to cause me any problems, but I find it quite amusing to watch a doctor who hasn't checked my heartbeat with his stethoscope before, frown as he hears the irregular beat, then look at me and frown a bit more, moving his stethoscope. Funny as it is now, it wasn't so funny the first time, because the way he looked I doubted I would reach my teens. Anyway at sixty-odd all seems to be well in the ticker department. (Famous last words, see Medical Matters Chapter 24)

I seem to be a bit of a medical anomaly all round as most medication I take seems to have side effects - from flu jabs giving me full blown flu to the so-called wonder drug statins which reduce your cholesterol. That one nearly killed me and took me over two years to get over the severe side effects they can have.

I was one of these strange children who called my mother and dad by their first names, just like the yellow cartoon character Bart Simpson who calls his father Homer. It seemed only natural to me as that's what my mother and dad called each other.

My parents would not have corrected me, just for convention sake even though they may have had funny looks from their friends. They were quite unconventional in their own way.

'Ah nostalgia isn't what it used to be!' Looking back it's as if I'm watching it happen to someone else,, and to this day I'm approached by people who say, 'Ah tha must be Larry and Stella's lad.'. They were known as Larry and Stella by all of their friends.

— 2—

MOVING DOWN TO THE FARM

AFTER THE WAR my parents ran a general store in a little village next to Haworth of Bronte fame called Oxenhope. My memories are rich in the colours and smell of the shop, its wall-to-wall, and ceiling-to-floor clutter of every conceivable household requisite stacked on shelves or hanging from the ceiling. It was all there, and the smell! Soap, paint, candles, wood, all intermingled to give a rich colourful aroma that you just don't get now in a modern supermarket, probably due to the advent of cellophane which prevents the smell permeating other products. Generations now will miss out on the emotive smells of a general store. Even the brown paper bags which the shopkeeper used to pack your purchases in had a smell and sound all their own for that matter.

Playing in the small living-room at the back of the store I had a little blackboard and easel with a box of chalks. These were very fragile for a small child and when they broke in half I discarded them to pick a new one. I could not quite get the idea that each half of the chalk would still work. I was soon put to right on the subject after three trips to the shelves for new boxes of chalk.

Just around the corner from the store was my grandfather's blacksmith's forge where he and my uncle worked repairing and making farm machinery and household implements and, of course, shoeing horses. Regular shoeing of working horses was the main activity as they were still a common sight on the roads and in the fields. Picture the scene for a small child peering into the large doors of the smithy; the smell of hot iron and steam, with an enormous cart horse standing in the middle of the floor on three legs with the fourth held on my grandfather's knee; the acrid stench of burning hoof as my grandfather fitted the red hot shoe to the raised foot of this giant gentle creature; the sudden hiss of steam as the shoe was quenched. Peering through the smoke and steam there would be the bright glow of the forge. The whitewashed, sooty, cobwebbed walls hung with blacksmith's tools resembling a medieval torture chamber, or a sorcerer's cave. That must have been a big influence on a small child, the sort of experience that used to inspire children to want to be engine-drivers on seeing their first steam train. Not that I became a blacksmith. That was a dying profession when I came of working age, but I have a definite passion for mechanical gadgets and a cluttered workshop.

Over the years as I go back to visit the village, the change is striking. The smithy was changed to a garage, then a house made into flats, and our old shop and house is now a bank.

One day when I was only about four years old, I was standing watching a similar scene, although this time my grandfather and uncle were working on what I can only imagine from later experience was a large agricultural machine. My attention was focused on a slowly cooling piece of iron bar on the floor in front of me. The bar was turning from bright yellow then orange to dull red through to black. I was fascinated. Looking up I saw my grandfather watching me gazing at the cooling metal. Looking down again I bent and reached out for the bar, there was a sizzling noise, pain, then I drooped the bar. The next thing I knew I was being dragged into the depths of the smithy. I was bent over and my hand was thrust into a tub of murky cold water. It was held there till the pain of the burn was replaced with the numbing cold of the water. Still in shock after I was placed on my feet, my grandfather bent down and examined my now blistered palm with his rough calloused hands, looked me in the eye, and said in his gruff but kind voice, 'Tha warnt be pocking up hot metal, ony moor will tha?' (translated to, 'you will not be picking up hot metal any more, will you?') And with those few words of advice he gently picked me up in his arms and carried me next door to my mother in the store. Passing me over he explained to my mother in his eloquent economical manner that, 'Young' uns been having a lesson in smithing.' Nothing more was said as my mother comforted me in her arms while rubbing butter on my burnt hand. But looking back I suspect my mother had a few choice words later with my granddad for she guessed that I had been *allowed* to pick up the hot metal as a 'lesson in smithing.'

I hold no animosity towards my grandfather although I know without a doubt he could have intervened to stop me picking up the hot iron. But I look on it as a lesson well learned, as thanks to my grandfather's 'lesson in smithing' I mostly remember not to use my bare hands when working with all the pieces of metal I've heated up over the years since for various reasons. ''

Soon after that event my parents bought a farm as my father yearned to get back to the land so we moved away to the farm about five miles across the valley. My final memory of leaving was of a little girl in a white flowered dress crying as she waved goodbye, as we drove away for the last time. She had decided that we were an item, for we often made mud pies together in the street out of horse droppings. Sad to say I cannot remember her name and have never seen her since.

The farm was an amazing place for a child, although a little primitive. There was no running water, just cold water from a well in the yard supplied from a spring. No electricity just heaps of wax, where the candles had burnt out.

The farm was in a general state of disrepair through a lack of money. As hill farming was a poor living and still remains so to this day, it took a few years before all the modern amenities were installed.

Unfortunately the inside loo was one of the last improvements. The toilet was situated outside in a small outhouse shared by a calf pen, for rearing newborn calves. The winters were worse, trekking through snowdrifts across the yard to the loo at night in the dark is no joke especially for a small child. The shed was quite warm however as the calves gave off a lot of heat, albeit a little humid.

The toilet was a large bucket (affectionately known as a bucket and chuck it) with a rather splintery wood seat, that had to be emptied when full, on a patch of ground at the back of the house that grew luxurious nettles, which was fortuitous as this prevented me as an inquisitive child exploring that particular patch. The smell of the bucket/toilet was somewhat modified by the calves, for their dung in my opinion is not offensive, cows being herbivores eating sweet grass and hay. It’s the meat eaters of this world that have stinky, pungent, waste products. However the calves didn't appear to complain about the smell of sharing their toilet with a carnivore and would reach over their pen to give you an affectionate lick as you sat on the throne.

The previous owner of the farm was reputed to have kept a pigeon in the house to keep the cobwebs down as it flew about the rooms. There was no mention whether he cleaned up the pigeon pooh on a regular basis.

The farm was called White Field which I think sounded poetic and rather romantic. We assumed that the name was given it because of the milkmaids, and cotton grass that grew profuse in the meadows. Sadly buttercups now abound, the only survivors of modern farming. Yellow Field Farm just doesn't have the same ring about it. Mind you it still sounds better than Nut Head Farm down the road. I must assume it had a different meaning two hundred years ago when the farms were built on this hillside.

When electricity was eventually installed it seemed like a miracle. It transformed the house from a dark scary cave into a proper home, and all the ghosts seemed to be exorcised. I have never felt frightened at all in the house, living there to the present day. One incident much later as a teenager did make me wonder if it was just a lack of imagination on my part or perhaps I was insensitive to any ghostly vibes. Some friends and I were experimenting with a Weegee (Ouija) Board at the house as they were all the rage in the sixties. For anyone that is unaware of the concept, it’s a circle of cards of the letters of the alphabet on a table with an upturned glass in the centre. Participants sit around placing a finger on the base of the glass and take turns to ask any spirits present questions. The questions are then answered by the movement of the glass spelling out the words by moving to the cards in turn.

It's rather spooky when the glass starts to move even though you get the nagging feeling that it's one of the sceptical participants having a laugh, and that the glass has a lot of assistance in certain directions. Anyway after some questions with gobbledegook answers it was my turn. I asked the classic question 'Is anyone there?' To everyone's surprise the glass moved forcefully and spelt out 'YES'. A little spooked but undeterred I pressed on with 'Who are you?' The quick and positive response was 'JOSEPH PECKOVER I LIVE HERE.' There was something about the response that stopped the game, it was the sudden personalising of the presence or 'the chill that pervaded the air' (just thought I would throw that in for effect, although we all did feel a little chilly and uncomfortable). Later research revealed no former owner dead or alive by the name of Joseph Peckover. So there you go, no such thing as ghosts, at least not on the farm.

The installation of electricity to the farm was rather spectacular, well at least to a small child. We had our own electricity poles marching across the fields to our farm. The final one, just yards from the buildings, had a large green box at the top which was called a transformer and it had twenty thousand volts going through it. The engineer told me I must not climb up and touch it, and I never have, for those words reminded me of my experience and lesson from my grandfather about hot metal, luckily!

My father did test the power of twenty thousand volt though albeit by accident. He was ploughing a field which the poles ran through; when for the fourth time that morning a piece of buried rusting fencing wire got caught up in the plough blades. After a lot of sweat, swearing and sore fingers he managed to free the length of barbed wire and in a fit of pique he hurled it into the air. Unfortunately that particular tangle occurred directly under the overhead wires. He later described a spectacular flash as the fence wire vaporised in a shower of hot metal and sparks that rained down on my terrified father as he ran for cover. The overhead wires were severed, cutting off electricity to our house, but thankfully not to half of Keighley. I distinctly remember my father returning home to my mother standing on the doorstep telling my dad that 'the electricity had gone off, Larry,' with my father looking rather pale and sheepish saying he knew. 'Ay it wer me', he confessed. After my father had described what had happened, my mother decided that an indignant phone call to the electricity board was necessary, undertaken by herself. She could be quite forceful and as attack is the best form of defence she said that our electricity had inexplicably gone off and it was desperately needed to milk the cows that evening and what were they going to do about it! My mother, as they say, took no prisoners and power was soon restored in time for milking but we did get some enquiring looks from the engineers who came out to repair the damaged overhead cables, as a large section had just disappeared.

My father's description of the fireworks display from the vaporised wire sounded rather good, and I decided to try it for myself sometime. I never did may I add, but much later I did set fire to the electric pole next to the house, but that's a confession for later.

CHAPTER TWO

At the time the electricity was brought to the farm house we could not afford the cost of the installation with the poles and transformer so my parents came to an agreement with the electricity board whereby we paid for it over five years with rather a strange clause that payments were part of a standing electricity charge to the farm. No matter how much electricity we used or didn't use the repayments remained the same. That meant for the first five years our house was lit up like Blackpool Illuminations. I think we got our money's worth, although, after the five years and the first proper bill, a sudden 'lights out' economy drive was launched by my parents, reminiscent of the wartime cry of the air raid wardens, 'Put that light out!'

Although the house wiring at the farm was done by a proper electrician it was a little suspect as I vividly remember as a child sitting in the bath and reaching for the soap. As the back of my hand touched the wall I received a bit of what I now realise was an electric shock albeit a surprisingly mild one considering I was sitting in the cast iron bath half full of water, I complained to my mother that 'the wall bit me.' My mother told me not to be silly walls don't bite and touched the wall for herself, screamed, and dragged me from the bath. It turned out that the whole house was live and there was a distinct lack of an earth. This was so serious it had to be rectified by the electricity board, delaying my next bath night by a fortnight. I think that early close call with electricity sealed my long association and fascination with all things electrical, especially the more spectacular high voltage kind. Again another story!

In the living room cum kitchen we had an open fire, in which we burnt anything from coal to logs and coke, which is processed coal that the gas board had taken the gas out of but still burns well and is cheaper than coal. When I was deemed old enough to handle ladles of red hot lead my father brought out a box of moulds for making things out of lead. As a lad he used to make his own lead soldiers. There were also moulds for making toy aeroplanes and farm animals and all sorts of things; some were difficult to work out what they were until you actually cast them and it became obvious. At nine I was deemed mature enough for my dad to show me how to first take small chunks of lead piping that we found around the farm, melt it down on the open fire (lead has a relative low melting point) and pour it into the moulds. Easy peasy, no problem, well not many anyway. One problem was to get the best results the moulds had to be hot which necessitated them being balanced on the edge of the fire, then lifted off onto the hearth and then the two halves of the mould held tightly together while the hot lead was poured in. Now as much as the moulds were already hot, they became a lot hotter after the molten lead was poured in. There were screws sticking out from the back of the mould that my father had fixed bits of wood to but these had rotted off. But I found that bobbins from my mother's sewing box were ideal, and I only had to unwind a couple as there were already some almost-empty ones at the bottom. My dad was very impressed with my ingenuity with the bobbins but my mother was a bit annoyed about the balls of cotton in her sewing basket. It was a bit tricky to pour the liquid, hot lead at the same time as holding the two halves of the mould together but was achieved with only a few accidents. The little accidents luckily never involved flesh but my mother's hearth rug suffered a few burnt patches from hot moulten lead splashes. I did see a TV programme once where this guy poured moulten lead over his hands without any harmful effects, a bit like these Indian Fakirs who walk on hot coals. Didn't fancy either myself.

The soldiers were a great success and I even sold some to my mates at school. So all the lead was soon depleted and I moved onto less dangerous hobbies like gunpowder and rockets as you will read in a further chapter.

My mother and father were always trying to modernise the farm both inside and out, my mother inside and my father out, with help and suggestion from each other.

One modernisation was a telephone, which took a little negotiation with the then GPO because the farm was a little off the beaten track. The only way they would agree to install the poles to carry the wires to our farm was only if we shared a party line with the next farm. It worked by our phone having a button to cut out the other farm's phone when we needed to make a call, and our neighbours having the same button on their phone when they needed to make a call. This was OK in those days as a phone call a week was an event. Until they installed a gadget years later, we had to take it in turns with the neighbours to make calls. After that there was no problem until, that is, forty odd years later when

I needed broadband for my computer and the gadget was still installed. It took innumerable phone calls to the provider to get it sorted.

Although a little isolated it was what I consider the perfect place to grow up, and in retrospect a grand place to live for the rest of my life.

— 3 —

LIFE ON THE FARM

AS THE YEARS went by the farm grew, new outbuildings went up and land was improved with ploughing and fertiliser, but it was always an uphill struggle. Both my mother and father had to go out to work to supplement income from the farm. My mother worked for some years in the weaving shed at the woollen mill down the road, where the noise was so great from the looms she learnt to lip read so she could chat with her friends on other looms. I think this caused her to be deaf in later life (not the lip reading, the noise) as the TV was always at maximum volume. The upside was that the lip reading came in handy.

My father would do work on other farms. This would mean double the work as our farm was never neglected. In the early sixties my mum and dad were offered a job of delivering milk for a farmer in Riddlesden, an area of Keighley, and, money being a bit short, they took it on. It involved getting up early, milking their own cows, then collecting the milk from another farm in crates of bottles and delivering it to houses in Riddlesden. A milkman's job is quite hard but my mother and father were quite fit and coped well even taking into account the milk round is on a steep bank, with virtually every house having a long steep driveway and steps to make Whitby's one hundred and ninety nine look like a walk in the park. After delivering sixty gallons of milk, (that's four hundred and eighty pints) they came home and had a nap, although not for long as there was always work to do on the farm.

It was very hard working the farm and having a milk round as well but the extra money was very useful and the farm went through a programme of new building, and more livestock. This continued for some years and my parents made friends with their milk round customers and were well liked. Then came a big shock. The farmer was having financial problems and decided to take over the milk round himself to save money. My parents were given a month's notice and were devastated and angry for they had built up the round and made it very profitable. During the following days my parents told their customers what had happened and a lot told them that they would change their supplier. This gave them an idea. We had the milk from our own cows, all we needed to do was bottle it. It was an amazing feat but by the time the month was up they had installed a small second-hand bottling plant which supplied all the customers who had stayed faithful to my parents. They walked away with half the round and overnight more than doubled the price they were being paid for their milk from the Milk Marketing Board. Within a few months, they had their name on the bottles and had a viable business.

It was really hard work doing the and running the farm, as not only had it to be delivered, it had to be bottled, and it became my job to get up early, bottle milk before going to school, and bottle some more after school in the evening. I was also coerced into helping to deliver the bottles to the customers' doorsteps at weekends and holidays from school. My recollections of the milk round was every house having incredibly long paths, and steps, mostly uphill, carrying the full bottles up, with a lighter load back down with the empties. It always seemed to be winter in my memory as I always remember having cold feet and hands, even though I must have helped in summer as well. It's tough being a farmer's lad!

Even with the extra money coming in from the milk round we were still quite poor but there was always good food on the table and plenty of it, and a warm house. There always seemed to be big pans steaming on the cooker and the mouth-watering smell of baking. Apart from cooking and the milk round my mother helped on the farm. She could drive a tractor better than most men, learnt from her land army days. I can picture her now in a flowery summer dress driving the tractor with a trailer full of hay.

During the war as a land army foreman my dad's job was to go around all the farms in the area finding out what they needed doing to increase their crops or how to plant new ones needed for the war effort to feed everyone on our little besieged island. He would assign land girls with the appropriate machines to do the job. He also had the dubious notoriety of ploughing up the lovely common in Harrogate, known as the Stray, for extra crops. Soon after the war it was restored back to grass as it had little impact on the war effort, it being unsuitable for crops.

Well after the war when the land army was dispersed my father bought some of the machinery that was being disposed of and that set us up when we bought the farm. We were one of the first to have a tractor on this hill side. It's strange now to think there were still mostly horses working the fields in my lifetime. All the farms around us had stables and tack rooms full of harnesses for the big working Shire horses, which were slowly replaced by tractors and heavy machinery.

One of our much later tractor purchases was a mega machine called a Field Marshall. It was painted green with red wheels and trims. To me as a child it seemed like a gigantic steam engine you see at steam rallies. It was actually diesel with one massive cylinder the size of a dinner plate, my dad taking it to bits one time to repair it as I looked on fascinated. It had a massive starting handle sticking out the front, which was virtually a two man job to turn. The alternative to the handle start was a hole in the side of the engine with a screw cap which you unscrewed and inserted a blank twelve bore cartridge. When you screwed the cap back on there was a button in the middle which you hit hard with anything to hand, like a spanner. That fired the cartridge and amazingly turned over the engine and started the tractor. This fascinated me but annoyed my father as the cartridges were quite expensive. Consequently another nail in its coffin and what led to it finally being sold was the fact that if you drove it for more than half an hour or so you came home with black freckles, I Imagine a bit like the Black Death! This majestic tractor had this annoying problem of kicking out specks of oily soot from the exhaust pipe which stuck out the top of the engine, in true tractor fashion, right in front of the driver. Despite my father dismantling the engine twice he could not cure it. And it became such a problem it had to go. I did suggest he wore a mask like Batman whose comic, I used to read at the time, but all to no avail. I was very sorry to see it go as it was an impressive beast. We replaced it with a relatively boring grey Ferguson.

One of our early tractors ran on a concoction called T.V.O. which was short for tractor vaporising oil. It was used during the war as a method of saving fuel as it used low grade petroleum like paraffin that ran agricultural vehicles. High grade petrol was saved for our aeroplanes. The T.V.O was so low grade that you couldn't start a tractor on it when the engine was cold, as it was not volatile enough. You had to start it on proper petrol first to warm up it up, then there was a little two way tap under the duel tank to switch it over to T.V.O. If you were a little impatient and switched it over before the engine had warmed up properly it would stall, and the carburettor had to be flushed out, which was in my father's own words 'a bloody faff', one of the few times I ever heard my dad swear.

I was eventually installed at the local primary school, a large hall surrounded by four class-rooms and a staff room, which pupils were not allowed to enter under pain of death. Even to knock on the door for a legitimate reason heralded a scary scowl when answered by a teacher with a cup of tea in her hand. The cloakrooms were dark and always seemed to smell of wet coats, carbolic soap and disinfectant. They had huge pot sinks at one end where we had to wash our hands, three to a sink before meal times, water fights were inevitable.

Getting to school was a real pain as it was about two miles away with no buses. So apart from an occasional lift from either my mother or dad in our battered old Ford van, it was a long walk for a five year old, and never seemed to get shorter for the rest of my school life.

The farm was at the top of a very steep hill. Going down in the morning wasn't that bad but I hated the long climb back up in the evening, especially in bad weather, with snow a foot deep and no chance of getting the car down to pick me up and get back up the hill. Thankfully in really bad weather my mother would come to pick me up from school with the tractor. With the big tyres and tread it had no problem with deep snow, and it certainly impressed my classmates and probably some of the teachers too.

Even our tractor was ineffective in the year of nineteen sixty three, when the road into Keighley was blocked by massive snow drifts for over six weeks and only then cleared with a JCB digging out the snow to make a narrow passage. Luckily the road into the village was opened after a week or so, and for that time we had to pour milk away down the drain as the Milk Marketing wagon, who we sold it to at the time, could not get to the farm.

Farmers are notorious predictors of weather as a lot of work on the farm was dependent on predicting adverse weather. There's the classic 'red sky at night, shepherd's delight, red sky in the morning, shepherd's warning.' The one my dad was always quoting was, 'If there's snow still under the walls, there'll be more to fotch it.'

In good weather our old Ford van used to plod up the hill. It had no fixed back seats, just an old car seat from a different car thrown in the back for me to sit on. I remember one day my father changed gear into first going up the really steepest part of the hill and let the clutch out a bit sudden. My seat shot to the back of the van, as it was not fastened down, being only a temporary fixture because the van was mainly used for ferrying farm products. The back doors flew open and I shot out. Left deposited in the middle of the road, still sat on the chair, I don't know who was more shocked, my mother, father or me. It was a good job that the road was a little-used single track country lane, and no-one was following close behind. Although tarmaced it had tufts of grass growing up the middle, it was so little used.

Over the years it has now grown to a fully tarred two way busy road, the deep ditches either side filled in, which is a bit of a shame. It was a constant form of amusement as cars would often slide into those ditches when passing another car and we earned a substantial form of income pulling cars and wagons out with our tractor when they ended up in the stranded in the ditch.

Looking back over the last fifty years or so makes me realise just how much has changed. Not just the big obvious things like television, computers, cars and aeroplanes. Most were all about when I was a child, just a little cruder and less of them, but how our lifestyle and work has changed.

Take farming, you would think it has changed little over the years, but I was recently talking to a youngish farmer about 'How it was in my day.' He thought I was telling him something out of a Victorian novel, or a Constable painting. He could not believe that as a child I milked cows by hand, turned whole fields of hay with just a crude wooden rake, forked loose hay, not bales, onto a cart to bring it into the barn or made haystacks next to the farmhouse, when there wasn't room in the barn. As I've said before, our farm was quite advanced having a rusty and knackered old tractor, but there were still working cart horses on farms about us. Within their financial limits my parents tried to keep up with farming technology.

The war in a way helped modernise farming. During the war the land army was created, and modern machinery was funded by the government and used on farms for the first time. Even the farmers entrenched in the old ways could eventually see the advantages of tractors over horses.

Then soon after the war-industries which were geared to weapons of war were switched to other products, as in 'swords to ploughshares' so it was tanks to tractors and farming slowly moved out of the dark ages.

A lot of the farms round about kept bulls to service their dairy herd so that they produced calves for the market, to swell the herd and replace old cows whose milk yield had dropped. Also cows have to give birth every two years or so to keep producing milk. We on the other hand used the AI, short for artificial insemination. This was a governmental organisation that kept a herd of prize bulls of different breeds which would produce calves for beef or dairy. For a reasonable fee they would come and fertilize your cows with long glass tubes of frozen bull's sperm. This produced the very best calves. Preferring the AI we didn't keep a bull, my father said they were too dangerous. Bulls are immensely strong with a mean streak especially if separated from their harem of cows. I've seen a bull hook one of its horns under a heavy Land Rover in a field and lift it nearly on to its side. The only thing that prevented it being turned over completely was our dog being sent into the field to chase it away, by swinging on its tail by its teeth until it was called back.

When we first started to build up our dairy herd all the cows had horns. Never mind bulls, a cow with horns can be quite dangerous. A cow doesn't have to be malicious to do you damage or another cow for that matter, just a sudden turn of the horned head when you are working in close contact like milking and feeding. My mate Mick tells how, when he worked on a farm as a young lad, he lost his two front teeth to a cow that spiked him in the face as he was putting a bucket of feed down in front of it.

As we slowly increased our herd with calves we de-horned them with a gadget we borrowed from the farm next door. It was an electric iron with a dimple on the end that became red hot, the method was to hold the calf down and press the hot dimple over the horn bud. This burnt off the horn before it could grow and cauterised the wound at the same time. This sounds pretty horrendous but after the initial shock, it shook its head and would be OK. They did try various chemicals to burn the horn away but they were so toxic if another calf licked the poison or it dropped into its feed it was fatal. You could eventually get an anaesthetising injection and most farmers use it nowadays. Even more horrendous was when the horn was removed from mature cows. The cow would be restrained in what was called a crush that held the beast immobile during the procedure. The horn was then sawed off, but this must have been very painful for the cow for the horn not only contained blood vessels which bled profusely, nerves were also present. We did have one cow de-horned in this way, but it was so horrendous that my dad never had another done and put up with the danger until all his herd was replaced with our own de-horned calves. They did try to breed hornless cows but it was unsuccessful and they do have a nontoxic chemical nowadays that removes the horn bud on new born calves but most farms still use the hot iron method, with the addition of anaesthetic I'm glad to say.

You will have to travel up to the highlands of Scotland to see a cow with horns nowadays and then they will be on big shaggy Highland cattle where they let them have horns for show.

Sheep have tails but are docked as lambs. This is done as they tend to become a bit shitty at the back end which attracts flies, can get maggots and become infected, so it's in the sheep's own interest to lose its tail. This used to be done with a quick cut with an axe on a block of wood, but we were a little more sophisticated than that as we used little elastic bands that were pushed onto the young lambs tail that cut off the blood supply and after a week or so it would just drop off with little discomfort to the lamb. It always amused me to find a lamb's tail in the field with a little red elastic band on the severed end.

Our dog had a bit of a reputation for its fearless attack on wayward bulls. She was a black and white farm-dog whose name was Meg in the best Yorkshire tradition, of course.

We also had a dog called Bess. She was a slimmer version of Meg but just as fearless. Unfortunately, neither Meg nor Bess were there to come to the rescue one early spring morning. Before it was fully light, my father opened the milking shed door for the herd of cows waiting to be milked. He was standing just in the door greeting his herd one by one when the third one happened to be an enormous bull squeezing its muscular bulk through the door. Now bulls don't normally back up, but this one did. With a lot of swearing and a constant bludgeoning with the muck shovel from my dad, it beat a reluctant retreat.

What had happened was that the bull from next door seeing our tempting, unprotected herd had decided to add them to his harem. This was achieved by just virtually walking through a stone wall. I personally have seen a large bull walk into a gate and carry it forward with the uprooted stone posts till the gate was trampled under foot the bull not breaking step. I have also witnessed a bull jumping a metal five-bar gate, not quite making it and landing astride the gate and crushing it.

Bulls now have been bred for their placid nature and are mere shadows of their aggressive ancestors. The ones you see being led around show grounds with a rope are not the same beasts from my youth at all, but I would still give them a wide berth if there was one in a field. Anything that weighs well over a ton and a half, with a mind of its own and mean ancestry has my total respect. Even cows can be dangerous if they have a calf and will attack a dog or a human if they think their calf is threatened.

Our herd consisted mostly of Friesians (that's the classic black and white ones you see on TV butter adverts) but we did have four Jersey cows (they are the fawn-coloured, bony ones appearing to be wearing lots of mascara on big doleful eyes). They produce very creamy milk which boosted the overall fat content of the milk we sold to the Milk Marketing Board, so we were rewarded with a premium for our milk. I have it on good authority that the reverse is now the case with the increased popularity of semi-skimmed milk, due of course to our obsession with diet and low cholesterol.

The Jersey milk also provided us with a bit of a luxury, for some of the milk from the Jersey cows was placed in a large stainless-steel bucket and left overnight. Then in the morning the cream had risen to the top, like cream used to be on your daily 'pinta' that would arrive on your door step. The dairies decided some years ago to put it through a process called emulsification meaning cream and milk are mixed together so they do not separate out.

The cream which formed on the top of our Jersey milk was very thick and was almost the colour of the cows themselves. The cream was decanted off the top of the milk with a large flattish spoon, the handle bent to make it like ladle. Then it was scraped into a brown terracotta-glazed pint jug with a crazed yellow inside. What was left was poured into the rest of the milk to be sold. When the cream jug was full it was then taken into the house for the three of us and that would last us about a day.

I can only believe by modern medical understanding that we were either blessed with a gene that dealt with the effects of massive amounts of cholesterol in our bodies. Or was it that these natural foods without any additives protected us?

One of my favourite uses for the Jersey cream was on my porridge for breakfast. For a start my mother made the porridge with Jersey milk not water as was usually recommended so it was quite rich to start with. When it arrived on the table I immediately added a large overflowing tablespoon full of golden syrup which would form a moulten liquid pool in the centre. To this I would add a few large dollops of thick Jersey cream. The porridge apart, I would enjoy eating the cream and moulten golden syrup on its own, the true legendary ambrosia, such an exquisite taste that I very occasionally indulge in it to this day if the ingredients are to hand. I would then gently stir the remaining syrup, cream and porridge together, not totally mixing the mass as to appreciate the taste of each. Then strangely enough, as if I had not indulged my cholesterol tolerance to the limit, I would add a decent size nodule of home-made butter, again courtesy of our Jersey herd. This would melt and form a greasy, bright yellow river around the edge of the bowl. Having completed this ritual I would tuck in to this culinary extravaganza, my own version of the full cholesterol breakfast. Needless to say, protective gene or not, my morning porridge nowadays is a little less rich.

Our herd was quite healthy as my father was a firm believer in vets, for if there were ever any problems the vet was soon called. He wasn't cheap but it paid off in the long run as our cows were always happy and healthy giving a good yield of milk. They always passed their bovine tuberculosis test so our milk was always safe to drink.

We did once have some infection in our cows. They developed a cough and diarrhoea. The vet said there was nothing to worry about and it would clear up in a week or so. I found it quite dangerous actually because if you walked down the cowshed behind the cows who were infected you ran the gauntlet of projectile, warm, runny cow shit, for when they coughed the diarrhoea was splattered across the walkway onto the wall, or on to you if you weren't quick enough!

All our cows gave birth to healthy calves, only occasionally having the vet in attendance as my dad was quite proficient at bovine midwifery, and also sheep, eventually, for that matter. Although I do remember one time the vet was called as a poor cow seemed to be struggling to give birth. It turned out that when he put his arm into the cow's womb to turn the unborn calf around as he thought it was a breach birth, that the calf was coming out bum first instead of head first. He got quite a surprise when he felt two heads but only one body!

The cow was incapable of passing two heads at once, so he had to saw off one of the heads with a wire saw inside the cow's womb. I'm afraid the calf didn't survive the operation but the cow did and went on to produce many more healthy calves. This was about the time the Americans and for that matter us Brits were setting off atomic bombs all over the place. Just makes you wonder doesn't it!

My mother and dad decided to diversify into sheep as well as cows as the land began to improve through my father's expertise and hard work. It would support a few sheep as well as our dairy herd. We started off in a small way as much through lack of skill in sheep husbandry as finance. Sheep were not something my dad had ever had much to do with before, so instead of going out and buying a whole flock he asked around at lambing time for lambs which had been abandoned or their mothers had died with the trauma of birthing. Sometimes farmers manage to place them with other sheep who had lost their lambs. This can be difficult as sheep don't easily take to other sheep's lambs and let them suckle. Some of the tricks to get them to accept another sheep's lambs can be a little extreme, for example holding the sheep down and rubbing its nose with the orphan lamb to try to blank out the smell of its lost lamb. Or the dead lamb of the potential foster mother would be skinned and the pelt tied onto the back of the orphan lamb to try and fool the sheep into believing that it was her lamb alive and well. If all this failed and the sheep would not allow the orphan lamb to suckle, hand rearing with a bottle was the last resort. It would be impractical for a farmer with a large flock to bottle-feed all his orphaned and abandoned lambs. That's where we came in. My dad bought, for a few shillings, two lambs from a farmer who had no surrogate mothers to place with the lambs, and had neither the time nor inclination to hand-rear them.

When my dad brought them home he announced that they were now mine and it was my job to rear them. This involved first to gently warm some watered down cow's milk as sheep's milk isn't as rich as cow's milk, fill an old pop bottle, push a rubber teat on the end and try to get the lamb to suckle. It's amazing how quickly they caught on. Mind you, the poor little buggers were starving by the time I got them.

Within weeks they were not only gently sucking the milk from the rubber teat they came running when they saw me and with a bottle in each hand, I had a problem staying on my feet. At first we kept them in a shed out of the weather, with a heat lamp in one corner as a warmth substitute for their mother. They had to be fed milk every four hours at first, that meant getting up at two in the morning, which thankfully my father took care of, but I was expected to do the six o'clock feed before going to school. My mother did the daytime feeds and I took over again after I got back from school. It was very rewarding because they grew up to be big healthy sheep who produced fleeces and lambs for the rest of their lives. I named them Tip and Top and they would always come running to me even when they had lambs of their own. They were the beginning of our small flock of sheep.

At the end of the farm's financial year my mother would present the accounts to the Inland Revenue, with the profit from the fleeces for my two sheep separate and as a child I did not pay tax. This was queried by the Inspector with my mother having a stand-up battle with him over it. My father kept quiet, as knowing my mother, he knew that the Inspector was on to a loser arguing with her, as my dad knew she could be rather forceful and scary when roused. Sure enough my dad did not pay tax on the fleeces. Every little helped in those hard times.

Health and Safety was not a much used phrase in those days. I regularly was perched precariously on the tractor driven by my mother or father, or even on machinery being towed. By the tender age of ten I actually drove the tractor towing heavy machinery. It certainly set me up for life for towing and reversing a trailer or caravan with a car on the roads.

I can only remember one accident I had with the tractor. I was transporting some clay pipes across the fields from the farm where they had been delivered to a man who was laying drains for us to dry up a wet patch where we kept getting our tractor stuck. The pipes had been loaded into a box fastened to the lifting gear at the rear of the tractor, and before I set off the box was lifted up off the ground with hydraulics. A school friend who was helping me scrambled onto the box, sat on the load of pipes, and we set off. When we arrived at the site I duly lowered the box to the ground to unload. Before I could start unloading, the man doing the draining asked if I could back up a bit and get the pipes closer to where he was working. So obligingly I dropped it into reverse and let out the clutch. It might, in retrospect (wonderful thing retrospect), have been advantageous to have lifted the box back up to its travelling position. As I reversed, the back of the box dug into the ground, up-ended and turned upside down, trapping my school pal under the box with the pipes on top of him. I can't say that I panicked, I just went into a catatonic state at the sight of my mate's shocked and agonised face peering out from the wreckage. Luckily the draining guy was a rock and completely unflappable and took charge. How we managed to extricate the lad from the pipes and box is a bit hazy, but within ten minutes, he was sitting on the grass looking a little dazed but unharmed except for a few minor scrapes and bruises. After that he lost all interest in helping down on the farm, but we still remained friends.

The drainage man never did tell my father so saved me a long lecture on being careful with machinery. He was the type of Yorkshireman who, if a spaceship full of aliens landed next to him in a field, would just saunter over to them and say something like 'eyup lads can I help thi?'

One of the stories I've heard about him was when he was in his teens. Him and his mate were riding home one evening on a bus when four rowdy young lads got on and started to cause a nuisance. They refused to pay the conductor or get off when the bus was stopped.

At this point Bob said in his usual quietly-spoken voice to his mate, 'Shall we sort em owt, Bill?' 'Ey, Bob, else thell mek us late for us tea.' Now Bob and his mate weren't big lads by any standards but were strong as oxen with working on farms from childhood. They each grabbed two of the trouble-makers by the scruff of their necks, dragged them off the bus, kicked their arses with big working-boots and threw them over a small wall. With a nonchalant brush of their hands to signify a job well done, they climbed back on the bus that had waited for them to a standing ovation from the rest of the passengers.

Bob was also into folk medicine, well sort of. He had one particular remedy that worked as a repellent to mosquitoes that at certain times of the year could be a real pain when working outside. Bob's remedy was to soak his hanky in the nearest sheep dip which was used for killing parasites on sheep by immersing them in the strong smelling liquid and wipe all his exposed skin with the lethal brew. How he survived into a healthy old age, which he certainly has, is a miracle.

You could write a couple of books about his life, no problem. Characters like Bob seem to be few and far between nowadays.

Another reputedly true story I have no reason to disbelieve was when the local lads had their annual fishing trip to Whitby. When they arrived the sea was a little choppy. The local fisherman whose boat they had hired warned them that it was quite rough out of the harbour and did they still want to go out. Well, being Yorkshire lads they didn't have much choice. Apart from the expense of travelling all that way and paying for the boat, they had no intention of appearing wimps. So they assured the fisherman who was taking them out that it was no problem as they were all seasoned sailors! Not that any of them ever set foot in a boat from one year to the next! After loading all their fishing gear on board which included essential provisions like five crates of beer between six of them, and a pack of sandwiches each, they set off.

The instant they left the protection of the harbour they realised just how rough it really was. Nothing dangerous or the fisherman would not have risked his precious boat, but sufficient to cause at least four out of the six lads to spend a large proportion of their fishing hanging over the side shouting 'huwee'. This necessitated consuming large quantities of beer to calm their stomachs. This continued till one of the older lads slumped back in the boat after a rather monumental throwing up session over the side to complain that he had lost his false teeth over the side into the water. This caused great amounts of sympathy interspersed with Yorkshire dour wit and merriment. When the lads had settled back to their fishing, one of the lads surreptitiously removed his own false teeth, hooked them to his fishing line, and dropped them into the water. With a cry 'of 'Hey Jim, are these your teeth?' he swung his line with his own false teeth dangling on the end, over to his toothless mate. Jim grabbed the teeth unhooked them, inspected them minutely and said in a rather disappointed voice, 'No thems noorn mine' and threw them overboard! Too late the original owner cried out, 'Tha daft bugger. Them wer mine', as he watched his false teeth sink without trace.

These fishing trips were a regular annual event. An excuse for a booze-up with the lads and a day at the seaside and were always a source of adventure stories that were told in pubs and clubs right up to the next trip.

Another time when they hired a boat, and went through the routine of loading provisions and setting out to sea, about a mile offshore the boat started to take on water and began to sink. The boat-owner calmly radioed for a boat to come and rescue them. The boat-owner assured his passengers that there was nothing to worry about for rescue was imminent.

It wasn't as imminent as he thought, for by the time the rescue-boat arrived, their boat was about to go down. As the rescue-boat drew alongside they all jumped aboard to safety and started to congratulate each other on a narrow escape. Then there was a sudden cry of horror as one of the lads leapt back onto the sinking boat, 'Mi ruddy beer,' grabbed two crates of beer which were now floating on the bottom of the boat, threw them to his mates, and then leapt back into the rescue-boat just as the sinking boat went to the reputed Mr D Jones' Locker. Priorities that's what it's all about. The crew of the rescue vessel looked on unbelieving as the rest of the rescued lads congratulated their hero for a brave act of unselfish heroism, toasting him with the rescued beer.

Another episode involving Yorkshire eccentricity and false teeth was the story about a seventy- year-old local lamenting the loss of his dentures down the toilet when he flushed at the same time as sneezing, (although the general consensus was he was drunk and was throwing up down the said toilet.) One of his mates stood at the bar who worked at the local sewerage works, suggested jokingly that he come down to the works and look at a collection of false teeth that he had dredged out of the sludge along with other nondegradable flotsam that he didn't go into detail about and see if his teeth had turned up. To the worker's surprise he turned up at the small sewerage works some days later and was directed to a wooden hut where the two sewerage workers had their tea breaks. On a shelf at one end there was the gruesome display of about a couple of dozen sets of dentures. Ten minutes later the old lad emerged with a toothy grin on his face and told the worker to his horror that none of the teeth were his but, after trying them all on, the pair he was wearing were near enough! Did he kiss his wife when he got home?

That reminds me of a joke I once heard about two men working down a sewer, and one takes off his coat to hang up when he drops it in the stream of sludge flowing past. He immediately attempts to fish it out to the protests of his mate who says, 'Tha's noorn barn to weer that now ista?' 'Of coors not, what dost tha think I am. It's just that mi sarnies are in mi pocket fo mi lunch break.'

My father and mother had many friends and neighbours, all great characters in their own right. Names like Ratty Joe who was the local rat catcher named not only for his profession, by all accounts. My dad once saw him eating his sandwiches out of his lunch box and was appalled to see it was where he also kept his little bottle of rat poison. 'More Or Less' was another character named for his repeated use of the phrase. I never did know his real name and as far as I know neither did my father.

There was the local grocer who was a little on the mean side, who earned the nickname 'Nip Currant' for his reputation of when weighing out currants nipping one in half to achieve and precise weight with not a fraction of a ounce over.

There was the man with the exotic name of Orion Peek (his proper name). He had a reputation for curing dogs that where a little under the weather. It was usually owners who had overfed their dogs for years. His remedy was to take them up to his allotment for about a week and not feed them. A little harsh perhaps, but when they were returned to their owners they were jumping for joy to be returned and fed, looking a lot healthier. Orion also had a country-wide reputation as a pedigree dog-breeder. This was achieved not by having a collection of breeding pedigree dogs, but by asking around for puppies from litters that the owners didn't want. Then forging pedigree certificates and even dyeing their coats to improve their looks, then selling them on to people who paid exorbitant prices for virtual mongrels.

All gone now, replaced with rather bland, but probably as dishonest, non-characters with names like Wayne, Dean, and Britney.

There were some tough characters out there. A good friend of mine described how, when a packet of five Woodbines cigarettes fell out of his pocket at the gym where he did training with his elder brother. On seeing the ciggies, his brother who was a professional wrestler collared my mate, opened the packet. Finding one half smoked, my mate was made to sit down on a bench at the side of the gym and eat the four and a half remaining cigarettes!! Tough therapy but my mate never smoked another cigarette ever again, and, by the way, he never ate another one either.

One of the more unbelievable stories I have been told but definitely true was about the boiler man at the local bobbin mill manufacturing bobbins for the woollen industry. He had to start earlier than the rest of the workers to stoke up the boilers ready to power up the machines for the day, probably about six o'clock or earlier. No great hardship you may say as some people today start work that early, the only difference being this guy walked from Brighouse which is an astonishing twenty miles, that's forty miles a day round trip in all weathers; summer, winter, rain or shine. It was reputed that if he got wet on his journey in the rain he would take all his clothes off and dry them on the steam pipes, tying old newspapers around himself with string till his cloths dried.

CHAPTER THREE

Some of my chores on the farm were looking after our free-range hens; letting them out first thing in the morning, feeding them, and collecting the eggs before I went to school, then shutting them in before dark so the foxes couldn't eat them. Now for some reason I am still at a loss to explain our hundred-odd hens were separated into six huts. This was fairly straightforward as the huts were relatively small and would only hold about fifteen or so hens, but why they had to be one to a field spread over six fields stretching from the farm to our farthest field about quarter of a mile away, God only knows, for my father was rather vague about the reason. When I asked, on the occasions when I had fought my way to the farthest field and back again carrying corn out and eggs back in hail, rain, wind, sleet, and snow, I would receive very unsatisfactory answers saying they needed plenty of space to lay well. They certainly were provided with plenty of opportunity as I calculated that each hen had about half an acre each. Overall it was character building, I suppose. The hen-houses were a motley collection of wood huts adapted with perches and shelves for the hens to lay their eggs in boxes filled with straw. One was even an old aluminium wagon-body, probably a mobile signals-truck left over from the war gutted of its paraphernalia and sold off. It still had black Bakelite signs etched in white with things like 'Generator cut off switch' and 'Wireless antenna connection point'. These always fascinated me and over the years I would prise them off and take them to show off at school.

We had names for all the fields. The field with the wagon-body hen-hut was surprisingly enough called the ‘Wagon-body field’. The field next was called the ‘Hollow’ field as the hut was situated in a hollow that ran down the centre of the field, reputed to have been carved out by the reservoir bursting its banks many years before we came to the farm. I always thought it was a little dangerous having the hut at the bottom as it could happen again but my father said it gave the hut shelter from the wind. Inevitably the hut in the farthest field was called the ‘The Far field.’ We were simple folk!

Another one of my duties was to mix the food for the cows at milking time. Hot water was poured on a product called sugar-beet. This was usually done the day before it was fed to the cows to allow it to cool and swell up. This was then scooped into individual buckets with corn and a mixture of sweet smelling ingredients that are probably lacking in today's manufactured cow fodder. The mixture was stirred and then placed in front of each cow as it was being milked. The room where I used to mix the cows’ food was inevitably inhabited by rats, and it was always advisable to carry a stick to deter some of the larger of the species from taking cow-food from the bucket you were mixing at the time.

The milk straight from the cow was warm and had to be cooled by running it over tubes with cold water running through them. When the milk was cooled it was poured in to large milk churns holding ten gallons, we called milk-kits for some reason? These had to be trundled out to the stand by the roadside to be collected by a wagon from the Milk

Marketing Board and taken to a central dairy for distribution. When I was strong enough it was my job to take it to the stand. It was far too heavy to lift and carry so it had to be rolled on its bottom edge while holding the lid. There was a knack to this. If the lid came off it was a disaster as the churn fell over leaving you with the lid and a lot of spilt milk. The stand by the road side was about three feet high so that when the collection wagon pulled alongside, the kits could be easily lifted onto the wagon. Lifting the kit onto the stand for collection was quite a feat for a young lad. The churns had to be hoisted up, requiring great skill as well as brute strength. It's all done with tankers that draw the milk from tanks on each farm. Back then it was character building, and muscle building too. I was left alone by most of the bullies at school as I developed broad shoulders but, I'm afraid, never developed a six pack, something to do with the Jersey cream and my mother's wonderful cooking perhaps?

Life on the farm was not all work, well not for me anyway, although my mother and dad might have queered that statement. One of my favourite pastimes in summer between hay-making was swimming in the 'Res'. This was a small dam of water that was wonderful to swim in. It did have large notices declaring it was drinking water but we all knew that was a lie as it was just a reserve supply for the dams that used to drive the water-wheel to power the mill further down in the village. By then anyway, steam had taken over as a power source and the dams were unused and eventually drained and our 'res' was unsuitable as a drinking-water source as it was fed from a run-off from the moors and was brackish with peat. So it was a perfect bathing venue for dozens of youngsters, far safer and cleaner than the river. Even though today the river Aire has fish swimming in it again and strict pollution laws have done miracles, I have no desire to take a dip in the river. I have only swum in one local river, that's the Wharfe way up in the dales above the first sewerage works at Grassington. With what seemed like endless summers, I became a proficient swimmer with my own local pool next to the farm.

I also was a keen rambler, or actually it would be more accurate to call me a Lone Wanderer. I would go off over the moors even as a young child. One of my favourite spots was down into a local wood at the edge of my father's land called Brighton Wood. It gave me a deep appreciation of nature, flowers, wild life, and the countryside in general which influences me to this day. The story goes that it was called Brighton Wood because after it was abandoned as a stone quarry which had probably supplied stone to built half of Steeton, some of the local lads built a dam across the stream that runs through the middle to form a pool in the centre which became a great bathing spot, and as a trip to the real Brighton was only an annual event, if at all, the locals had their own seaside venue. The pool had disappeared by the time I came along, but I used to enjoy build mini dams across the stream and then destroying them by throwing rocks at it, pretending to be Barnes Wallace of Dambusters' fame.

CHAPTER THREE

Although I was a bit of a loner I would go exploring with school friend on occasions. These exploring trips would last all day, usually on a Saturday. They were arranged among my class- mates in the boring drawing lesson on a Friday afternoon as we were allowed to talk as we drew the teacher in the nude ... I mean a vase of flowers. We would gather early morning with our provisions for the day which consisted of jam and bread sandwiches and Popalol to drink. What is Popalol you may well ask. Well it's a home-made pop, because when your pocket money was only a shilling a week pop was a bit of a luxury. We used to call in at the local shop on our way home from school and buy a penny's worth of liquorice sticks and as soon as we got home we would drop them into an old pop bottle filled with water. The liquorice would dissolve overnight providing us with a cheap refreshing drink for our day 'layking out'.

There were lots of interestingly named places surrounding the farm. One was a strip of moor just off the road that no-one seemed to own, called 'Irish Moor'. By all accounts it was used by the Irish navvies as a site for their temporary huts that they lived in, when they were building many hundreds of miles of dry stone walls in the area, which are such a feature of the Yorkshire Dales. They were employed for years in this area and must have been a regular sight working in the fields. It's fascinating when rebuilding the odd wall that has fallen down to realise the skills of the original Irish builders, considering they have stood for hundreds of years. Sometimes you come across broken clay tobacco pipes that the navvies were very partial to smoking as they worked. These were dropped into the middle of the walls that they were building when the delicate, long, thin tobacco pipes got broken.

All this wandering was done in Wellington boots, affectionately known as wellybobs, as these were standard issue on farms, being rather muddy places even in mid summer. Gates where cows congregated were particularly bad, and you were not advised to sweep and muck out the cow shed in shoes.

This habit of wearing 'wellies' has left its mark literally as I still have hairless calves to this day where the hairs have been permanently worn away by the tops of my wellies.

My mother would always insist I always wear my wellies. But it was as a teenager when a similar phrase of 'don't go wading without your wellies' took on an all new different meaning of always 'wear a condom for sex.'

Wellies were essential on the farm in navigating vast seas of mud. The down side was when your wellies got stuck, this could be particularly disastrous when running, as you tended to leave your boots behind in the mud and carry on running in your socks, which was rather unpleasant to say the least.

Another down side of Wellington boots was that things tended to go down the tops, like corn when feeding the hens or snow when walking through snow-drifts. This paled into insignificance compared with the stories my dad used to tell about rats trying to escape by taking refuge down your wellies. Not even pulling your trousers down over them was the answer. It takes little imagination to see the frantic rat going up your trousers, then down your wellies! Or, perhaps even worse, carrying on up your trousers.

A rather rude aspect of Wellington boots I found out much later was the perverted sexual practices of lovelorn, sexually frustrated, farmer/ shepherds who allegedly were in the practice of stuffing the back legs of sheep down their wellies to restrain them during bestiality intercourse. Gross or what!

About the worst thing I had down my wellies was when I was about six and attempted to walk over a smouldering garden fire. (Haven't we all done that? No?) I fell through the crusty ash on the top into the hot embers in the middle. Luckily my dad was close to lift me out, but not before hot ash had fallen down the tops of my wellies. It's quite difficult but urgent to remove Wellington boots with burning hot ash when they are jammed on, but my dad quickly managed to pull them off leaving rather badly burnt skin on one leg. I was rushed to hospital by my dad with my mother in attendance and carried into Accident and Emergency. The nurses and doctor were very good and soon had me cleaned up, but my leg was in a bad shape with about nine square inches of bare flesh where the skin had been burnt away. The doctor told my father and mother it wasn't very serious and it would soon heal especially if they used this revolutionary treatment for burns. He instructed a nurse to scatter this special powder on the burnt area with a little shaker like a large pepper-pot explaining that the 'asbestos dust' would dry up the wound, forming a temporary skin so the wound would heal quicker and keep out infection. Yes, that's right, asbestos dust! There was a cloud of the stuff as the nurse liberally scattered what is now recognised as lethal dust over my leg with her little pepper-pot. Thankfully that little gem of revolutionary treatment was abandoned before either the parents, or more likely the nurse, went down with asbestosis. To be quite honest the treatment was successful as my leg soon healed and I'm glad to say at sixty plus now I'm not suffering from the dreaded asbestosis.

It always amazes me how good ideas and inventions that have been hailed as wonderful, revolutionary, and even to have health benefits turn out to be downright bloody dangerous and even fatal. I seem to remember smoking was reckoned to be a healthy habit when I was a child.

One such thing that was discreetly taken out of circulation without much official investigation was an innovative shoe gauge! I remember being taken into a shoe-shop by my mother to get me a new pair of shoes for my first day at school. I chose a pair that was a compromise between what my mother wanted and what I would be prepared to wear. The shop assistant then stressed the need for plenty of space in the shoes for growing children and suggested I try a new gadget that allows the child's foot to be viewed inside the shoe. It was a large box in the corner of the shop. Leading us over to it the assistant told me to insert my shoe into a hole at its base. As she threw a switch on the side of the box there was a green glow and she told my mother and me to look through a little window on the top. There was my bare foot in the outline of a shoe all in an eerie green and, sure enough, the green toes moved in unison to me wiggling mine. The assistant pointed out how my foot was snug, but with space to grow. How many shop assistants were sterilised or developed cancer with constant use of this lethal piece of kit, God only knows, not to mention the children who used it a number of times per visit to the shop every year. From what I know now of X-ray machines housed in what appeared to be wood rather metal, there was no concept of the dangerous radiation for those who used it. So much for the brave new world of technology that was going to cure all the world's ills and free us from diseases and drudgery.

I never had pets as such; the dogs we had over the years were working dogs, black and white Border collie sheep-dogs mostly. And of course the cats we had, sometimes up to half a dozen, were working animals too, as the farm was always pestered by rats and mice. I did have a grass-snake once but it got out and frightened my mother as she opened a drawer where it was hiding and it had to go. We did have a Mynah bird in a big cage next to the phone. It really wasn't a pet in the usual sense but it was a lot of fun. It was an amazing mimic and soon learnt to shout 'come in' when any one knocked on the door. This was a little annoying as people would knock and walk in on the bird's request. It soon progressed to making its own knocking sound, which was worse as we were continually having to answer the door with no-one there. I think the nail in its coffin came when it perfected the telephone ring that was situated just below its cage, it was so good that both my mother and father were continually picking up the phone only to hear the dialling tone. The bird eventually went back to the pet shop!

I did have a tame magpie which, I suppose, could be called a pet but it was very independent. It would fly onto my shoulder for food and if none was on offer would clean out my ears with its beak hoping for a tasty morsel. I took it as a fledgling from its nest, which I had been watching being built all spring. I even climbed up to it to observe the eggs and then the chicks and observed the parents coming with food. A magpie’s nest is domed with just a small opening big enough for the adult birds to squeeze through or for a small boys hand to enter. I watched as the fledglings left the nest one by one until there was just one left. I had already noted that one of the five chicks was definitely a runt and was not as well developed as the rest. After a day with no sign of the young bird making an exit, and the parents seemingly abandoning their parental responsibilities, I removed the chick. It was very bedraggled and cold so I took it home and reared it by hand.

Amazingly it flourished despite everyone's predictions that it would be dead in the morning. It eventually lived, free to fly away if it wanted to but stayed around the farm. Initially I was afraid one of the cats would make a meal of it as it wasn't as wary of their predatory nature as other wild birds around the farm. My fears were unfounded as I observed six of the largest, most vicious moggies who were sunning themselves on the windowsill being attacked and sent scattering in all directions by my now fully-grown magpie. It then strutted up and down, king of the sill, proclaiming its territory in its harsh call. It loved to ride in the car. It would perch on the dashboard squawking at dogs and cats as we passed them. I'm afraid that its love of car travel was its downfall as one day after a ride in the car, it tried to make an exit as the door was being closed, was crushed and died instantly. I was heart-broken that something so alive and with such personality could be snuffed out and gone forever.

Overall life was good on the farm and the healthy life, good food, and a positive attitude to hard work set me up for life. I think myself very lucky not to have been brought up in a town in some back street. Mind you, I've never known anything different!

— 4 —

THE FORMATIVE YEARS

I WAS NOT enamoured with school, when people brag about which grammar school they went to I tell them 'well my school was approved.' It seemed an endless blur of teachers talking about things I could not understand and, at best, had no interest in. There were spelling tests at which I always achieved a miserable score, usually one and two out of ten, and only a high score when we were trusted to mark our own. Also, abject embarrassment when we all had to pass them on to the left to be marked and ridiculed with phrases like 'you will never guess how the dumbo spelled this one.' Kids can be very cruel, and there was no support from the teachers who were not beyond a little sarcastic comment of their own.

My way round my embarrassment of my nonexistent spelling ability was to write illegibly so no-one could make out the crap spelling. This was compounded by one of my first teachers who at the time should have been teaching us joined-up writing decided to go for italic writing in a big way. While a very artistic form of calligraphy, it was useless for everyday use as it's not joined-up writing. This has dogged me all my life as I had to single-handedly adapt italic into my own form of joined-up hand writing, doing it very badly may I add.

The advent of word processing on computers transformed my literary life and gave me a way of putting down my aspirations in print. With a spell checker I was set up, but that was no help for another forty years, and then people could actually understand what I had written. A new experience for me, to be able to write a letter. The world was suddenly my oyster, and when I went on the web with e-mails, I did not even have to misspell the address on the envelope! Ecstasy. Needless to say as I write this the page it is a mass of red underlined misspellings as my spell checker goes into overdrive, and sometimes can't even get close to the word I want. Of course forty-odd years ago home computers were still a distant dream. Then computers were virtually still mechanical devices with cogs, and cams, with a hint of valves, and relays still in the future.

What do I remember of my school life? I made a Tyrannosaurus Rex dinosaur out of papier-mâché' which I was very proud of until it was put on display with the rest of the school, and mine looked pretty dreadful. Just why I was not very dexterous as a child is difficult to say as I've grown up to be quite good with my hands at making things. I must have been a slow starter.

I seemed to be the last one to go into long pants in my class! How cruel was the world to young children sending them out in short trousers in winter. My mother said I could have long trousers as soon as I stopped getting scabby knees. I don't remember putting the logical argument forward that if I had long trousers I wouldn't get scabby knees as the long trousers would protect them. But I am sure I did. Thinking back, it must have been something to do with the prospects of constantly having to patch up the knees on my trousers that made my mother reluctant to put me in long pants. I seem to remember living up to expectation, with raggedy knees on a regular basis when I finally made it into my long pants, and still having scabby knees. My first long trousers were called Cavalry Twills, which I thought sounded rather fine and not too naff to wear. My mother, always on the look out for a bargain, bought a job lot at a sale. They were all too long for my little legs so she altered them over the years but I eventually grew into the final pair, saving my mother the job of altering them.

I always look on history as being a very cruel time of swords hacking people to bits, rape, pillage, and such, Victorian workhouses, slaves, and wars. But in recent history sending small boys out in short pants is on a par with sending small boys up chimneys with brushes to sweep them - definitely should definitely go down in the history books as 'man's inhumanity to man'. This is reputed to have been said by Sean O'Casey, a famous Irish writer, over a pint of stolen Guinness! Really tragic that. It's also said about the Irish, 'For every solution the Irish have a problem.'

Also later in my school career, an echo from the past was our ex-sergeant major of a PE teacher making me stand in goal during football matches in skimpy, thin cotton shorts and tee-shirt with frozen snow on the ground. The goal post or net offered no shelter from the cruel wind and little opportunity as goalkeeper to run about to keep warm, I'll have you know.

It was a time of free milk in little bottles, and daily doses of cod liver oil capsules. I quite liked the milk which we all drank by spearing the silver top twice with our dirty thumbnail; one for the milk to come out, one for the air to replace the milk. Although great in theory, milk up your nose and down your front was a common occurrence as the fragile aluminium cap could so easily come off. This could be achieved by prematurely loosening the cap of a few bottles, before most of the other kids picked theirs up. Or, alternatively, a heavy pat on the back of a drinker as he was half way through had a similar effect. This necessitated drinking your milk with your back to the wall, and checking your tops carefully for sabotage. The teacher always made sure we all had our daily quarter pinta, kids with lactose intolerance being no exception, if it was even recognised in those days. The teacher reckoned all the crates had to be emptied, so he made all the big lads have an extra bottle till they were all used up.

I was never given any cod liver oil capsules but there was a large jar half full in the teacher's cupboard. Their bright yellow colour in the large glass jar always used to fascinate me as someone in our class said they were cyanide pills for us pupils to take during the war if German soldiers captured the school after they invaded. Vivid imagination or what!!

Apparently I wasn't a very bright pupil and did not pass my eleven-plus, which surprised me for I thought I did quite well. Again it was this problem about scribbling illegibly so they could not read my spelling mistakes. So even if I got the answers right no-one would have known.

I was to go to the local secondary modern, which had the reputation of being a good school, and if only I had done my homework I might have done better than one GCE and an RSA. I did not hand in any homework in my entire five years there and I occasionally still have nightmares about the wrath of the English teacher at the pristine condition and blank state of my homework book, with only the occasional scribbled paragraph hastily compiled or copied from a friend on the bus to school.

There were three streams; A.B.C. The 'A' group were the cream and were groomed to take GCE's. They took French and played cricket as well as football! (which I never understood, do you have to be cleverer to play cricket?). Of course the real crème de la crème had been creamed off for the grammar school at the eleven-plus. So it was not expected for any of the 'A' lot to go to university, technical college at best. But a few percent actually did make uni.

The B stream, which I managed to achieve, were your factory fodder and plumbers, bricklayers, and joiners, and were encouraged in practical subjects. The C stream, of course, were written off from day one. No-hopers who were just managed, not taught. This was partly their own fault as their behaviour was appalling. They had one saving grace as far as the school was concerned, a good proportion were very good at sports and winning cups for the school. One exception to the no-hopers from the C stream was my friend Mick. He was not only a superb athlete, but became head prefect and took walking trips up the Dales on his own with a dozen or so younger kids! Just to put that in perspective. School trips of that nature today would have to have a minimum of two fully-qualified in outdoor pursuits teachers. Mick was very highly respected but it would not be contemplated today. Mick also went on to run his own business for forty years. No mean feat.

My passage through secondary school continued in the B stream until the year before my final year when my mother, bless her, demanded that I be allowed to take GCE's. It was pointed out in a condescending way that only A stream students could take GCE's, but they didn't appreciate my mother's ferocious determination. She just looked the headmaster in the eye and replied, 'Well put my son in an A stream then'. So they did. I consequently spent my final year at school in the 'A' stream. She did not stop there though, she wanted me to take separate sciences i.e. physics, chemistry, biology, instead of just general science, as I was keen on science and it did not look like I was going to take any other subjects. My mother did lose that one though, as the school was just not set up for the separate sciences. That was the exclusive preserve of the grammar schools and I had missed that opportunity at the eleven-plus. I think I eventually did thank her for trying to get the best for me but it wasn't an easy time. To make up for the not taking separate sciences, the Head recommended I take religious studies which would potentially give me a further GCE. What? What the hell was that about! I had no ambition to be a vicar, and anyway I failed it!

Another way I feel there was an anomaly of our education system at the time was when all the class except your truly was entered for the technical drawing GCE exam. Some time after the exam the class was discussing the results of the technical drawing GCE exam with the teacher. He said he was disappointed that they had all failed. He then came out with the bombshell that there was only one person in the class capable of passing the exam and that was me! I did point out that he had refused to put me forward for the exam. Somehow he failed to understand the irony, and, embarrassed, he changed the subject. Although I did mention it when I met him twenty years later, he said he positively would not have said that. But he bloody well did!

Everyone in the school was divided into houses, even the teachers. This was a way of creating competitiveness in everything from sport to how many house points each house received in the year. I think this still only survives in a few select public schools nowadays, as the philosophy today is we are all born equal and competitiveness creates winners and losers. Yes well? Allegedly we were all given our house at random when we first went to the school, but there seemed to be some form of favouritism as it was the same house won year after year and my house always came bottom. That couldn't be totally put down to my lack of sporting ability as there were quite a few other losers in the house.

The four houses were Rivok, Pinnor, Gib and last and most certainly least Hawshaw, the one I was lumbered with. These were all hills around the school, and recently I actually climbed one. Funnily enough it wasn't Hawshaw!

During my final year I was also made a science monitor responsible for tidying up the lab during lunch time and breaks. This I'm sorry to say only lasted three days as I used a certain chemical I borrowed from the lab to make a snow storm in the class-room over lunch to impress my mates. I think the science master was quite impressed too, but was very firm that it was rather inappropriate and he felt I had betrayed a trust. Perhaps it was for the best as all those wonderful dangerous chemicals in the prep room were definitely too much of a temptation.

The long walk up and down the hill was still there, although the time to the bus stop in the village added another fifteen minutes to the journey to school. My parents applied for a free taxi because of the distance involved but to no avail. The farm was a few hundred yards short of the minimum regulation distance. But the real injustice of it was the next farm was just a few hundred yards into the regulation distance and the taxi made a pick leaving me to walk while the taxi drove past me to the same school with one passenger in the back. You really need to believe in fairness at that age and I often found the world distinctly lacking in that department at times.

I made quite a lot of friends at school. Some of them even walked the distance up to the farm to play out with me, although I am only on nodding acquaintance with just two or three nowadays. One of the big attractions for school friends was hay-making, although when they found out it was proper work most of them usually only came once.

Playground games were very popular in my day; 'Kick-can', 'Ralio' 'Conkers' 'Pig in the Middle' 'Split ye Knackers' and, of course, 'British Bulldogs'. The latter involved lining up as many lads who wanted to play. Girls didn't play as it involved physical contact, not that they were averse to physical contact it was the lads who had problems tackling them. There could be as many as fifty or so, at one end of the play ground with one poor sod standing his ground in the centre. Then en masse the entire line would run past him. The object of the game was for the person in the middle to drop to the floor one of the lads running past by any means, fair or foul, then that person would join the centre position. They would then each aim to drop another runner or 'twoing' any big kid who put up two much of a fight. This would go on until all the runners had been converted to the centre position of catchers. It was not a game for wimps, how no-one was ever killed or seriously injured

I'll never know, because we all played very rough and for keeps.

Kick-can was a rather gentler game with no physical contact but still played in dead earnest. It was a variation on hide-and-seek but while the seeker was looking for the hiders if one of them got back to a tin can strategically placed in an open area and kicked it as far as he could before he was tagged by the seeker, all the hiders who had been tagged up to that point were released to go hide again, while the seeker had to retrieve the can. And so it went on until all were tagged without the can being kicked or it got too dark to see the can.

Names for our street games often changed from village to village only the rules being set in stone.

A game that I think is still played today is 'Pig in the Middle'. although perhaps by a different name. Kids today just don't have the imagination that we did, or maybe they have too much. The game was to pass a ball back and forward between two players with a player in the middle (the pig). The object of the game was not to allow the pig to catch the ball, usually by devious means like bouncing the ball just by the pig, or even through his legs, to the other player. If the pig managed to catch the ball the person who missed the ball became the pig, and the game continued.

Conkers must be a universal British game whereby you thread a piece of string through a horse chestnut , after piercing it with an appropriate instrument; anything from a bradawl from your father's tool-box or, rather ineffectually, a knitting needle from your mother's sewing box. A proper hand drill was usually unavailable unless you could sneak your conker in to woodwork class and drill it while the teacher was distracted by a friend asking him a technical question. When appropriately strung you would take it in turns to smash your opponent's conker while he holds it up for the assault. Smashed fingers were not uncommon during a game and a long piece of string was a real advantage, although the swinging conker after it had been thwacked also posed a threat to life and limb. Soaking the conker in vinegar was an acceptable ploy to harden the nut as athletes were reputed to do to harden their feet. One had to be careful in this practice as too long immersion in the vinegar tended to leave the conker rather brittle, making shrapnel a definite eye hazard. Baking in your mother's oven on a low heat had a similar effect if overdone, a real life threatening experience for both participants. Not! So nowadays children are required to wear safety goggles. That is if they are allowed out of their cotton-wool lined, little glass boxes!

Another very un-PC game was 'Split your Knackers.' Again girls were excluded! This was a game played with knives, can you believe! This was an innocent time (well almost) when most lads carried pen-knives, even to school. Not as weapons to protect or to intimidate, more to get stones out of horses' hooves or as the joke went 'to get boy scouts out of horses' hooves.' The game involved standing opposite your adversary facing each other, about three feet apart. You started off with your feet together and took it in turns to throw your knife to stick in the ground within a foot or so of the opponent's left or right foot, and he then had to bring one shoe up to the knife. This was repeated by each of you till one of you was so stretched you fell over or quit with the pain. One of the few rules was that if you stuck you knife in your opponent's foot you lost! (Fair doos).

Proper games like football and cricket were also played but these were supervised by teachers although impromptu kick-abouts were played with four piles of coats substituted for goal posts. I very rarely played as our gym teacher always put me in goal dressed only in a thin T shirt and shorts. Have I mentioned this before? It's a very sore point, probably as it scarred me for life! It always seemed to be freezing with a cruel wind and not even being able to run around to keep warm cured me of any interest in football for the rest of my life, and luckily cricket was reserved for A stream, rather above us B and C plebs, so I never got into that either.

There were less savoury and far less healthy games boys used to play in my youth, although I may add I never anticipated in them. One was putting drawing pins on the latch-sneck, the type you use your thumb to press down on to open. A far grosser version of that was to cover it in dog shit so when you pricked your thumb you automatically stuck it in your mouth. No wonder parasitic worms were rife, not to mention blood poisoning, and they say kids today are horrible! Knocking on doors and running away before the occupants could answer was OK, but a refinement on this was to suspend a small stone on a length of fishing line so it was in front of the door, then a further longer length to a hiding place. A few jerks on the line knocked the stone on the door then pulled out of the way before the occupant answered. This could be repeated ad infinitum or until the line was spotted and followed to the perpetrator who had to make a quick exit to the accompaniment of 'I know who you are. I'll tell your dad of you.'

Another rather cruel game involved scaring the shit out of townies who were ignorant of rural ways. First you would show them the large patches of wild rhubarb. These are spectacular plants with leaves over a foot across and form dark cave areas under the dense foliage and usually grew in dense patches by streams. These were affectionately known as rat leaves, so we would tell the townies they were inhabited by giant rats and if you bent down and peered into the depths you could see their red eyes in the dark. If they showed some reluctance to get close, we would assure them the rats would only attack if you ventured into the leaves themselves as they would not come out in daylight. When they bent down to look under the leaves we would give them a hefty shove on the backside with the boot, sending the unfortunate townies careering deep into the middle of the patch. Then there would be great amusement at the lads screams as they tried to scramble out while they imagined being consumed by giant boy-eating rodents. These little pleasures were so rewarding! Of course we never did it to girls, not even townie girls. Nothing to do with the lads having respect for the fairer sex, you understand, it was just they tended to go hysterical and beat you up.

The classroom was always a rewarding place for practical jokes. The collapsing chair was always a favourite. Broken wooden chairs were usually stacked at the back of the classroom for eventual removal by the caretaker. With care you could prop one up at a desk to resemble a safe resting place. This usually got an uproarious laugh from the whole class when the child collapsed in a heap among the splintered chair. This was usually done to fat kids as they went down with the most noise and disruption. A bonus to this was when the fat girl or boy got a telling off from the teacher for breaking the chair. It may come as a surprise to dieticians today but we had fat kids then too, without the supposed convenience foods.

The toilets at our primary school were incredibly crude affairs. Outside in the playground with no roof on the urinal and only a leaky slate roof over the sit-down jobs. No electric so it was a dark, unsanitary, damp and uninviting place with three-quarter doors which when closed left you in near total darkness, with your feet in full view with your trousers and knickers down around your ankles. The dark was an invitation for another cruel trick whereby you spread stinging nettles on the seat for the pleasure of hearing the screams and bad language, when the unsuspecting bare bum was placed on the nettle-garlanded seat.

The urinals were against a five foot high wall next to the 'Rec' (recreational ground). After our morning bottle of milk a competition would ensue to see who could piss over the wall while standing at the urinals, especially the lads who had been made to consume the extra bottles. A large patch of well nourished nettles growing on the other side of the wall was proof that a substantial number of us managed to achieve this. This was perhaps fortuitous as it discouraged any unsuspecting person from sitting under the wall. And, of course, it did provide ample stinging nettles for toilet seats.

The girls' playground (girls and boys had separate playgrounds and separate entrances to the school in those days) also sported an outside toilet-block although I never ventured in there personally. I was informed by the more adventurous lads that when they had run through for a laugh to make the girls scream, their condition were as grim as ours.

Once a year the school had a party with food and music and dancing. This was before rock and roll of course. Most of the rock stars were, along with us, still in short pants.

We were all encouraged to do a bit of waltzing with girls, rather awkwardly may I add. It was another twenty years before I held a girl in the waltz-hold as the twist became a dance craze after leaving school. A compensation for having to dance with girls at the party was the opportunity for a prank. If you were quick you could shave the bars of carbolic soap out of the wash room into the sandwiches. This was particularly rewarding if one of the teachers ate one.

There was some weird unsavoury characters I remember from my early school days, and that was just the teachers. Well the kids were pretty bad too. In all my time at school as a pupil and working in a school I have personally known four teachers who have received accommodation from Her Majesty for crimes ranging from embezzlement to having inappropriate relations with their pupils. As I was saying that some of my fellow class mates were pretty gruesome. Some of the farmers' lads smelt strongly of cows from working on the farm. That wasn't too bad as I might have had a bit of a whiff myself, but some kids were positively pungent, and did not even have the excuse of mucking out the cowshed before coming to school. Some of the really bad lads were destined to spend a good deal of their future life in prison, as even at primary school they were positively evil and I'm sure most of them achieved their full potential. Some had disgusting habits like wiping their nose on their sleeve so most of the time they had silver and green sleeves. Also picking their noses and wiping it on anything close to hand, under their desks or a passing kid or even worse chewing it. I can only think this last form of disposal was an attempt to supplement a protein or vitamin deficiency. Gross or what?

We just missed out on personal little chalkboards, but not pen and ink. Although there were Biros about in the shops, their use in school was totally banned, and in the immortal words of our headmaster they 'degraded our writing skills and would never catch on.' Just as a piece of useless information, Biros were invented in the second world war as a response to aircrew experiencing great difficulty with fountain pens to write notes while on bombing missions. The varying air pressure tended to empty the ink from the little rubber reservoir, and blot their copy book.

Our desks did still sport inkwells with actual ink in them, to use in our copy books with scratchy pens with crude nibs that blobbed ink all over the place. I never did master use of pen and ink. My pen nib was always crossed or akimbo, and caused raggedy inky groves and holes in my copy book. My little three by three square-inch of blotting paper, issued once a week never lasted even a day before it turned blue, soggy and fell apart.

Ink monitors regularly filled the little white porcelain receptacles inset into the top of the desk. The ink was mixed from powder and was of such poor, weak, runny constituency that Bob Cratchit would have struggled to write in his ledger, for it was far worse than the ink Scrooge would have provided. The ink was made up and distributed by designated ink monitors, chosen mainly to keep them out of mischief rather than chosen for their competence. (It didn't work!) The designated monitors would go around each desk once a week and fill all the inkwells from a big jug. You could always identify them as ink monitor, even after several days, as their hands, and sometimes their faces if they had been partially slap happy (which they inevitably were), were stained a rather dirty blue. The rest of the class were not exempt from the occasional blue freckle.

The inkwell did have some use though apart from making my copy book illegible. They were very handy and well placed to dip the pigtails of the girl sitting at the desk in front. But of course I never did such a thing, mainly because you would get beaten up after school by the girl with the blue hair.

I'm not quite old enough to go back as far as individual pupil chalkboards but I do remember a stack of them in a cupboard at the back of the class-room along with the cyanide tablets. It's mind blowing how in my lifetime we've progressed from chalk boards to computers.

Another designated duty was board monitor whose job it was to wipe the blackboard at the end of each lesson. This not only saved the teacher valuable coffee time in the staff room but saved them getting silicosis from the chalk dust to boot. But it was some time off in the future before it was realised the unhealthy potential of chalk dust. Needless to say I should imagine there may be a few board monitors with persistent coughs about today.

Out of school there was always the apple orchard to raid, usually before the apples were ripe, and before the owner did his own gathering. A tell-tale stomach-ache gave the game away of the previous days visit to the vicarage orchard.

Not many kids had bikes but for those kids whose parents could afford one, they tended to be second-hand, ill-fitting for the size of child, and very old and ramshackle, and would have been a death trap in today's traffic. One definite taboo was for a lad to have a girl's bike, no matter how desperate he was for a bike. Bikes were never a priority for me, although I did have one for a while. With living on the top of a hill, there was always a long push up the hill back home which outweighed the fun of riding down. I always fancied fitting a small petrol engine on the back wheel. There was a gadget you could buy, but my dad never came across one that he thought was a runner or one he could afford for me. My only option was a square of stiff card taped to the rear strut of the bike that caught on the spokes as the wheel turned, making a sound like a motor bike. If anything this made it marginally harder to pedal but was an incentive to keep pedalling uphill as you imagined the sound was an engine propelling you. Yeh!

All these little horrible games were preformed in a small community were everybody knew each other and their kids, so a word with the father of the offender was usually quickly punished by a clip around the ear, no supper, and dragged around to the victim to apologise and it was all forgotten. Even the local bobby was encouraged to administer a clip around the ear with the full approval of the parents. Those days are well gone, dare I say more's the pity. There would be lawsuits, prosecutions and, of course, the dreaded Social Services involved if there was a hint of that today.

In all, I think one of the lasting memories of school, which doesn't say much for the education system, or ten years of my life at a impressionable age and haunted me into my working life, was Norman Wisdom!. Not that he ever came to the school, or I even met him but the deputy head was a big fan of Norman's films and subsequently for our Christmas, Easter and summer break, on the afternoon before we broke up, lessons were cancelled, and we all gathered in the hall to watch one of his films. Even at that tender age, he had limited appeal and certainly for most of the staff who apart from the fan club of one, the deputy head, sloped off to the staff room for tea, leaving the deputy head and a couple of ambitious staff who were looking for promotion, to control the escalating bored and unruly mob. As I said I was still haunted by Mr Wisdom years later when I went back to my old school as a technician, for one of my jobs was to set up the projector for the obligatory last day of term film and guess what! It was the same old Norman Wisdom films I was made to watch fifteen year earlier, and I was still a captive audience , only this time I was being paid to be at my post.

— 5 —

THE BOX

TV WAS INTRODUCED into our family for the Coronation in 1953, when I was five. The world and his dog seemed to pop round that day; aunts, uncles, cousins, neighbours, strangers! It seemed that we were the only ones on the hillside to have this new fangled contraption and people seemed to come from miles around to ogle. We all crammed into a small, snug living room with a small, but powerful, coke stove. There was a small space by the door where passers-by would come and go and copious amounts of tea and home-made cakes would be passed into the room. Every now and then someone had to move away from the stove for fear of passing out or catching fire, so there was a constant shushing and grumbling as someone blocked someone else's view of the tiny screen. The Coronation did not appeal, so I mainly played outside watching the comings and goings that day with the occasional peek in at the door. But everything else on that amazing little box from then on was magic to a five year old.

The TV itself was a huge wood veneered cabinet standing as tall as I was then with a tiny round porthole for a screen with three knobs arranged symmetrically underneath. The knobs in black, shiny Bakelite were labelled in gold lettering; 'Volume/on/off', 'Contrast', and Brightness.' That was all you needed. Upon investigation, there were two little ones at the back marked horizontal hold and vertical hold. These were definitely out of bounds for adjustment by untrained personnel, absolutely not for a five-year-old, although by seven I'd given them both an experimental tweak. There was, of course, at least one visit by the engineer to adjust the horizontal or the vertical hold, as they were mysteriously in need of adjustment. 'No, it wasn't me dad honest.'

There was only one channel then, BBC, and it was marvellous. It was a number of years before ITV appeared, received with a little wooden box on top of the set with a dial having about ten numbers in anticipation of lots more channels which I used to click round to see if any had appeared. I nearly wore the switch out before BBC 2 arrived. In fact we got a new telly to celebrate.

The TV always smelt rather hot and of burning insulation, and a funny pungent nose-crinkling odour that I always associate with electric. All this was long before the remote control gets stuck down the cushion on the sofa. The nearest thing we had to a remote was my dad telling me to get up and turn the volume up as I was a lot younger and fitter than he was. Or my grandmother trying to turn the volume up with her walking stick and only partially succeeding. Although she said she had trouble getting up, it was mainly because she didn't like touching it in case she got an electric shock.

The picture was very grainy, jumpy and had funny white horizontal lines across the screen. The picture also had a strange little half picture down the right-hand side, which the TV engineer rather confidently pronounced was a ghost, which I had nightmares about until it was explained to me it was a signal bouncing off the hill over the other side of the valley, and getting to the aerial a little bit late. That made good sense and the nightmares changed to other childish worries. The aerial was a massive 'H' on a long pole, strapped to the chimney with steel cables, which would regularly blow down in winter gales, as we were so high up on the exposed hillside but, perversely, behind another hill which blocked the signal from the transmitter.

We were told by our expert knowledgeable TV engineer that we were in between the two transmitters, 'Winter Hill and Emley Moor and neither were adequate to give us a decent picture because of all the hills, but I thought the names sounded rather magical. I remember asking my grandmother who lived with us at the time if she owned Emley Moor as her name was Emily. Her enigmatic reply was, 'No pet, my surname isn't Moor.'

The TV engineer became a regular visitor to 'change a valve' or 'adjust the aerial' or 'change a resistor or capacitor.' One of his classic excuses in spring, and beyond, when changing a valve didn't improve the picture, was, 'The sap was rising in the trees and blocking the signal.' This being all new technology my parents had to believe him, although they were a little dubious about the phrase being bandied about in winter until the engineer changed his tack and said it was snow on the transmitter.

TV reception was always very poor in certain places in the Aire valley because of all the hills, so an enterprising firm in Keighley thought they would bring TV to poor areas by cable. This was years before the cable TV we see today and was rather crude but effective and only went out of business when they installed a booster transmitter on a hill overlooking the valley in the late seventies. You can still see some of the cables stretched along house fronts where they have never been removed.

All this fascinated me and I would try to peer around the engineer into the dark, dusty interior with its red glowing valves and tubes when he had the back off. Some even had blue electrical discharges around them, which the engineer warned me about, saying, 'Yeh wont even have to touch them to get a very nasty shock young'n, it'll come across and get ye if ye get close enough.' Luckily, unlike my grandfather and the red hot metal, he told me first before the practical lesson!

All this must have inspired me in some way as I eventually became a TV engineer apprentice, at least for a time, but that's a later story.

Some of those early programmes are still vivid in my mind, even after nearly half a century: Muffin the Mule, (I had an actual puppet of Muffin, probably worth an absolute fortune now, but God knows what happened to it) Hank, (was that the real name of the programme? It was a ventriloquist dummy dressed up like a cowboy sat on a fence, and he sang as well), Bill and Ben (with Weed asking if it was Bill or Ben that had been naughty? Mind you I think that's still running, or until very recently, it seems.), Torchy the Battery Boy, Watch with Mother with Daphne Oxenford (what a quaint old fashioned name), 'Crackerjack' with Eamonn Andrews and 'Double Or Drop'. Then progressing to programmes like Robin Hood, William Tell just as naive and historically incorrect as Rawhide and Bonanza, and many others probably stretching into adulthood which I won't admit to watching. Their memories all act as a time machine that transport me back, sat on the chair in the front room silently watching the tiny screen. My mother in the kitchen preparing dinner, my father coming through the door from milking the cows. The not unpleasant smell of the cowshed on his clothes mixing with the smell of cooking food from the kitchen. Now I find it difficult trying to remember what I had for breakfast by lunch time, even though it's still porridge, and yet I can remember the smell of cows, and leek and kidney pudding cooking fifty years back!

Then along came ITV with the impressive add-on box on the top of the set with the dial on the front with ten positions! Optimistically heralding the advent again of multi-channels, then forty odd years later we have four. As I write this, we still don't have Channel Five, around here and no cable, (too far out) and satellite doesn't count, for the simple reason it seems to be all the good stuff brought from other channels with crap films thrown in.

I can even remember my first advert on ITV, which was for Murray Mints, the 'too good to hurry mints'. Apart from remembering the jingle, I never bought any. So much for the power of advertising. Can you still get them?

It was definitely a time of innocence, well as far as some were concerned. I watched 'Captain Pugwash' in total innocence with millions of others. With parents secure in the belief that the broadcasting authority's censors had removed any sexual innuendos like 'Master Bates', 'Seaman Staines', and the rather horrendous concept of 'Roger the cabin boy', but were obviously as naive as we were.

Perhaps less sexually provocative and probably done in true innocence were Looby Loo's intimate encounters with Andy Pandy in that large wicker basket with the lid down. I'm not so sure about the innocence of the content of the Magic Roundabout but that was French and we all know what the French are like.

I was once related a story that rather amuses me about the early days of the BBC. Their sound- mixing desks were custom made and a little unusual as the volume sliders were upside down. Unlike all other sound desks that went up for maximum and down for minimum the BBC's sound desks were the opposite. These had to be ordered specially from the manufacturers. This was fine as there was an agreement established, and the volume controls were affectionately known as AOT sliders by the respective parties. But as time past and the parties retired, the slides appeared in the official catalogue as AOT. The abbreviation was eventually surreptitiously removed when it was discovered AOT stood for 'Arse over tit.'

In my mid twenties, we had our own TV but a couple we were friends with were a bit radical and scornful of our telly saying it was a time waster and they didn't need to be entertained in their home. One day when we called on them they took a long time to answer the door and we were worried we had caught them having a bit of a 'love in' on the sofa. When they finally came to the door looking a little flushed we confronted them with our suspicions. They eventually admitted we had caught them watching TV, and in their embarrassment they had bundled it up stairs and hidden it under the bed. That is along with the cannabis plant they had growing in the corner of the living room.

Unlike the kids today (oh no I'm doing that 'now when I was a lad' routine and I may as well tell you now there might be quite a few of those to come. Were was I? Oh yes) unlike the kids today my time then spent in front of a TV screen would only amount to at most a couple of hours a week if that, no daytime TV and even in the evening at odd times a big sign would appear saying intermission, with some guy in an apron working at a potter's wheel. Also my dad's assertion that if I watched too much television I would get square eyes, and I didn't want that as I wasn't the most good looking kid at the best of times.

There was a whole world out there to explore, play rough games, biking and making things. TV was not bad but not the real thing. There was also the cinema with cowboy films to inspire rough necking, fighting, and killing! Well perhaps things haven't changed all that much after all. But at least we did get fresh air and plenty of exercise with restricted TV and no computers.

— 6 —

HAYMAKING TIME

FOR ALL YOU townies out there, with pictures of Constable's idyllic Haywain on their wall, I don't go that far back (not quite). Nor is real haymaking idyllic. It's bloody back breaking hard, sweaty and dusty work. Basically grass is cut, left to dry in the sun (hopefully), then brought into a barn or made into a haystack outside if you were unable to afford an extra barn or if the one you had would not hold enough hay to feed your number of cows you had over the winter. Not forgetting the cows had to spend a good five months in the barn not only from the cold but because there was no grass growing in the fields.

The drying part obviously relies on sunshine and no rain, which can be a scarce commodity in the Yorkshire Dales, well at least the sunshine. So it was all hands to the job in an almost frantic panic when the sun shone between showers. First the grass had to be cut by a mowing machine, a lethal looking contraption with a four-foot arm out from the side, much like a giant hedge trimmer, which would chop off fingers and was quite capable of cutting off legs of the unwary.

A friend of my father who was a regular visitor to the farm had that happen to him. I always remember he used to laugh uproariously when our sheep dog Bess made it her aim in life to sneak up behind anybody entering the farm yard and have a nip at friend or foe. Bess tried her usual sneaky rear attack, on my dad's friend's leg and lost a few teeth on his pot legs.

The story goes that this gentleman was cutting down a field for hay with a particular lethal combination of Fordson tractor and mower, whereby the Fordson tractor had a rather novel clutch and brake system which shared the same pedal. You first pressed down the pedal for the clutch then further down it became a brake. This was quite easy to use as one action disengaged the gears and stopped the tractor, except that it was also the parking brake, for there was a small catch that held the brake on. My father's friend pressed the clutch pedal, leaving the tractor in gear, locked the brake on, raised the cutting blade to above knee height, and leaped off the tractor to clean the blade that had become clogged. The small catch slipped off the pedal, the brake came off, the clutch engaged, the tractor surged forward and severed both his legs. This by all accounts was not an uncommon event. In future models that particular innovation was not a feature. Little consolation for the hundreds that were crushed and mutilated by this apparently user-friendly design.

Although we had a mowing machine from the start I have seen a field cut by hand with a scythe but it was very rare as, after the war agriculture moved on in leaps and bounds. We did have a scythe though, one like Old Father Time carries to reap the dead. It was used to cut the grass in the corners of the field where the cutter could not reach. Nothing was wasted!

Once the grass was cut it was left to dry for a day or so, depending on the weather, then turned to dry the other side. Initially, till we bought a machine to turn it, it was done by hand. A very time-consuming labour, with your arm not belonging to you after completing a five-acre field. I recently was discussing old haymaking times with a young farmer. As I was relating the joys of turning a whole field by hand with a wooden rake, he gave me a quizzical look and told me I was joking! 'Yer not that old. That was how they did it in Victorian times, you'll be telling me next that you forked loose hay on a flat cart drawn by a horse.' What could I say but no, we had a tractor pulling the cart and left it at that. When both sides of the grass were dry the whole lot had to be shook, and fluffed up with a pitch fork to let it dry completely.

All this depended on four or five days of sunshine and if at any stage it was to rain, the whole process had to be repeated. It was imperative that it was as dry as possible, otherwise, when it was stored inside it would go mouldy and spoil at best, or at worst, heat up to a very high temperature and catch fire when stacked in the barn or stack. My father always had a long metal rod which he would insert into the hay moo to check its temperature. When pulled back out if it was too hot to touch, the whole stack would have to be pulled out before it could spontaneously burst into flames. This never happened to us but on odd occasions we would see a barn fire on the other side of the valley of a less cautious farmer, particularly after wet summers, and thank our lucky stars it was not ours.

For a long time we could not afford to have our hay baled, and we could not justify the vast cost of buying a baling machine on such a small farm, even if our small tractor was capable of pulling it. So for many years we had to laboriously load the hay loose with a fork onto a trailer, which was pulled by a tractor back to the barn. There it was forked off up into the barn, sometimes in as many as three stages to get the hay right to the top of the barn and so make maximum use of the space. This was all carried out in a hot, dusty, dark barn, with twenty to thirty tons of hay each year. All with the weather as the deadline.

We eventually could afford to have our hay baled by contractors. This was a great labour saving innovation as you could quickly stack a trailer with much more hay than when it was loose. Although some caution was advised as if you got carried away and went too high in stacking the bales, or were a little slap-happy in packing, a bit of a bump in a rutted gateway would bring down the stack, passengers and all, as the stacker's tended to ride back to the barn on top of the stacked bales to unload them.

Another labour saving device with baling was a sledge towed behind the baler, so instead of the bales just being dropped all over the field, the sledge was stacked with about ten bales or so and dropped in one place so the tractor and trailer could collect all the bales in one place. I say labour saving, not for me it wasn't! I was usually the poor sod that rode on the sledge, stacking and tipping them off. It was hot, sweaty, dusty, work as the bales were coming at you at one every twenty seconds or so. I suppose I made life harder for myself because I would try to drop the bales off in a straight line across the middle of the field. That involved stacking the bales high so the stacks were dropped only twice in a complete circle of the field. Sounds simple but it was a matter of honour to line them up. It developed muscles that I still have today and a work ethic that in my opinion is a little lacking in most of the youth of today.

In the meantime it was loose hay gathered in the traditional way. One innovation for fields close to the farm was designed by my father. He constructed a large wooden sledge-cum-fork that fit on the front of the tractor to scoop up the loose hay. He had seen this on a farm during his land army days and with a little help from my uncle who was a joiner they had made a copy. It was a real boon as one person on a tractor could clear a field of loose hay in a fraction of the time it would take three men with a tractor and trailer with forks. The loose hay still had to be forked onto the trailer but at least it was all in one place.

With the old method one person had to slowly drive the tractor up and down the rows while one forked the hay up, and another stacked the hay on the trailer. Stacking and forking loose hay was a real art; forkers had to avoid stabbing the stacker with the lethal prongs of the hay-fork and the stacker had to avoid being stabbed by novice forkers while grabbing the forkful of hay and stacking it. The hay would be as high as the man forking the hay from the ground could reach. That was as high as ten foot, and had to stand the test of being driven back across the bumpy fields without dropping off. The hay sledge conversely would be driven up and down the rows of hay scooping it up into a bundle and trundled straight back to the farm from some fields that were close enough then would be forked up into the barn. In hard times when my parents could neither afford paid-helpers, nor find any willing relations or friends, the whole family got stuck in my mum, dad, and me.

There were a lot of farms far less ‘advanced’ than we were, run by generation after generation of farming families especially further up the dales. My father had made a lot of friends when he worked as a land army foreman and would go and help out when we had finished our haymaking if they were short handed and take me along. The money was not good but the workers were always well fed at lunch time. A welcome sight would be the farmer’s wife who would march across the fields towards the workers with a basket in the crook of her elbow and swinging a large enamel canteen of tea. She would never come directly to the workers but set out the meal some distance in front where she estimated they would reach by the time she had set out the picnic on the grass, time was short between showers at hay time.

When all the haymakers had arrived and sat on the grass, they would be issued with a bowl which would be filled with the main course which was inevitably shepherd's pie. You learned to eat it all up and scrape up your gravy with the piece of home-made bread you were issued with. For as soon as the farmer's wife deemed it was time for the sweet, it was dumped into the same bowl. Again you had to be careful to not leave anything (not easy with no bread to clear up you custard) as the tea was poured soon after, yet again in the same receptacle.

My mother wasn't only in charge of catering, as I said she could drive a tractor better than most men. She would be out there bringing the hay back to the barn or using the little machinery we possessed. I have a picture in my mind's eye of my mother in a cotton, summer-flowered dress riding the tractor across the field, none of your overalls. My mother liked to remain feminine even on a tractor.

It never ceased to amaze me how my friends would actually volunteer to come and help at hay time. I suppose it was only for a few weeks a year and was fun and exciting for them whereas I was there all year round and if felt like bloody hard work. I'm not complaining. It was a great life, really.

— 7 —

MY FIRST JOB

I really like poking screwdrivers in and getting lots of nice sparks

ON LEAVING SCHOOL my first job was at a TV sales and repair shop in my home town. This was thought by my parents to be the up and coming career for a young man who had shown some aptitude with electricity, even though this involved lighting a torch bulb with two wires and a battery. This used to impress my mother and father who were easily impressed by things like that. Receiving excruciating shocks from the mains when my experiments progressed from batteries to mains electricity, was far more worrying for my parents as they were concerned about my well- being as parents do for their offspring, but they assumed with the proper training I would survive.

I even constructed an electric ray gun at the tender age of ten. That consisted of a plastic tube with a live and neutral exposed with a trigger that brought them together. The theory was that the electric would shoot out of the end of the tube as a ray, like that fired by Dan Dare, a character in a comic book that I was keen on at the time. Once plugged into the mains I should be able to deal with any unfriendly aliens that should happen along, assuming the mains lead would reach the infestation. Even my dad, who was not very knowledgeable about electricity, ray guns, and unfriendly aliens for that matter, was adamant that it wouldn't work and was liable to kill me and not the aliens. The ray gun was confiscated and I went on to less dangerous hobbies like gunpowder and rockets, but never lost my fascination with electric - hence my first job.

Actually I didn't know what I wanted to be when I grew up, still don't for that matter, but at the time a TV engineer seemed OK so I went with the flow. The TV repair shop job came with an apprenticeship, which all the best jobs did in those days, and a day release to the local Technical College. Funnily enough over the five years I spent in TV repair a revolution in electronics was taking place. At college we made up circuits with valves, used in all TV's. If you peered in the back you would see a hot and dusty fairy tale land of dull red, glowing, glass tubes, with the occasional blue aura discharging from very high voltage tube that was required to produce the picture, and would take about five minutes to 'warm up' before the picture appeared.

The revolution of course was transistors and then silicon chips, which were a lot of transistors all scrunched up in a single block of plastic with pins for all the connections. This was the start of the trend where by if it went faulty, the repairman would replace whole chunks of the inside of your equipment, to repair it, which you could just about teach monkeys to do. Then as electronic equipment became even more reliable, even this was not cost effective, so the age of built-in obsolescence was born, Rather than have it repaired, instead customers bought the latest models, so the TV repairman died, or at least were severely reduced in numbers, and resigned to attending little old ladies who had forgotten where the on/off switch was, making it not a good career move.

No problem, I hated it anyway, although in some respects it gave me a good grounding in electricity and electronics, which has secured me work over the years although in other fields than TV repair may I add.

Repairing TV's in people's houses was very character building, to say the least, with a liberal helping of psychology. As an apprentice, I would go out to repair TV's with an experienced engineer, and into some of the worst council estates in Bradford, when not making tea for the shop manager that is. You could always tell a 'bad' house by the state of the garden, not just unkempt,- we're talking dead dogs here! - with lots of rubbish and the occasional burnt-out car. The smell when the owner opened the door would be indescribable, although I feel it my duty to tell you, and describe in detail. Urine, stale cooking fat, unwashed bodies, and all this trapped in a room that has not seen ventilation or light since a brick smashed through the front window probably about a year or two ago last Christmas, and has been boarded up with cardboard and Sellotape ever since. The main living room where the telly was would be piled high with heaps of unwashed clothes, cardboard boxes spewing everything from broken toys, more unwashed clothes, beer cans, newspapers, broken ornaments and part-dismantled electric appliances. Once I even found a large furry mouldy dog turd behind the TV I lifted out to repair, well I assume it was a long- deposited dog turd, as there was a dead dog in the garden! The carpet was usually indistinguishable from the garden and would probably sprout weed on the less trodden parts with a little more sunlight. Wiping ones shoes when leaving the house, not entering, was a necessity. This is where experience of the engineer came in and was probably the reason I was under his wing. He had already taken a blanket from the van after one look at the garden, and partially cardboard boarded-up windows. Before entering he would take a deep breath, quickly approach the TV, throw the blanket over it, unplug it, pick it up and while carrying it to the door breathlessly tell the customer that it would have to go back to the workshop. On placing it in the van the blanket would be raised momentarily to spray the set with air freshener purposely placed in the back of the van for just such an emergency. As we made a quick dash back to the work shop, I inquired why he had not even switched it on he replied. 'No time to wait for it to warm up, I was holding my breath, weren't you?'

The offending TV would be brought in with blankets still over it and have a very quick turn- over in the workshop. So quick in fact that the engineer in charge would tell the guy who brought it in to go have a cup of tea and it would be ready in half an hour. It was the smell you see, no amount of air freshener could mask the smell when the set warmed up with all those valves, and the engineer stirring it up, prodding about in the back of the set. It was quickly repaired and returned back to the customer, short shrift.

Not all customers were like that, sometimes we would even drink the offered tea. Although you had to be careful even at the nicest houses. Sometimes strange-tasting tea that was indistinguishable from coffee, and sludgy brown stains at the bottom of the cup usually meant you would have been better off saying, 'Thanks luv I've just had one,' even though you were gagging.

Sometimes you wouldn't see the customer at all as they would leave a key with a neighbour, although in this case I am about to relate, we did eventually meet the owner. We had retrieved the key from next door, gone into the house and turned on the television. The engineer I was with suddenly felt the urgent need for the toilet and trundled off upstairs leaving me standing by the TV. Not a minute had passed when the customer walked in, and I was just about to explain his presence upstairs when he bellowed down to me, 'There's no sodding bog roll up here, bring us something up to wipe my arse with.' The customer and I just looked at each other, she winked and said, 'I'll take him some up.'

What could I do? A very red-faced TV repairman, who had been handed the toilet roll by the customer while he was sitting on the throne, repaired the TV and we left quickly. He mumbled continually to me the rest of the day about the lack of loyalty in young people nowadays especially apprentices. Although he eventually must have seen the funny side of the situation as it soon got round the workshop. Not by me, may I add, as I was sworn to secrecy on pain of death. Well I may have let it slip over tea break!!

The guys in the workshop were a mad lot. I have often seen them playing catch throwing a glass TV tube between half a dozen of them. The one to drop it had to pick up the pieces, if he survived! Or when he came back from A&E, as a TV tube is under high vacuum and goes with quite an impressive bang. Adding to the fun it tended to store a rather high voltage if it was just removed from a TV, and if caught in the wrong way, this discharged through the catcher, almost inevitably resulting in him dropping it from the electric shock. Health and Safety was, in those days, only applied to children under 5 years of age working down mines.

As an apprentice you went through the usual initiation ceremony. Nothing serious involving boot polish, feathers and treacle, mind, you were just being sent to the stores for things like left-handed screw drivers, a long weight and a long stand. Long wait, long stand. Get it? With an hour or so standing outside the store with people walking past smirking at you.

Of course TV servicing apprentices got far more sophisticated initiations than mere plumbing or engineering apprentices. We would get a charge-up component called a capacitor with a couple of hundred volts, throw it at some victim shouting, 'Here catch this,' giving the catcher a nasty jolt. I remember my first few week as an apprentice getting some quite nasty electric shocks, and receiving an even greater one when I tried to do the same and charge up a capacitor from the mains, exploding the capacitor in my hand, and blowing out the entire shops fuses (quick lesson in electronics, you can't charge a capacitor with AC mains electricity).

A story I was once told was about an apprentice on a building site one of whose duties was to make tea for all the lads on the site. There was this big water boiler and the lad used to just throw a handful of tea bags in and boil it up. One day there was a general consensus among the lads sitting around in the rest hut on site that the tea had got so bad as to be undrinkable and the apprentice was summoned to account for the disgusting taste of the tea. The lad was a little pedantic saying he made it just the same as he always did, just throw some tea bags in and boil the water. One of the lads gave him a quizzical look and asked him if he emptied the old tea bags out first. The lad's reply caused a bit of an uproar when he declared, 'Yeh, of course, probably about once a week!' This instigated one of the lads to pick up the tea urn and tip it upside down, depositing a large pile of soggy, mouldy tea bags on the floor, and, to the dismay of the gathered tea drinkers, a rather stewed very dead mouse, that had climbed in looking for nibbles and a warm hidey hole. The said apprentice kept his job, just, and never had to make tea again but he got some pretty lousy, horrible jobs for the rest of his apprenticeship.

I worked at three TV shops during my relatively short foray into radio and TV servicing and at one of them I was expected to help install aerials. This, of course, involved clambering about on roofs, an occupation that holds no joy, and an awful lot of dread for me, especially with very dodgy ladders and no safety equipment. Health and Safety would have a fit nowadays. It was probably the equivalent of the Victorians sending children up chimneys to sweep them. In my case with my poor head for heights, and sometimes freezing rain, snow and hail to contend with, the inside of a chimney would have been preferable to the roof outside.

Quite a lot of customers were concerned for your well-being even if the boss showed none. Cups of hot tea were usually waiting for you after coming down from the roof, and were usually gratefully accepted no matter the state of the house. Although sometimes the concern was a bit misguided, as some customers would flatly refuse to let you switch on the TV with the back off as it clearly stated in big red letters, 'Do not remove this cover when switched on'. This proved a little difficult to comply with as it's fairly essential to do both to repair the thing. One had to try and convince the customer that you really knew what you were doing. Sometimes a little unconvincing when at the previous house you had perhaps inadvertently brushed ones hand against a hot valve or touched a live wire with something like 20,000 volts on it and had to pick yourself up from the other side of the room, looking distinctly pale.

There was a lot of psychology involved in TV repair, as well as technology. One of the engineers I worked with was a master. It was a time when most people rented TVs because of the initial expense and the poor reliability. People felt cheated paying rent year after year if it didn't break down, so they would call you out anyway. The trick was to convince them that you had serviced the set, changed lots of components and improved the picture one hundred percent. One of the ways the 'master' achieved this was to position himself behind the set with the customer in front watching the screen. He would role the picture with a control called the vertical hold (not found on modern TV as it's done automatically with clever electronics). As a series of identical pictures rolled over the screen, the engineer would get the customer to say when the 'best' picture appeared; he would then adjust it so the picture locked on to what the customer had picked as the 'best'. Hey presto one happy customer.

It didn't always work. So out would come the impressive valve case with its clusters of neatly packaged glass valves. After rummaging about in the back of the set and extracting a couple of dusty valves at random, he would then fit the new shiny ones and switch on. The picture would be much the same. However they were a happy customer and the rental firm did not lose out too badly as the extracted valves were dusted off and used for the next customers who needed a little therapy.

I was privileged to be present at the unveiling of the first colour TV to go on display in a shop window in Bradford. It had been made at the Baird factory just up the road and our TV shop had been chosen for its premier.

All the engineers gathered round, had the back off in minutes and were avidly going through the workshop manual seeing what they would be up against when they were first called out to repair the beast. One rather rotund bumptious engineer elbowed himself to the front, took one look at the blue glow around the tube, and exclaimed, 'Bloody hell.' He referred the manual, quoted an astronomical figure for the voltage feeding the tube and shouted, rather dramatically, 'Everybody stand back, the bastard is radioactive.' Then, with no other explanation, ran out of the shop. There was a stunned silence in which everyone took a step back nervously smiling at one another. The silence was broken by the shop manager who was having none of this nonsense on this special occasion and shooed everyone into the back workshop, only instantly to troop out again on the return of the rotund dramatic engineer waving a Geiger counter. Parking the instrument on the top of the TV, he then made a theatrical gesture of turning on the machine and waving the detector head around in the back of the colour TV. Even from the distance that we had all retreated, we were in no doubt of his previous claim to the toxicity of the blue area we had seen. The manic clicking of the Geiger counter with its little meter needle hard over into the red. Even the less technical among us had seen enough atomic disasters movies to take a good two paces back this time.

Within thirty minutes a van had pulled up outside the shop and two strong men had bundled the offending colour-set in the back and burnt rubber back to the factory.

A colour TV was not on display for another month and actually for some considerable time after that. When it was returned it was extensively modified and shielded, perhaps a little too enclosed in retrospect, for within an hour it had caught fire in the shop window nearly burning the entire shop down. It was some time later over tea break the question arose, 'Why the hell did that engineer have a Geiger counter in his car?' For some reason no-one dare ask the engineer in question!

As you may have gathered TV engineers were all a bunch of loonies and con men. I can say con MEN as it was a totally male preserve! Because women were scared of electricity in those days? Probably more to do with gender fixing as most girls did domestic science, typing, or child–care. The sciences were for the boys. Anyway the TV repairmen I met were all barking mad, some more than others, possibly due to the radiation from the sets they repaired.

One turn of fate was that one of the more sane engineers introduced me to amateur dramatics and this had a profound effect on my life. Not actually acting as such, may I firmly note, but the technical side of theatre certainly fascinated me. Although I did tread the boards, as they say in theatre for going on stage, it was usually with either disastrous results or a very discreet appearance right at the back as part of the chorus. And sometimes even walk-on parts with no lines and miming the songs as I did not wish to spoil the harmony.

Following on from my first profession, I progressed to progress-chasing in a large factory which made switches! That involved wandering around this huge factory looking for lost switches. This turned out to be as riveting as TV engineering, well no, make that far less riveting!

After that I went for diversity. There followed a series of jobs among them were cement mixer at a works that made concrete lintels, (my predecessor having fallen into the large mixer and died!) lab technician, photographer for a car-sales magazine, wedding photographer, with a few baby portraits in between, burglar alarm installer, plumber, gardener, greeting-card salesman, audio- visual technician, (sounds grander than it actually was), and school nurse! Interspersed with buying junk and selling it at antique fairs and car-boot sales. I have been gainfully occupied all my life!

Now I'm retired, hopefully an author!

— 8 —

AMATEUR DRAMATICS

AT THE INNOCENT and tender age of seventeen I became a Thespian. It was certainly an eye- opener for a young man. There were men dressing up as women and women dressing as men, and that was just backstage! Yes, the roar of the crowd and the smell of the grease-paint definitely have an addictive appeal. It was in the genes as my mother in her youth played leads in the village hall productions in Oxenhope. I have a picture of her in an old newspaper cutting, sitting on a moon, singing and smiling at the audience, looking a lot younger than I remember her.

Although my attraction was more on the technical side like lighting, sound, pyrotechnics, and general backstage work, I eventually did have a yen, albeit, misguided to tread the boards. Misguided for a young man who could not dance, sing, and with no acting ability at all, cruelly but accurately referred to as equivalent to Eddy Edwards' skiing ability. He was famous at the time for his enthusiastic but disastrous Olympic skiing performance.

Why they let me on stage at all was a complete mystery; possibly a lack of young men willing to dress up in silly costumes, sympathy, or just hoping I would be vaguely unnoticed in the chorus, right at the back just to fill a space. Come to think of it, the director did tend to position me well at the back for most productions, usually the third villager on the right, and the musical director would scowl at me from the orchestra pit if I got carried away and actually sang instead of mimed.

To give the Society its due, they did try and encourage me by giving me a named part once. The musical was the 'King and I' and I was the king's son's chief courtier called Phra Alack, would you believe.

One of my more memorable lines was to rush on stage shouting to the king's son. 'Master, master your father's deeing.' In moments of stress I do tend to revert to very broad Yorkshire, (as opposed to only mild broad Yorkshire for my normal speech). Luckily this was in rehearsals. The director took me on one side with his arm around my shoulder and explained, in a rather patronising manner, that, inasmuch as it would be difficult to conduct the musical in Siamese even if Rodgers and Hammerstein had required it, a broad Yorkshire accent was perhaps a little inappropriate. To further complicate matters I was rushed into hospital with appendicitis after the first night, and in the true spirit of the show must go on, I made it back on stage for the last two performances four days later, much to the disappointment of my understudy, and the director, for that matter, who I am sure would have preferred the understudy, as I did tend to revert back to my broad native tongue again on my return.

That was my first and last named part, but I did kind of get my own back. Some shows later I was given the part of a gorilla in the pantomime 'Robinson Crusoe'. This was nothing to do with my acting ability, it was just that I just happened to have a gorilla suit, (but that's another story).

Everything went well at rehearsals, I was to appear behind the two main comedy actors and then disappear when the audience shouted, 'Behind you' and at one point I had to eat a banana held by 'Sammy,' Mrs Robinson's lodger, (my director friend). All went well till about the second night by which time I had gained a bit of confidence. I was about to eat the banana out of his hand but it fell off onto the floor. Undeterred he picked it up, placed it back in the skin, and held it out so I could eat it. The only thing was that it was now covered in dust muck and I definitely spotted a hair grip from one of the ladies of the cast embedded in the banana. Even with a gorilla mask on the audience could spot my reluctance to consume this now-contaminated inedible fruit. Being panto the audience thought it was all part of the act and rolled in the aisles. So I hammed it up a bit, to more laughter as I exaggerated taking bits of debris off my tongue. The next night, thinking he was getting the laughs, Sammy flicked the banana onto the floor on purpose going through the same routine. With his back to me he could not tell I was getting the laughs, not until the final night when someone told him. When he stopped dropping the banana, spoiled my impromptu comedy sketch, and told me to 'stick to the script!' I thought it prudent not to mention the gorilla was a nonspeaking part so had no script and, as far as I knew, his script didn't involve dropping his banana. That was definitely the last 'major' part to be offered, even in panto.

As well as being the gorilla in 'Robinson Crusoe' I was volunteered to black up and wear a grass skirt and hold Robinson prisoner in the desert island scene where Robinson, played by a rather gorgeous long-legged lady, is captured by savages. The native chief did a rather spectacular war dance, threatening Robinson with being eaten. Well, as much as I could empathise with the chief as Robinson was rather tasty; his war dance got a little scarier every night. By half way through the week during the scene Robinson whispered to me that she was terrified that the chief was really going to stab her with the knife albeit a wooden one. The only consolatory words I could muster were, 'You and me both, pet, and I'm supposed to be on his side.' To complicate matters further the tension of holding Robinson made me pull her arms a little too far behind her back, popping the buttons on her jacket but luckily only revealing a perhaps rather inappropriate feminine blouse. We both survived the week with only minor lacerations and splinters, and no further revelations in underwear. We all had a good laugh about it at the end of the week.

Perhaps about that time I decided to keep to backstage, which was more fun anyway. Backstage was always teaming with scantily clad young ladies in tight ballet dresses, or exotically dressed chorus ladies who were not opposed to passionate kisses and cuddles behind the scenes. If you were really lucky you could be sent on an errand to the front of house, which involved having to walk through the ladies' dressing room during a major costume change. Some of the sights were a huge eye-opener for a young innocent lad. The principal's dressing room was a definite no-go, after one night during a pantomime when I saw the ageing male dame in nothing but padded bra and panties. Did he really have to wear female underwear under his costume? Yuk! Enough to put a young man off sex for life. It didn't though!

One rather gorgeous young dancer who I quite fancied but, at seventeen, was far too young for me, always had a smile for me. I used to take photographs of some of the cast posing on stage in their costumes during the interval and give them copies. I took some great ones of my favourite little dancer and duly gave her them at the end of the show. She was very pleased with them and asked me what I wanted for them. Pushing my luck I pointed at my cheek and asked for a kiss. She smiled sweetly at me and said, 'If I try to kiss you on the cheek you'll turn your head at the last minute and I'll end up kissing you on the lips. That's just what my pervy uncle does.' I tried to look hurt and shocked about the insinuation but could only grin sheepishly as I had been sussed.

Affairs backstage were always an interesting topic in the Society and there were some very tangled relationships going on. Some were discreet and some very blatant. Some were spectacularly revealed as in the two married principals (not to each other) who were whispering what they were going to do to each other after the show, in a quite corner backstage. Unfortunately for them, their radio microphones were still switched on and their licentious indiscretions were shared by the audience and backstage alike, through the sound system. On another occasion a radio- microphoned principal had a rather noisy turn, out in the backstage toilet which added richly to the show's sound effects, albeit a little out of kilter with the impassioned love song being acted out on stage between two principals.

One radio microphone incident in which I became involved in indirectly was when one of the minor principals in a panto developed a bit of a sore throat, probably as a result of nerves, on the second night of the week-long show. She approached the sound engineer for a radio mic to get her through the rest of the week for her 'very, very important solo'. Perhaps her approach was a little demanding, so being a little peeved and not having a spare radio mic anyway, he gave her a duff one he just happened to have in his tool box. Her performance and song for the rest of the week went well, despite her lack of amplification. On the night before the last performance, the sound engineer and I were having a bit of a laugh about the mishaps during the week's show, when he divulged the secret of the lady with the broken, silent mic. Now this is where the story gets a little hazy as I cannot remember for the life of me, passing this on to a third party, especially the lady in question. Just before the final performance the sound engineer became painfully aware that his little deception had been revealed, as the lady left him in no doubt of her opinion of his professionalism, his integrity and his legitimacy. Then he blamed me for blabbing! I must say, with my hand on my heart and swear on my mother's grave, I didn't, well at least I don't think I did! Anyway he reminds me about it on a regular basis as we are still friends and I promised faithfully not to mention it in this book. Oops!

Soppy panto love songs are always a source of amusement to me. I was once witness backstage to an especially comic incident when a rather sweet but sickly love song was being acted out on stage in front of a packed audience. The scene was set whereby the principal girl and principal boy, also a girl as principal boys in panto traditionally are, were approaching one another across the stage, having rose petals scattered from above over them by the stage manager sat astride a girder over the stage. At a crucial moment when they were about to touch hands, the shoe of the guy who was scattering the rose petals fell off and dropped between the lovers, with a resounding thud and a little fountain of rose petals, rather spoiling the ambiance. But being true professionals they carried on their love song to each other with barely a falter.

By the way, have you ever wondered how two girls can sing sickly sweet love songs to each other on stage while gazing into each other's eyes and keep from giggling? The only way, I have been told on good authority, is that they stare fixedly over each other’s shoulders, avoiding eye contact at all costs. Especially I should imagine when a shoe falls among the rose petals between you with a loud plop!

Another time I was innocently lounging backstage between scenes of a pantomime which traditionally has lots of custard pies and wicked genies appearing in flashes and smoke. The scene was set for the pie to blow up after the dame left it in the oven too long. It was a good ten minutes before it was scripted to go off, so I assumed it was safe to sit on the reinforced barrel that the theatrical explosive, maroon, was to be electrically detonated. Well it would have been, if the same one-shoed stage manager hadn’t decided to prepare for the detonation by switching on the gadget which fires the explosive, while pressing the firing button by mistake. Wow was that a shock! I was staggering about backstage in a confused and shell- shocked state when, to add insult to injury, the stage manager rushed up to me and told me off for sitting on it. Mind you he got his comeuppance. When the dame came off stage at the end of the scene, my telling-off paled into insignificance compared with the roasting he got as he ruined her ham perform ... sorry I mean his dazzling performance. Mind you that particular stage manager was definitely accident prone. One show required the stage to have a fog effect drifting across stage. This was achieved by dropping dry ice into hot water. The container for the hot water had rather a narrow neck and a large chunk of dry ice got stuck, the stage manager in a bit of a panic, as usual when something went wrong, tried to push the ice down with his foot. The inevitable happened, the ice dropped and our beloved stage manager's foot splashed down in the near boiling water. As far as I remember he managed not to swear, but he did howl and joined the dancing girls on stage as he hopped enthusiastically through the now impressive fog, out of step and almost drowning out the orchestra's rather delicate rendering of the Sugar Plum Fairy.

Another incident with theatrical maroons was during a play that needed a large explosion during a dramatic scene. Again a large dustbin was used with mesh on top and the maroon dangled in from the top. The lid was always left off to allow the not-insubstantial explosion to dissipate out. However a very tidy minded theatre chairman thought dustbins should always have their lids firmly secured at all times. The consequences being that when the maroon was detonated remotely at the appropriate time, the ensuing explosion was pretty spectacular. Three old ladies on the front row died of a heart attack (no, only joking). But the dustbin lid was nowhere to be found until eventually someone looked up and discovered the lid embedded in the ceiling.

My own management of theatrical maroons came when I was deemed responsible to handle dangerous materials, (really!). It was at the theatre when a play required an explosion at the end of Act One. I decided that the dustbin didn't have the proper bass acoustics, so I brought in an old water tank. I was quite pleased with the results at rehearsal and waxed lyrically about the deep, full acoustics of the explosion in the tank. Although the director didn't show quite the same enthusiasm, he eventually expressed no objection. The prompt on the other hand whinged it was damaging his delicate hearing and made him jump every time it went off, nearly dropping his script (wimp!) Admittedly it was on his side of the stage as he sat in the wings, but he was at the front and the tank was a good fifteen feet away towards the back of the stage. By the final performance the whining by the wimpy prompt was getting to me (not recommended to piss me off, but he didn't know me all that well). So, it appeared I had slightly over-ordered on the explosives and had three spare maroons on the last night. It felt a shame not to use them, so I wired all four together. I probably could have found a use for them eventually, but there was always another play to over-order for. Just to add to the effect and to piss off the prompt as much as he'd annoyed me all week, I moved the tank a little closer to his chair. Well when I say a little closer actually, it was three feet away, just far enough so he didn't see it behind a piece of scenery! I did quite regret my excess of revenge, but not a lot, it was sweet! The wimpy prompt fell backwards off his chair and needed to be helped to the kitchen and given three cups of hot sweet tea, before he stopped shaking, and it was touch and go if he could prompt the second half of the play. Not that he would have been much good at prompting the actors as he was quite deaf (which only lasted three days I was relieved to find out later). He could not hear the silences when the actors forgot their lines and was required to prompt, so kept adding his prompt every now and then anyway. The director took me on one side and voiced some concern about the violence of the explosion. I explained that I had connected four maroons together because I just happened to have some left ... no way! I lied as I was rather looking forward to still being in charge of pyrotechnics for future plays. So I explained that the maroons are quite variable and it must have been a particularly potent one. I'm not sure I convinced him, but it was the last night and the play had gone well so I got away with it, but sadly it was quite a while before I was in charge of pyrotechnics again.

I eventually managed to order some maroons for myself, and I'm afraid I was a little irresponsible with their use (surprise surprise). I used to connect them to friends' cars' ignition under the bonnet. Surprisingly most of them are still friends. The effect was quite spectacular when they came to start the car. After the explosion, smoke would drift up from the bonnet as the driver sat catatonic in the driving seat or leap out of the car and run away. I always tended to be close at hand to administer CPR if there were any accidents, and of course to prevent any unnecessary calls to the police (pre bomb squad). I usually didn't have to explain my part in the explosion, for, when they saw me, they understandably recognised my trademark humour, tending to express their feelings. They were then able to relieve their pent-up tension. Luckily I was never threatened with violence - well not seriously.

My theatrical sense of humour nearly did get me decked one time by a person I really didn't expect. He was a very quiet, unassuming kind of guy, never raised his voice or actually got excited about anything, almost to the point of being boring really. However I managed to stir him quite unintentionally by a simple clap of the hands. I was standing behind him as he had his head in a cupboard, connecting some electrical wires in a joint box. As I watched, I could tell he was a little unsure about two wires that seemed to be spare to requirements. I waited my moment till he touched the wires to terminals then clapped my hand loudly just behind his head. Withdrawing rather suddenly from the cupboard he failed to clear the frame by quite a few inches, severely banging his head in the process. On staggering back from the cupboard, slightly concussed, he questioned my parentage, grabbed me by the collar and attempted to lift me off the floor. Luckily he came to his senses, realised that this was out of character and, before I could even try to defend myself, put me down and stormed off. I did apologise later with a straight face, and it was accepted with a curt nod.

I've done a few stints as stage manager. For some small shows it can involve numerous duties including seeing all the cast are in the right place at the right time.

One time I was stage managing a revue involving various acts and compered by a rather famous TV newsreader. He was very professional, as you would expect, witty and eloquent on stage, but still friendly backstage chatting to us all. All was going well, a singer was just coming to the end of her song and the next act was dutifully waiting in the wings to be introduced. Then blind panic, no compère! I quickly scanned backstage, behind scenery, in among large props, no compère! Down a flight of stairs to the dressing room, and there he was holding an intense conversation with one of the acts in the second half of the show. By this time I could hear the act on stage coming to the end, so no time for 'excuse me or pardon me' but it was 'YER ON!' He just turned to me, said 'OK', and carried on with the conversation. I just looked panic-stricken and ran back to my post just in time for the singer to take a bow and walk off stage. Then with perfect timing the compere strolled on stage, waved to the departing singer and calmly introduced the next act. Immaculate timing, professionalism, or just luck. Well apart from giving me apoplexy, I'll give him ten out of ten for ultra cool.

A bit of a follow up from that story was some months later the wife and I were shopping in the local supermarket when someone passing said, 'Hi.' I hope I carried it off well by saying 'Hi' back, smiling, but I certainly did not fool my better half for, when we had passed, she looked at me incredulously saying, 'You didn't know who that was, did you? It's that famous newsreader. He recognised you!' Fame is a fickle thing, for the famous and non-famous alike.

Another embarrassing incident happened when I was assistant stage manager for a play. We had just arrived at the interval and there was a rather hectic scene change to achieve. So as soon as the stage manager had pulled the curtain we dashed on stage to get stuck in with the scene change. The first thing I knew that there was something amiss was when I cannoned into the back of the stage manager as he had stopped rather suddenly and was staring at the audience! The curtain had only half closed. The audience was in the throes of applauding the actors at the end of the scene, which quickly died on the exclamation of the exposed stage manger. In hindsight a rather loud ‘oh bloody hell’ by the said guy could have been a little more professional, but hindsight is useful, in my opinion, only for a laugh in the pub afterwards and professionalism does not apply when neither of us was used to appearing in front of an audience.

My home town was not only blessed with a successful amateur dramatic and operatic society, it also has a playhouse putting on seven plays per year, as opposed to the just one musical and one pantomime from the amateurs, which gave more scope to get involved, and I was one of the few who were a member of each.

Again I was slightly hampered by my lack of acting skills but soon found a niche backstage with lighting and stage managing. Although an opportunity did arrive, in a play called ‘Habeas Corpus’. One scene involved one of the actors being hung on stage, with a harness that prevented him from receiving permanent neck dislocation and asphyxia. The harness did not seem to fit all that well and tended, during rehearsals, to actually fulfil the noose's original purpose of hanging. With no time to order another one, someone less concerned with the possibility of brain damage had to be found. Being a bit of a daredevil at the time I took on the part. It was a black comedy, and the scene was where I was standing on a chair with the noose around my neck and the rest of the cast ignoring my suicidal attempt. As the cast sit down for dinner, someone takes the chair away, leaving me hanging, and then the curtain closes. I must admit it was quite heart-warming that the entire cast rushed to support me and return the chair once the curtain had closed completely, but I must admit to some moments of panic when the curtain seemed to take an hour to close. Needless to say I survived the entire six performances with only minimal brain damage and spinal cord dislocation.

I seem to have had quite a few near death experiences in my life. The other one at the theatre was when we decided to put a fan in the ceiling of the auditorium in a trap door that gave access to the loft. The ceiling was very high but fortunately the hole for the fan was above the balcony which made it a little less daunting. So we set up a scaffolding tower at the front of the balcony and another intrepid playhouse member and I climbed up. As high as the tower seemed perched on the balcony, it was about seven feet short, and as we were both well under six feet tall it was a bit difficult to reach. So my co-fan installer decided to climb onto the safety rail of the scaffolding tower, grabbed the edge of the hole and was going to pull himself up into the hole and climb in. As I went to the edge of the scaffolding to help him, he pushed off with his feet. This was rather fatal as my weight at one side combined with his kick made the tower start to topple. It was not so much as my life flashed in front of me, rather, frantically deciding as I glanced down at what precise spot I was going to land in a crumpled heap. At this point I was not all that concerned, well perhaps a little, as the balcony we were on had quite a steep rake and I was going to land at the top. As much as I was pretty focused, I inadvertently screamed, attracting the attention of two strong men who dashed from some distance to the rescue, as the tower majestically toppled. They grabbed the tower and pushed it vertical again. Great! However! While the scaffolding was at sixty degrees the legs down the side which were in the air had fallen off! My saviours returned the tower to vertical, and walked off congratulating themselves on a timely rescue, discussing what drink I was going to buy them in the pub afterwards for saving my life. The tower, now deprived of legs down one side, majestically started to fall the other way. Only this time towards the stalls which were fifteen feet further down over the balcony's edge. No warning scream this time, involuntary or not, just catatonic panic. Is the inability to move during a panic attack an advantage? At least it gives the brain time to mull over the situation without having to control the body while it runs around like a headless chicken. Perhaps I squandered this opportunity with the image of a cartoon! This was it, my life really flashed before me this time. The stall's seat-backs jutted up like the jagged rock at the bottom of a impossibly high cliff from which the cartoon character, Wile E. Coyote, was about to fall after being pushed by Road Runner. Then thump! The tower hit a support bar that ran from side to side across the auditorium and stopped at a precarious forty-five degrees. At this point I did not wait to be 'rescued' again by the knights in tarnished armour. I shimmied down the leaning tower and clutched the floor, passionately kissing the slightly soiled carpet. Luckily the rescue squad had now returned and re-erected the tower at its vertical best with all its legs connected as my mate had been left dangling from the hole in the ceiling unaware of the drama unfolding twenty foot below, a little preoccupied with his own problems, just clinging on for dear life to the edge of the trap door. I know this sounds a bit like I plagiarized this from Stan Freberg with his classic tale of pulleys, ropes, and barrels of bricks, but I swear it's true, it's kind of etched indelibly on my memory in fine detail.

My inventive gadget and special effects skills were exploited by the theatre on some occasions. One memorable time was when the playhouse put on Dracula.

I had a field day! There were fires that suddenly flared up, chairs which moved by themselves, cushions which sank as if the invisible man had sat on them. But best of all was a bat that had to fly out over the audience and, not just any stuffed bat as in the unimaginative script, mine would flap its wings, scream and its eyes would glow red.

Well it did, with a lot of gears, electric motors, a sounder out of a car alarm, two red bulbs and of course, to power all this, a rather large heavy battery, which in retrospect was its downfall, literally! All this was encased in a rather realistic scary, black furry coat. It had black silky bat wings, fangs, and talons. Do vampire bats have talons? Well mine did. This was then suspended on a fishing line which ran across and over the audience and was pulled from the back of the auditorium with a draw line. Well, rehearsals and the first night went great. There were suitable exclamations of fear as the bat flew out over the unsuspecting audience as Dracula disappeared with a flash and smoke effect giving the appearance he had turned into a bat. The second night didn't go too bad except the winding device got tangled leaving the bat hovering over the audience for excruciating seconds, still screaming, flapping, and transfixing the audience with bloodshot eyes, as I watched helplessly backstage. Only an heroic effort by my co-technician, John, saved the day by snapping the reputed unbreakable fishing line with his bare hands and reeling it in manually, (a feat I have always thought of as on a par with mothers lifting cars off their trapped child).

Mind you, this pales into insignificance compared to what happened on the third night when the line on which the bat ran broke, allowing the bat to free fall from about ten feet landing on the lap of a little old lady on the front row. At this point the curtain closed leaving me no option but to crash through the curtains into the auditorium to retrieve my still screaming, thrashing, bloody- eyed bat from the lap of the now catatonic old-age pensioner.

Fearing the demise of the little old lady either through concussion or heart attack, I plucked the offending bright-eyed, thrashing, still screaming, bat from the pensioner's knee and mumbled, 'Sorry luv' and 'Are you all right?' To which she replied, rather weakly. 'Mmm.' When I had recovered from my potential heart attack, I spoke to her again at the end of the show. She told me in a typical true Yorkshire understated manner, 'Eh lad, it was a bit of a shock you know, but it'll make a good story for my grandchildren.' I'm happy to report no further incidents accrued for the rest of the week after the bat wires breaking-strain was strengthened by a three grades increase.

One year the Society put on Paint Your Wagon and as a publicity stunt I decided to enter the Keighley Gala procession with a Wild West covered wagon. Not having one to hand I had to make one, and borrow a horse. As much as I'm pretty handy I decided to at least borrow, rather than make, the wheels, chassis and shafts for the horse. That in itself was no mean feat as I did not know anyone who had one and living in a farming community you would think they were ten-a-penny. But alas, plenty of tractors, no horse and cart, a sign of the times. Word did get around and eventually I found one and, to my surprise, it came off a large council estate in Keighley. You would think people with carts would be reluctant to lend their carts to strangers, but with an explanation that it was for the Gala procession, he readily agreed, the Gala being a well-supported tradition.

So with some plywood for the sides painted to look like planks, metal hooped over the top for the canvas in the form of a couple of bed sheets sewn together which was then stretched over them, much like it would have been constructed in the Wild West, only a little less substantial as our covered wagon only had to get us across town not half a continent. If I do say it myself it looked pretty good and, with buckets, barrels, axes and an old tin bath strapped down the side, it really looked the part. Now just one thing missing? The horse!

Now we still do have horses in the countryside, albeit usually owned by young ladies with a yen for the equestrian. Unfortunately not all riding horses take to having a lumbering great cart strapped behind them. Luckily I found one with experience with a cart, and an owner willing to lend it to me. It lived just down the road and I got the added enjoyment of riding it back home.

Then came the day of the Gala. My good old dad volunteered to take care of the horse with his experience as a carter as a young man. I had arranged with a bunch of lads and lasses from the show to dress up in their costumes to be waiting for us at the assembly point. The lasses were all geared up as saloon can-can dancers and all six of them piled onto the wagon. One sat with my dad on the front who had a big grin on his face and the rest hanging out the front and back, whooping it up. The lads, dressed as cowboys, walked along the side of the wagon, and I led the horse. The horse was great, it wasn't phased by all the commotion going on around us, and finally we set off. We were positioned in the procession behind the Gala Queen in an open-top Rolls Royce. It's slightly down hill at the start and all went well until we were on the flat and the horse seemed to be having a little difficulty pulling the cart. It seemed to slip and then it reared up. Apart from anything else, the Gala Queen in the open top Rolls in front became a little nervous of the flying hooves just feet from the back of her head, not to mention the, no doubt, very expensive polished boot of the Rolls. After calming it down we set off again but I could tell it was struggling. The next time the poor thing slipped again and reared up it actually snapped part of the harness. This took some time to temporarily repair and the procession had to stop behind us and could not overtake us but the rest of the procession moved off in front of us. This caused us some concern as the receding procession was nearly out of sight, but from the relieved look on the Gala Queen's face, as the Rolls departed into the distance, she at least was happy about the delay.

After a quick confab with my dad, it was decided that we had overloaded the cart with our six albeit slim dancers, so they got down and pranced about alongside the cart, which was actually better as it showed off their costumes and encouraged them to do an impromptu can-can dance. The lighter cart seemed to do the trick and we set off at a good pace, trying to catch up with the rest of the procession, although I kept a strong hold of Ned's harness.

The next trauma loomed as we passed a rather rough pub with its raucous, drunken clientele spewed out onto the pavement. Our can-can girls were an obvious target for rather childish comments although that wasn't the problem, as the girls were quite capable of dealing with a little heckling - especially backed up by six big lads dressed as cowboys carrying axes, shovels and rather realistic toy rifles. No, my problem was a drunken idiot who rushed out of the pub crowd carrying a young child, rushed up to the horse brandishing the child, and shouting, 'Stroke the gee-gee, stroke the nice gee-gee'. This is a horse that not a minute earlier had reared up, hooves flaring, for no reason and now it had a child, thrust in its face, shouting, 'gee-gee', with outstretched arms, nearly poking it in the eye. Luckily a policeman turned up and escorted the pillock and child back to the pavement, before either the horse or me had to deck him.

With the show field in sight there were no more incidents, although we had caught up to the Gala Queen in her Rolls and for the last hundred yards her royal wave to the crowed lining the pavement was interspersed with panicked glances over her shoulder. I did contemplate creeping up behind her and shouting 'NAAAAHHH' in my best imitation of a horse whinny, but I didn't.

What a great success all in all, we won a plaque for the most innovative entry. The society had bums on seats for the show and none of us were killed, or even members of the public for that matter. There was the little matter of delivering back the cart then the horse for the rest of the day but it was a sunny day and quite enjoyable.

Eventually when I took the horse back. The owner met me at the gate shaking his head. And then he laughed, 'Interesting day lad?' I replied it certainly was. Then he explained that he was standing in the crowd when the horse reared up and explained that it should have had special shoes for that weight of cart and its load of saloon wenches but he said I seemed to be coping well so he kept out of the way and went back into the pub. I thought thanks a bunch! But just thanked him for the loan of the horse.

I did do another float for my musical about the Cottingley Faeries but not quite as elaborate and no horses involved. It consisted of a flat-bed lorry that we built a framework on the back of and covered it in leaves and flowers so you could only just see inside. My faeries from the musical stood inside peering out and waving at the crowd. A great success and a good time had by all and I got a plaque for that one too.

Aye, lots of happy memories being a Thespian.

— 9 —

PHOTOGRAPHY AND AWAY WITH THE FAERIES

I'VE ALWAYS LIKED to paint and draw, the big problem is I'm useless! I can copy cartoons, you know Donald Duck, Goofy, and a funny dog that I think might be original but I could never publish it as my own, all usually drawn on steamed up windows with my finger. So as a frustrated artist I latched onto photography. The usual stuff to start with, holidays, life on the farm, then girl- friends, and that's when it dawned on me - my forte was a people photographer. I rather daringly, or more accurately naively, took a friend's wedding photos. It wasn't a total disaster. Mind you, you wouldn't call it the social wedding of the year but they did pay me, and were well pleased. So I became a part-time wedding photographer. And reasonably successful if I do say it myself, with very few cock-ups, I am willing to bet few photographers can truly say that, as things can so easily go belly up. There are a lot of stories there, some rather amusing.

Like the groom whose best man wrote HE-LP on the soles of his shoes. So when the groom knelt at the altar the guests seated in the church saw the supposed plea, to the amusement of all except the bride's mother. She beat the groom severely around the head, up and down the graveyard when they were out of the church, while shouting in her best Keighley accent, 'You've ruined my daughter' which I thought was a little unfair for as much as he may well have deflowered his bride-to-be before the wedding day, the poor lad's only crime was that he had not read the soles of his shoes before putting them on that morning, as you should always do of course. Meanwhile the real culprit, the best man had sneaked off to the pub with one of the busty bridesmaids.

The most laid back wedding I ever did was for a really nice West Indian couple but the groom and best man were so laid back they were horizontal. My itinerary for the day was to photograph the bride at home then go to the church to photograph the groom waiting expectantly. Well, on my way from the bride's house to the church I happened to see the groom wandering in the opposite direction in jeans and a sweatshirt. I was a little hesitant to stop but when I did he just said, 'Hi man, I'm running a bit late.' That had just got to have been the understatement of the year. So I rushed him off home to get changed and pick up his best man, managing to get to the church only seconds before his blushing bride arrived, and then I had to send her taxi around the block so I could take a picture of the groom and bundle him into the church. All in a day's work for a wedding photographer.

I've had my share of fainting brides and grooms at the altar, but none so bad that a glass of water and a quiet sit-down in the vestry with the vicar didn't cure. The service then carries on with the guests smirking and making comments about the stag or hen party the night before.

I remember the most tragic wedding which seemed to go so well during the day. When I took the photographs around to their house three weeks later when they had got back from their honeymoon, only the bride was there and the atmosphere was a little tense as she looked through the album. I got the sinking feeling that she was definitely unhappy with my photographs until she explained my photographs were great, it was just that her and the new husband had separated and were living apart. I dared not ask what the hell happened on the honeymoon. Whatever it was, it sounded pretty terminal for the relationship. On a purely monetary basis it ended OK as I did get paid for the photographs but I felt desperately sorry for the couple.

There were weddings that were very formal and the bride tended to be very uptight and nervous, usually dominated by the mother who understandably wanted everything to be perfect for her daughter on her special day. These were all right, but the really memorable ones were those where everyone was relaxed and the bride and groom just enjoyed themselves. I always tried to convey this to the bride and groom when I was discussing with them how they wanted their photographs, just to relax and enjoy their day.

It was always important to establish who in the relations and friends at the wedding were to be photographed and with whom as there was nothing worse than asking for grandparents when they had died three weeks before the wedding. Asking for the parents of the bride and groom for the line up can have complications. You can end up with couples that don't want to stand next to each other, with a line up of six or more divorced and remarried parents.

Some wedding photographers I came across were rather rude and aggressive which I thought was not in keeping with the bride and groom's special day. They would order the bride, groom and guests around like a Sergeant Major drilling his troops, dominating the whole day, not just calmly arranging line up, then subtly moving the proceedings on when you have taken the photos. They definitely did not like the guests taking photographs, which I thought was very insecure as I assume it was from fear of them taking better photographs, Not allowing any of the guests to take pictures is crazy, although you can feel a little pissed off when they have a more expensive camera than you. I would just let them get on with it, even giving them opportunity by stepping to one side after I had taken a shot so they could click away to their hearts' content, just relying on my final presentation to show my superior photographic skills. Well sometimes.

Apart from the person doing the service either in a church or registry office, you've been part of more weddings than all the other people there. Years later couples would stop me in the street and chat with me as if I was an old friend. It's quite a responsibility to advise the bride and groom on how things are best done in your experience, and my main advice is to just enjoy the day and relax.

Guests do tend to get in the way (especial those with expensive cameras) or worst still disappear when required for a photo line up. The best man, if he was mistakenly chosen for being the groom's drinking buddy instead of a sensible friend, inevitably slopes off to the pub with an alcoholic uncle, just as he is required for the photo. This, along with small children, drunken uncles pinching the bridesmaid's bum just as you are about to take a picture, and, of course, the inevitable rabbit ears behind the head of Aunt Ethel executed by a cheeky cousin of the groom, (that takes you hours of painstaking delicate touching-up to remove from the wedding-guest line up) are just part of fun in being a wedding photographer.

That's not to say I took the competition totally lying down. There was always the desire to take a better set of photographs than guests, mainly because you were getting paid a not insubstantial sum of money to do so. There was nothing worse than when the newlyweds were inspecting your photographs for the first time with the comment, 'Well they are OK but Uncle Fred's pictures are a lot better!'

Once you had positioned everybody and got everyone smiling, taking the picture was easy. Unfortunately I would have the same picture as everyone else. One of my little naughty tricks was: if it was quite sunny, the classic procedure is to have your back to the sun otherwise you tend to get a line up of silhouette. You could line them up with their backs to the sun and use a flash gun. This lit up the subjects but everyone else taking pictures got the silhouettes. It also eliminated the line up squinting from the sun in their eyes which does nothing for a good picture. You could also position your line up to avoid things like gas works in the background when the sun was in the wrong place.

Weddings were not my only forte and I was once asked to take photos of the school sports teams for the school magazine. No problem there as the PE teachers were a fearsome bunch and had strict discipline. All seemed to go well on the day. The problem arose a few days after the photos were presented to the staff. I was told there was a problem with the girls' hockey-team's photos and could I do them again. When I was shown the offending prints it was not immediately obvious, until it was pointed out to me, that the seated front row of hockey girls were displaying a wonderful show of knickers, brilliantly white and clean but not the sort of display suitable for the school magazine.

On the second take each photo line-up was preceded by the gym mistress giving the orders, 'Knees together girls, and smile.' Advice that perhaps would have made good moral advice for some of the young ladies present. I was also asked to redo the boys' rugby team. I was a little perplexed as to the problem as none of the team, as far as I could remember, were wearing skirts so legs apart should not have exposed any knickers clean or otherwise. The rugby coach had spotted two of the team on the front row had their hands on each others knees, not on their own. It appeared they had seen a professional rugby team photograph with two players doing the same, and thought they'd try it for a laugh. The rugby coach was not laughing!

Overall it was an interesting business which paid for my other interests, one of them being photographing faeries!

It all started when I read about the Cottingley Faeries, this was about two cousins in 1917 Elsie Wright and Frances Griffiths, aged only twelve and nine respectively, took amazing photographs of faeries on a very primitive camera that fooled the world and caused controversy for years. They even convinced Sir Arthur Conan Doyle, the famous author of Sherlock Homes, of their authenticity and that faeries really existed. Which they do of course! Do I believe in faeries? Well it's not so much a belief as keeping an open mind. I read a lot of scientific articles, and even though they are written by eminent scientists discussing cutting edge research it sometimes reads like science fiction. There's the large Hadron Collider creating mini- black holes, anti-matter and recreating the Big Bang at the beginning of the universe, thirteen point seven billion years ago. One article in particular really blew my mind as it was talking of a theory that we are all a holographic projection of another, flat version on a two dimensional 'surface' at the edge of this universe. The writer of the film 'Matrix' must have read the article too. Or the scientist has seen the film 'Matrix', one or the other.

Anyway believing in faeries or at least keeping an open mind pales into insignificance compared to believing what some scientists' view of the world entails.

Back to the girls photographing faeries. One of the less metaphysical theories of how they did it was that they drew pictures of faeries (they were quite good artists), cut them out and then posed them propped on twigs and flowers secured with hat pins, then took photographs of them. Even with this deception explained the photographs are amazingly beautifully composed, and have a definite magical feel. I am further intrigued, having recently read the book written by Frances Griffiths the younger of the two girls and her daughter 'Reflections on the Cottingley Faeries'. It gives an amazing insight about her version of the 'Cottingley Faeries' She is adamant she actually did see faeries, and as much as four of the photographs were faked as a prank but the fifth was genuine. The book gives a fascinating account to what really happened in the dell and how Conan Doyle and others tried to cash in on the artistry and naivety of the young girls.

Now as I explained before I can't draw. So ... why not photograph ladies dressed as faeries. Now let's get something straight. This was not an excuse to photograph ladies in skimpy faerie dresses, I'm an artist. Seriously though, apart from the obvious perks, I took my hobby seriously and I was quite in demand, even when I taped wings to their backs with gaffer tape!

Most of these photos were taken in my studio, as this allowed me to take scantily clad ladies through inclement weather, with the added advantage of controllable lighting. Having developed the prints, and achieved reasonable pictures of pretty ladies (and actually one boy whose mother was a bit of a feminist and wanted both her daughter and son as faeries!), I carefully cut the ladies out of the background. Taking these cut-outs with wings and all down to the woods and positioning them in what I deemed to be appropriate mystical settings, I then took a photograph.

I was very surprised with the results. They were crap! The two girls aged about nine and twelve nearly a hundred years ago, with an incredibly primitive box camera borrowed from their father, on what was reputed to be their first attempt, created magical black and white pictures that stunned the world. Then there were mine! I had the advantage of working in colour. You would expect my pics to be more vivid and alive. In reality they were flat and obviously cut out and stuck in flora. I was a little disheartened. But I was all the more determined to keep trying!

The pictures looked faked, insipid, and contrived. Back to the drawing board. Using the same technique of pictures of ladies cut out and carefully posed in the flowers and rotting tree trunks where faeries are reputed to abide I tried again. Eventually with a little Taurus tenaciousness and an awful lot of film, I think I came close to at least the spirit of the originals.

This, may I add, was long before the digital age. Now I can create faerie pictures without the aid of scissors. I can create shadows and reflection that I could not have imagined twenty years ago.

My obsession with the faerie realm got around and I was approached for a two minute spot of fame on the TV programme 'Pieces of Parkin'. I was a little disappointed when I learnt that it wasn't 'the Michael Parkinson' but I went for it anyway and it was a bit of a laugh.

A film crew duly arrived at my house and wanted to film me in the woods. I was interviewed sitting next to a rabbit hole and was asked how did I know that faeries lived down there. Well you just go with it! Don't you? So I answered with as much sincerity as I could manage that I just have a feeling for these things. The next question did throw me though when the pillock of an interviewer asked me in front of the camera how do faeries keep their holes clean. I lived in fear for months after it was shown on out-take TV that they would show my reply as an out-take with bleeps, as I asked him, 'How the bleep was I supposed to answer that?'

I even went to the excess of making a fake faerie detector with a probe to insert down appropriate holes with a meter on the front which flickered as I stuck it down this rabbit hole. This was achieved by one of the camera crew shorting out two wires off camera.

I'm not quite sure who was fooling who, as I'm convinced only a very few viewers must have believed any of this, but that's entertainment!

After that they wanted to film one of my young models dressed appropriately in faerie dress and taped-on wings, sat on a three-foot high toadstool which I just happened to have handy (there's a story about why I just happened to have a three-foot high toadstool kicking about which I may relate later). The illusion was that she would wave her wand and disappear. This was achieved by filming her waving her wand then stopping the camera, then she climbs down off the toadstool and they start filming again. A little twee but reasonably effective. A few close- ups of my faerie pictures and it was done. Two months later it was shown on the box with only mild embarrassment on my part, as most people took it for what it was, tongue in cheek.

I did get rather a surprise about a year later when someone came up to me and told me I was on the in-flight entertainment on the Torremolinos run. Fame eh!

As a spin off from my dubious claim to fame I was asked to be advisor to another TV programme about the Cottingley Faeries. This was hosted by an American journalist by the name of James Randi who makes a living trashing the paranormal A bit of a creepy looking guy who would probably do better promoting the paranormal, I've heard rumour lately that a strange experience he has had has changed his outlook on spirits and things. I assume it wasn't the faeries as he was quite off-hand and sceptical when I was filming with him.

Anyway we went filming in the village of Cottingley and interviewed a selection of locals. They were asked if they believed in faeries, if they had seen any in the dell next to the village where the two girls had taken the photos. Also, when shown my photos of faeries were anything like how they imagined faeries to look like.

We got a variety of answers, mainly facetious as you would expect. All the time we were filming, there was a young girl of about ten hovering in the background. Eventually she was invited over and asked the big question, did she see faeries? Her answer rather caused the interviewer to raise an eyebrow, not as much for what she said as for her enthusiasm and obvious sincerity. 'Oh yes they're beautiful!' Then the interviewer asked her if my photographs were anything like what she saw. Her reply made the hairs stand up on the back of our necks. 'Oh no, they are just little balls of light that flit around among the leaves and grass.' She really meant it! There was no way on earth she was faking it. That young lady saw faeries! I didn't think at the time but I would have done well to give her my camera and send her off to the dell. Conan Doyle, eat your heart out!

It perhaps was inevitable with my passion for faeries and my Thespian background that I would write a musical about the Cottingley Faeries, so I did.

With a little help from some friends and long hours poring over lines, stage directions, and, of course, songs, a viable musical emerged. My biggest worry was writing the songs, does the music come first or the words? After consulting our musical director he told us to go away and write the words and he would add the 'dots' (musical score) later. With some trepidation we sat down and wrote lyrics, surprisingly enough it worked. Is that how A.L.W. does it? I've never met him to ask. We had a script, songs, music, a story and altogether a musical, just like that! (only two years of hard work). All we needed now was a venue and some actors.

It never ceased to amaze me how so many people had faith in the musical. People volunteered to put their reputation on the line. OK so the director, choreographer, lights, sound, backstage staff, props and even the prompt didn't appear on stage, just had their names in the programme. However the actors had to stand in front of hundreds of people and say my words and sing my songs. Now that's faith and friendship, they actually believed in me and my musical! Considering they were amateurs, they all were real pros. It never went beyond four nights at the local theatre down the road from the little village of Cottingley. Although there was an Hollywood film about the Cottingley Faeries suspiciously soon after I started passing a script about. There were a few very familiar scenes but what the hell, plagiarism is the greatest form of flattery.

I would put that down as one of the high spots of my life. Manic at the time as I took it on myself to produce it, which involved organising the cast, building sets, compiling the programme, and anything that cropped up like refereeing the slight disagreements between the choreographer and the musical director. 'Thespians!'.

The guy who took on director was absolutely superb and also played one of the leading parts, a double reputation on the line.

At the end of the day, it was a success I invited Elsie Wright's son and Frances Griffiths's' daughter to the last night, and they both attended, what an honour!

So if you are looking for a musical with magic, faeries, a good story with a hint of truth, get in touch!

So at the moment I'm just collecting faerie books, faerie figures, and creating a web site with some of my faerie photographs. I'm a little too old to get away with asking young ladies to get dressed up in skimpy faerie costumes and to have me photograph them.

I once had my slight obsession about faeries explained by a psychology student at a party. He suggested that my fascination with faeries began long before my reading about the Cottingley Faeries. The student reckoned that he could psychoanalyse people and tell us what influenced us in our lives by asking us all, as we sat around talking, what was the first book we had ever read or even just looked at the pictures. He explained that book would then influence us for the rest of our lives. There was a lot of scepticism, and a lot of us could not remember our first book, but a few could remember and it was amazing how it did relate to some of them and how it had affected their thinking, ambitions and traits.

I was one of the persons present who could not remember their first book, but it did make me look out my old books which I still had. Why I still had my first book, you may ask. The answer is I'm a hoarder but again that's another story. I found it, very tatty, missing its cover, but my first book. It was real nostalgia, my childhood came flooding back. Guess what? Yes, it was a book on faeries, pictures and all! So go digging out your first book, it could be a revelation! And be a little careful what you buy you child for their first book

Do I believe in faeries? Yes. Have I ever seen any? No. Have I seen an atom? No. Do I believe in atoms? Yes. Not a very satisfactory answer and there are a lot of clever people who would tear that answer apart. There are a lot of supposed clever people out there who believe in God! So where does that leave us? That's enough philosophy for this book. I might well write an intellectual book later on the belief of faeries, God, and the theory of relativity some time - but don't hold your breath.

— 10 —

BOMBS AND ROCKETS

THIS CHAPTER SHOULD also be headed **'DON'T TRY THIS AT HOME'** or anywhere for that matter, so please don't. I would also like to add this all took place well over forty years ago, well before 9/11 and terrorists. The nearest thing I get nowadays to explosives is lighting a few fireworks at Bonfire Night (not home-made ones may I add).

Apart from being a bit of a pyromaniac, I was also rather fond of space exploration and have, with the help from an old school friend who was as crazy as I was, created and set off home-made rockets of which one at least disappeared out of sight and have never been found! Although I doubt sincerely that it will ever turn up on the moon or even in orbit for that matter.

I started quite young on my quest for explosions and rocketeering, at the tender age of ten I was making gunpowder. I had found the formula in an old chemistry book and, with the help of a chemistry set I received perhaps naively from my parents for Christmas and with an extra ingredient I cajoled my mother to buy at the chemist, I was away.

The preparation was carried out on our kitchen sink, and the end product looked good. Now all I had to do was test it. So, separating a small pile on a tin lid, I struck a match and lit it. Well, with only being a loose pile, it just went a rather satisfying whoosh. That would have been fine but for two things, my mother entered the kitchen at the same instant the small pile spread to the big pile. This was really spectacular. Within seconds the kitchen had filled with smoke through which the bright glow of the kitchen sink becoming red hot could be seen from the far side of the kitchen my mother and I had retreated to before exiting the kitchen altogether, until the fog cleared. I didn't get into as much trouble as I was expecting as my parents were, I think, rather proud of their inventive son and were relieved I was unscathed. Also the house did not burn down even though the kitchen's stainless steel sink was a write-off due to the fact it had buckled and was permanently discoloured and had eventually to be replaced. I'm not quite sure at what temperature this occurs with stainless steel but imagine it's rather high.

Another unfortunate incident from that first experiment with gunpowder was that I found cutting my fingernails after mixing my gunpowder created mini explosions as the gunpowder under my nails were detonated by the scissors, surprisingly enough with no detrimental effect to my fingers. Although it did make me aware of its potency perhaps even more than the ruined kitchen sink.

Although I was banned from making more gunpowder I discovered much later that common chemicals from the kitchen and garden shed were even more potent that my rather inadequate chemistry set.

Our first attempts at space exploration were more bombs than rockets. They would make a loud rising screeching sound, lift two feet off the ground and explode. This was rather spectacular but not quite the orbital outcome we had anticipated.

This also got me in trouble with my father. A couple of days after a rather dismal launch, but a rather superb explosion, had made a foot-deep crater in my dad's field, my father asked me if I had been 'setting off bombs again'. To which I replied quite truthfully we had not, as they were definitely rockets! I discreetly mumbled this under my breath. 'Well what's this then?' he asked as he led me to the exact spot were the failed launch had taken place. At first I could not understand how he had located our launch site as we had taken great care to fill in the crater after the explosion. Then I saw the ten foot ring of dead grass which the scattering of unburned rocket fuel had killed off.

That was the end of the rockets. Well not quite, we changed the rocket fuel for a more environmentally friendly chemical and by coincidence had greater success as rocketeers.

The original stuff was a little deadly anyway, as my friend's older brother found to his cost. He was not as sophisticated as we were with ambitions of orbital rockets and was perfectly happy to just make loud bangs and craters up on the moor top. This particular time he and his mates had arranged to meet and set off the bomb on Saturday morning. They had prepared the explosive on the Friday night after school. That was the first mistake, as the stuff had a tendency to become rather unstable a few hours after being mixed together, and I do mean unstable! The second mistake was to hide the bomb under his youngest brother's bed.

Well, about two in the morning the young lad got out of bed to go for a pee. His bedroom door got caught in a draft and slammed shut setting off the, by now, very unstable bomb. The damage was amazing; it blew out the side of the house and put the bed up into the loft. Fire, police, ambulances, were all there (this pre-dated the bomb squad) but the bomb disposal squad who were usually just happy de-fusing World War Two bombs were called in. Yes there were definitely a lot of good reasons to change our rocket fuel.

Without going into much detail if you treat ordinary cotton wool with a few chemicals, you end up with a rather potent rocket fuel. It's really amazing stuff. It's what magicians use to make things disappear in a flash. You can place a piece in the palm of your hand and set fire to it and it doesn't hurt, the flame is so fast. (This is not recommended for old ladies and people with weak hearts. I speak from experience, trust me!). I have been told that you can do the chemical thing with an ordinary newspaper , with quite spectacular if you get someone to read it then set fire to it. But I've never tried that one.

I've got to confess that while our aspirations were directed to the noble art of space explorations I did make the occasional bomb, with the rather satisfying flash and a bang. I had read somewhere that the army enhance their combat training simulations and produce a mini atomic mushroom cloud by placing a pan of petrol mixed with Lux soap flakes (can you still buy them?) over the bomb. It's very impressive and could be seen for miles. You would definitely have various emergency services in attendance if you tried that one today. I must stress that the making of those bombs was the most dangerous, stupid, crass and unimaginative of the consequences thing I have ever done and believe me I've done some pretty foolhardy stunts in my time as you will find out as you read on. Apart from the obvious dangers of bombs in general there are unreliable short fuses, tripping up as you run for cover and perhaps not running far or fast enough. But the real big one was hammering the pipe flat that the explosive was encased in, yes hammering! How the hell I didn't blow myself to smithereens with the first hammer blow is beyond comprehension considering the unstable explosive. So hammers aside and my survival instruction:

DON'T TRY THIS AT HOME!

The treated cotton wool was marginally safer but still had the capacity to get me into trouble. There was the time I was supposed to pick up the leading lady on my way to the theatre. Having arrived and been asked if I had seen her as she was due on stage soon, that's when it dawned on me, I had forgotten her. I must confess to exceeding a few speed limits that evening, as I dashed back to pick her up.

Well she was in a bit of a state as you can imagine, stood on her door step looking rather worried, and sat shaking in the passenger seat, not entirely due to my rather reckless speed. Half way to the theatre she asked me if she could smoke. I'm rather against smoking but considering the circumstances I condescended. This might have helped calm her frayed nerves but for the fact that being a bit of a joker I had stuffed the ash tray with this explosive cotton wool, and forgotten about it. Yes, you've guessed it, the first flick of the ciggie ash in the car's ash tray and it erupted in a harmless, but rather scary, gout of flames, luckily not distracting my driving too badly, but doing nothing to calm the lady's nerves, as on top of everything else she dropped her cigarette and had to scrabble for that. I really do not know how she got through the play. It was a true display of professionalism. The only outward sign of her shattered nerves was the comment that she appeared a little more subdued than usual backstage, with an excessive consumption of cigarettes, dashing the ash into her hand with an ever so slight nervous twitch, not using the ash tray. She eventually did speak to me again and we had a good laugh about it, years later. Well, that was until there was a Ceilidh dance at the theatre, when during a rather enthusiastic dance called Split the Willow which I am particularly fond of, and attack it with gusto, I stepped backwards onto her ankle and snapped her Achilles tendon, resulting in her spending the next six weeks in a pot and on crutches. I do detect a slight wince and a very cautious side-step when we now meet at social functions.

The stuff we used for the rocket is very stable and easily made but the final process was drying the wet cotton wool. I would have normally left it to dry in the sun for a couple of days except my mate had turned this spectacular rocket out of aluminium on his father's lathe and we were dying to set it off.

It was about three foot long and very sleek with fins and all. It would take quite a lot of the special cotton wool, so I had come prepared with a large box of the stuff. But it wasn't dry enough when we were ready to load it into the rocket so I decided to use my mother's hair dryer. Now in retrospect that might have appeared a mistake as there is a heating element that can be seen to glow red hot inside the nozzle. But as this was safely encased I thought it would be fine. So it would have been, except the explosive cotton was rather dusty, and with the hair dryer blowing it about, then sucking it in, and passing it over the hot element. Bingo! There was this blinding flash and I was thrown backward! A burning feeling on my face, and then pain. For as much as a small piece set alight on the palm of your hand does not leave a mark, a pound of the stuff lit three feet away from your face definitely leaves a mark. Just to get some idea of the fieriness of the flash, an ornamental candle five feet away on my mother's sideboard was set alight, and a large proportion of polystyrene tiles on the ceiling were melted, dripping down like stalactites. At the time I had a beard (well we are talking the sixties) which was removed, literally in a flash, along with my eyebrows, eyelashes, my Elvis quiff, and a fair percentage of skin from my face. It looked like a bad- to-severe case of sun burn.

A thick application of my mother's cold cream was not sufficient to quell the pain so I made a reluctant trip to A&E. The doctor who examined me said it was only superficial and would soon heal, but wanted to know what had caused it. Quick as a flash (no pun intended) I told him I was trying to light a garden fire with petrol and it blew back in my face. The doctor pulled a face and said I was very lucky, it could have been a lot worse Too bloody true doc, you don't know the half of it. Months later I was fine, which is more than could be said for my parent's ceiling which had to stay like a grotto with the stalactites until they decorated, with my parents telling me it should serve as a constant reminder of the perils of explosives, as if my tender face was insufficient as a constant reminder.

I did eventually make a new batch for the special rocket and it went up and out of sight into the clouds. We never did find it, which posed the worry about what it could have landed on, but it must have buried itself in the ground, hopefully to be dug up hundreds of years later and put in a museum as an ancient artefact from space and proof that aliens had visited earth. So that was the last, an end of an era of space exploration.

Just recently I've attended three funerals of friends and relatives, and it sets you thinking. Not too morbidly mind you, as it's not my style but it did make me think how I would like my sending off arranged. I'm not religious in the conventional sense, so a kind of Irish wake with me propped up in the corner sounds good. You know, no miserable buggers saying what a great guy I was when they don't really mean a word, as they probably were thinking what a right pillock I really was.

So when I mentioned it to my friend John about him possibly giving me a eulogy at my wake, as he would tell it as it was and make fun of some of my madder exploits, probably more than I would like to remember, but I thought if it was relevant at my funeral it would liven up the proceedings, he readily agreed.

So I mentioned to my friend, John, about the possibility of him giving the eulogy at my wake. He would tell it like it was and make some fun of my madder exploits, probably more than I would like to remember. I thought it would be OK at my funeral as it would liven up proceedings. He readily agreed and also suggested a few refinements, As he was aware of my dabbling in the preparation in explosive cotton wool as a youth he thought it would be appropriate to have me prepared in a similar fashion. That way I could be cremated in a spectacular instant flash. Actually this tied in nicely with my own plans to be launched in a burning Viking longboat across the lake which I had dug out a few years ago, to an island in the middle, and my ashes scattered there. The explosion would save the trouble of having to scatter them, and it would add a bit of a modern feel to the ancient ritual. There's some doubt that this would be legal, I will perhaps look into it! Apply for the appropriate permission before I die...

Another rather spectacular explosive formula I found in an old text book for chemistry teachers. It could be easily made sourcing the appropriate chemicals required with a quick root through an old medical chest and the cupboard under the kitchen sink, would you believe. One of its drawbacks as an explosive also happens to be one of its attributes. This is the fact when it dries out it is so sensitive a fly walking over a small pile of it will detonate it. Even a minute amounts explodes with a load bang and a rather pretty puff of scarlet smoke which I found out much later was rather poisonous. It certainly made a rather fine fly trap on a piece of paper on the window sill, but of course I could not leave it at that. I found if you scattered it wet on the passenger seat of my car, when it dried the seat became rather alarming to sit on. Giving friends a lift opened up a whole new potential for practical jokes I was so fond of. Although, I struggled to find friends that appreciated it as much as I did. Scarlet stains on their trousers (and probably a few brown stains on their underwear) soon put an end to that little jolly wheeze.

I did at one time flirt with nitro-glycerine, again from my old chemistry text book. It was surprisingly simple chemical reaction with readily available ingredients, with only one slight minor problem, the reaction creates heat. This does not seem to be an insurmountable problem until you read the underlined warning that detonation will occur not far above room temperature.

Nitro-glycerine was used extensively in mining and demolition, being far more powerful than gunpowder but is unfortunately a notoriously delicate high explosive, the least knock or vibration will set it off. Thousands of people who used it on a regular basis, like quarry men, miners, and railway workers who used it for blasting rock for the railway track, made one mistake and died or were severely injured. A chemist named Nobel was so appalled by this carnage and human suffering he set about creating a safe explosive. With a little experimentation he came up with a simple answer, to mix nitro-glycerine with a certain kind of clay. The result was dynamite, a relative stable and safe high explosive which saved thousands of lives, although some say this was far offset by its use in war and terrorism.

Nobel not only had the satisfaction of being a great humanitarian it made him a very rich man indeed, and yes, he is the same Nobel who sponsors the Nobel Peace Prize. All that high power stuff was out of my league but I do find it fascinating.

It would appear that explosives are unnecessary for an explosion. Would you believe I can raise a reasonable bang just starting a tractor. The tractor in question was a real bugger to start. I had been trying for days, in-between charging batteries, so in desperation I decided the only option was to put the two batteries in series therefore doubling the recommended voltage from twelve to twenty four. That should get the sod turning over fast enough to fire even the most reluctant engine.

This involved a little extra wiring that caused me to experience some difficulty pressing the starter button and holding the extra wires on the terminals of the batteries.

At this point, enter the cavalry in the form of my good friend John and his son. After a little discussion he agreed that my plan of batteries in series, like slotting batteries end on end in a torch, to double the voltage was an excellent idea, as John is very knowledgeable about things like that and is as crazy as I am. So I delegated him to hold the wires to the terminals of one battery and his son to the other. At this point the son backed away saying, 'You two are dangerous when you get together, I don't want anything to do with it.' Well I called him a wimp, a pussy, and asked him what possibly could go wrong? He just smiled and backed further away. A little re-delegation of procedure was required with John holding two terminals and me holding the other two while pressing the starter with my foot. What happened next needs a little technical explanation for the explosion which knocked both of us off the tractor.

We worked out later was that we were subjecting the batteries to a little undue stress, causing them to give off copious amounts of hydrogen and oxygen, and as every first year chemistry student knows that gas is rather flammable, explosive even. So a small spark caused by the loose hand-held terminal was all it took to complete the reaction. The exploding shrapnel from the batteries did not actually do us any damage per se, although it came as a bit of a shock. But the sulphuric acid out of the batteries did cause us some distress, as it sprayed us in a corrosive even coating over both of us. When we had hosed ourselves down in the yard, that stopped the stinging, removed any nylon clothing that hadn't already dissolved and started laughing, I warned John's son in no uncertain terms that the phrase 'I told you so' would not be tolerated. But he said it anyway. Kids today, eh?

All this was a long time ago and I no longer mess with anything explosive as I've stated at the beginning of this chapter, except for the occasional fire work on Bonfire Night and I repeat those are bought not home-made.

— 11 —

PLAYING WITH FIRE

I MUST CONFESS again to being a bit of a pyromaniac. I've decided it's my dad's fault really, he always seemed to have a fire on the go on the farm, with me in rapt attendance from an early age. We also had an open fire, which a surprising number of children have never experienced in a living room nowadays. Gazing into the fire and seeing faces and people in the flames and red hot coals was a gentler time' before television and computers distracted kids' attention.

We always had a bonfire on the fifth of November, Guy Fawkes Night. My dad was an enthusiastic bonfire builder, a tradition I have carried on to this day. Progging was all part of the fun. I have only realised that the word progging (my spell checker comes up with some very strange configuration for this word) is a colloquialism and the world-at-large looks at you very strangely if it's used even in context. Even a few miles down the road they use the word 'chomping' instead. The meaning of the words progging and chumping, by the way for all 'offcumdens' (people not local), is the collection of combustible material to burn on the bonfire on November the fifth. Usually it is tree branches but can range from abandoned settees to garden gates not locked up ... sorry, I mean not required.

This particular bonfire had been constructed around a forty-gallon drum of old tractor sump oil which both my father and I thought would make the fire burn well as the previous day's rain had left the contents of the bonfire a little damp. Well we finally got the fire going with the aid of a little paraffin, which in itself is not recommended; well perhaps it's marginally better than petrol.

There was around thirty of us around the fire as our bonfires were quite popular and all my friends were there. The fire had been well alight for about half an hour when we began to hear a strange bubbling sound. My dad and I looked at one another and I just managed to say,

'You don't think that's the sump oil....', when there was this almighty whoosh and, yes you've guessed it, the boiling sump oil ignited, causing a spectacular flaming mushroom cloud from the centre of the bonfire. There was a mass stumble backwards and thirty people were laid on their backs around the fire. It would have made a very interesting aerial photograph and I think you get the picture. The most important thing was no-one was hurt and we all had a good laugh but both my dad and I got a roasting (not the most appropriate word) from my mother later that evening. We all must have memories of bonfires on cold November nights, cold backs and hot fronts perhaps not with as big a gradient as this particular bonfire caused.

A more recent incident, but not an actual Guy Fawkes bonfire, was when I accidentally set fire to an electricity pole (as you do). It all started when I was removing some old railings which a small tree had grown through at the side of a shed I was taking down. It's very difficult to cut down a tree that's reinforced with cast-iron bars, even with a chain saw, and especially with a chain-saw come to think about it. Having only produced a lot of sparks and ruined the cutting chain on my saw I decided to burn it out. The fact that a twenty-thousand volt wooden electricity pole was only eight foot away had not escaped my notice I just assumed it would not burn, (wrong!). It would not have been a bad assumption but for the fact the wooden pole had been covered in a tarry substance to protect it from rotting, making it rather flammable.

So I built a bit of a bonfire around the offending tree and lit it with just a TINY sprinkling of petrol, honest! All was going well. The bonfire was being consumed but the tree was not. More wood for the fire was obviously needed so I went around the other side of the house to fetch some more. Coming back with an armful of kindling I was rather surprised to find the electricity pole ablaze from base to about ten feet up. You hear of people going catatonic under stressful situations, well I think I was for about three seconds before dropping the wood and uttering a rather strong sexual expletive to the devil's abode, then heading for the hose pipe! Now I'm quite knowledgeable about electricity and its undesirable effects when mixed with water, but I must confess to being a little overwhelmed by the spectacle of the burning pole. Anyway fate took control and saved me, as it has had a tendency to all my life, for as I set off at a run pulling the hose, I wrenched the tap clean off the wall which no doubt saved my life. I still had the problem of the now blazing electricity pole. So my next thought was a bucket. Now as it was filling from the gushing pipe sticking out of the wall it gave me chance to contemplate the undesirability of putting out an electrical fire with water. By this time I had noticed the cables that carried the electricity down the pole and underground were burning and melting, and there was a definite glint of bare copper through the flames. So quick as a flash, I devised a cunning plan. If I throw the water from the bucket onto the pole in such a way that the water left the bucket before touching the pole, it would not create a path for the electric to pass through me. Well I'm living testimony to the fact it worked! Still not recommended but the fire was out after four such dexterous manipulations with the bucket.

After three or four days recovering from my trauma I inspected the damage, and sure enough the cable down the pole was definitely missing a rather prodigious amount of insulation. I didn't quite know what to do about that, taping it up with electric isolation tape seemed inappropriate and dangerous. The obvious thing would be to call the electricity company immediately, but I took the safer option and did nothing. Every time I passed the pole I became more worried and if I happened by it in the rain, there was a definite sizzling sound. So eventually after a few months (it had been a very dry summer) I did the right thing and called the electricity company. I was a little surprised at the speed an engineer came out to see it and even more surprised that a full team of riggers was on site in the hour. The chief engineer took me to one side and asked me how it happened, and of course I told him the truth, that it was some gypsies who had taken down the shed and burnt some rubbish that was left over, setting the pole on fire, then driving off. He looked at me and shook his head and said, 'Gypsies eh? Well I'm glad you reported it so promptly. It was very dangerous.' At that point I gave a vague smile and slunk away and made tea and biscuits for the workers.

Yet another rather more alarming incident was when I set the airing cupboard on fire and nearly the whole house! Not on purpose may I add, it was purely accidental, well at least you could say incompetence.

It all started when I went green, that's ecological green not envy. I decided to get a windmill, nothing massive just one with four-foot blades. I bought one off e-bay and stuck it in the field next to the house. How can that nearly burn your house down? Dead simple, read on. It was not going to do anything complicated like run the TV or fridge, as that requires fancy electronics, it was just wired into an immersion heater in the hot water tank and that would give me hot water when the wind blew. Initially it didn't work all that well as the immersion heater was a little too powerful for the power of the windmill, and it wasn't turning fast enough. So I decided to add a resistor in the circuit so the immersion heater didn't take as much power. A bit technical that, well the theory was, but the resistor was a little iffy. It was fine until the wind blew a bit strongly one morning and the resistor became rather hot, and melted, in turn showering sparks and hot metal onto the towels and blankets in the airing cupboard. Not a good combination, as the warm dry towels ignited. Now three things saved the house.

The first was a good fire alarm system that I installed; being an alarm installer once upon a time (I'll have to tell you about that part of my career sometime). If one of the alarms goes off they all go off and break into a siren song. I have to admit that my reaction to the alarm was not immediate as burning toast does have the same effect. The second thing that saved the house is written on the cover of the 'Hitchhiker's Guide to the Galaxy' - 'DON'T PANIC'. It really is a life saver, although a little adrenalin works wonders. Looking back it never crossed my mind to call the fire brigade. I just tackled the now flaming cupboard with the third lifesaver that was a big fire extinguisher. The best thing I ever bought, well scrounged off a skip actually, but it did work!

I'm not sure where this is written but the phrase 'where fools rush in, angels fear to tread' springs to mind as an afterthought. As I opened the cupboard that had flames licking around the edge of the door, smoke and flames engulfed me (this may sound a little dramatic but you will just have to take my word for it as they were my partner's words not mine, as she stood aghast at the spectacle). The only thing that saved me a severe scorching was, at the same time as I opened the door, I pressed the fire extinguisher button, and it slowly beat back the flames and smoke. Eventually there was only minor damage to the airing cupboard, the house, and me! However all the contents were a write-off.

A caution here. This definitely carries the warning I have used in previous chapters 'DON'T TRY THIS AT HOME'. The standard procedure of 'get out of the house and then call the fire brigade' is definitely the best course of action and just because I'm a lucky nutter, never follow my example.

— 12 —

GRAND DAYS OUT

MY GOOD FRIEND John was bloody ace at arranging amazing trips out, to what I can only describe as strange and exotic locations. At one stage in his career he was my boss, for his sins.

One such trip was to a women's prison. You may well ask! Well what happened was, his department had been offered some redundant computer equipment and never one to turn 'owt' down,' especially if 'it's for nowt', he arranged for us to go and collect it. Now, in the eighties, computers weren't very sophisticated but this lot was positively archaic.

There wasn't a transistor in sight, only relays, electric motors, punch cards and lots of switches but still it was impressive and interesting, and of course we didn't turn it down.

The story behind it was that there had been a government initiative to educate prisoners about modern technology, so that when they were released they would get well paid jobs and relinquish criminal behaviour. Nice thought, but for the deviance of human nature, or nurture, or even both, most of the cleverest prisoners, now with a greater understanding of the system and the technical know-how, turned from petty crime to more sophisticated fraud and embezzlement.

Perhaps this is a bit cynical of me to think what a waste of money, but it was one of the explanations given in confidence by one of the guards as we were removing the kit. The other obvious explanation for was that the kit was built at the very beginning of the computer revolution and things became obsolete as fast then as it does today.

Anyway, some of John's students may have been inspired later by dismantling this mechanical dinosaur, probably more into mechanics rather than computers.

It certainly inspired me, not into mechanics as you may think, but to avoid scary women (a lesson perhaps at times unheeded throughout my life). They were everywhere, leering at us as we carried the gear out of the prison. After the first trip we decided to keep all together carrying the stuff to the van. Even with a guard present we all felt rather intimidated. It gave me an insight into what some women complain about when being sexually harassed by men. The frustration and tension in there among the women inmates was electric just as portrayed in the TV programme 'Prisoner, Cell Block H'.

We found the security a little wearing too, as every time we took something out to the van we were searched on the way back in, and, after about twenty trips, this got very tiresome. But over all it was an interesting experience adding greatly to life's rich tapestry.

Yet another trip involved visiting Jodrell Bank. John was doing a project on weather satellites and, rather than buy the large expensive dish, we were going to build one. We were a bit unsure of the dimensions and intricacies, so we went to the best place to get the low-down on the optimum requirements. Yes, John talked his way into one of the world's biggest radio telescopes. I still don't know how he did it but he certainly has the gift.

As we approached you could see the large dish and its smaller companions but nothing prepared us for its actual size up close. As we parked the car and walked towards the centre, we saw that the whole place is surrounded by a high security fence with a gate for visitors. The only problem being that there did not appear to be a gatehouse and there was nobody about. The gate was locked with an impressive card entry system. After about ten minutes, we were rescued by someone approaching from the car park. He asked us if we were going in. We told him that we had no pass card. 'That's no problem,' he explained as he gave the gate a sharp kick and the gate swung open, 'The stupid electronic lock's crap anyway.' We followed him through, and made our way to reception. We were then directed to a low, concrete building to meet the man whom John had made arrangements to see.

We entered a long, low, concrete building to the impressive sight of the entire long wall filled with rather old fashioned dials, switches and screens with green pulsating squiggles flashing across them. A man in a white coat and a shock of white hair greeted us and after introductions began to explain the function of the wall of electronics. It appeared that this was the original set-up which detected the first Russian Sputnik and with only some slight modification over the years was still tracking most of the satellites to this day. Trying to ask intelligent questions we enquired if the signals were being picked up by the large dish we could see through a window, or one of the smaller ones. To this day we can't decide whether he was pulling our leg or whether he was really serious, but he shook his head, walked over to a small open window, pulled an ordinary piece of wire about three-foot long that was dangling out the window back through into the room, looked us straight in the eye and said, with no hint of a smile, 'No need. It's all picked up on this bit of cable.' And with that he poked it back out the window. He then proceeded to explain that the large dish was for astronomical observations, but for some years now, since a storm during which the wind lifted one side of the carriage that the dish stood on four feet up off its rails, it had been welded down to its rail track in a fixed position which rather restricted its use.

Soon it was time for lunch and we were taken to a very basic canteen on site. The food was OK but the real treat was that Sir Bernard Lovell was two tables along from us having his lunch. WOW!

After lunch with Sir Bernard, we were directed to a scientist working on one of the smaller dishes. For the life in me I cannot remember what he was observing. Some far distant galaxy perhaps? But what stuck in my mind was that the detector on the dish had to be cooled with liquid nitrogen. He asked if we would walk with him to the store while he talked to us, as his detector was beginning to warm up and it needed to be cooled with some more liquid nitrogen. He took what looked like an old, soup vacuum flask off a shelf and set off with us down a short path to a small building with lots of warning signs plastered all over it. He asked us to wait a second, as he slipped into the building and emerged minutes later carrying the flask bubbling, fuming, and spitting liquid nitrogen. Totally unconcerned, he proceeded back to his lab, explaining the subtleties of his work while swinging the flask back and forward, splashing drops of super cool liquid nitrogen on the path and grass verge. I could not take my eyes from the spectacle. He must have trodden this path many times previously as the grass from the store to his dish was in very poor health. Eventually he must have noticed our concern and pointed out that if he screwed the lid on, it would inevitably explode, as the nitrogen gas given off as it warmed slightly would build up enough pressure to blow the flask apart. Perhaps my inability to remember his lecture had something to do with the vivid vision of the eccentric scientist and the swinging, smoking flask.

On our return to school we eventually constructed a satellite dish with the information we got from the people at Jodrell Bank. An interesting project and a memorable day out!

Another grand and interesting day out was when my friend John needed a helicopter gyroscope (as you do!) for a science gallery exhibition at the museum he worked for at the time. So he arranged to visit this company which deals in ex-military equipment, and asked me if I would like to tag along (what a bloody silly question!).

Well, we drove down to this place from directions given by this gentleman John had spoken to on the phone, turning off a country lane along a tree-lined drive to what appeared to be a small detached cottage. This did not look right at all for a military equipment dealer, and we were just about to turn around thinking we had gone down the wrong drive when a large police van arrived and four policemen got out, went into the cottage, came back out arms full of what appeared to be riot gear and started loading it into the van. Shields, helmets, body armour, the works. We then assumed we had reached the right place, which was confirmed without a doubt, when we entered the front door and walked down this passage to a door marked Reception. Lined up along this corridor was what I can only describe as an assorted collection of missiles, in ascending order of size, point up, resting on the floor, balancing on their fins. There were about a dozen, starting at the entrance with one about a foot tall to one at the end of the corridor that was taller than me at about six foot. If these were displayed to impress it was a one hundred percent success, even if they were 'probably' dummies.

At reception we met a jolly little man who welcomed us enthusiastically, introducing himself as the owner of the company. Not really the sort you would expect to have missiles in his front passage if you excuse the expression. Anyway he was pleased to show us around. The first big surprise was that the small detached cottage was a Tardis, like the Doctor Who police box, and we could not work out how there were so many large rooms all full of very interesting gadgets. There was one room full of night vision binoculars which had a gyroscope in them. He demonstrated these by letting us look through them through a window. He then shook us by the shoulders, not too gently I may add, and instead of the vision going all wobbly what you were looking at stayed perfectly still, amazing!

Another room had a big video screen where he showed us a clip, taken from the bomber of a bombing raid on a large building in the desert in Iraq . It showed the missile going in. It must have been one of those guided jobs as it appeared to be off-target then homed in, bull's-eye in the centre. A massive explosion, a blinding flash, and the building disintegrated. Just like in movies. Till you realised there was probably people in there.

At the other end of the belief factor he then showed us a clip from 'The Bill' with him dressed in police uniform, smashing a door down with a hand battering ram for a drugs raid. Apparently he had supplied certain constabularies with the device and the producers of 'The Bill' had asked him to use one in an episode for realism. They are now seen regularly on police videos on drug raids, and we now know who supplies them.

This jolly little guy also showed us some bullets and boasted that there 'wasn't a bullet proof vest in the world that could stop them passing straight through.' We wondered if the bullet proof vests he was also selling carried a large tag warning about the possible danger of coming across one of these bullets fired in anger.

Eventually he took us to a room containing guess what? Helicopter gyroscopes. I think if we had been looking for Star Wars type laser guns there would have been a little room somewhere in this Tardis full of them.

Having inspected the gyroscopes with John choosing one, we were invited to a very nice pub lunch down the road and after we were suitably fed and watered, he then offered to take us to a local Air Force base where he had purchased some odds and ends we might be interested in. My mind immediately went to Jeremy Clarkson and his purchase of a Vulcan bomber, and how I would explain a similar purchase to my wife. I envisaged about as much trouble as he did, but it was a great fantasy anyway! John told me a wicked joke about Vulcan bombers, Jeremy Clarkson, (who John has worked with) and the mess his purchase of one did to his lawn as it was dragged across it to its final resting place in his garden. John swears it's one of his original jokes and I believe him. The joke goes ''What's the connection between Jeremy Clarkson's lawn and Spock's mother from Star Trek.' Answer - 'they have both been shagged by a Vulcan'. If you don't get it, ask a Trekkie.

Well perhaps thankfully there were no Vulcan bombers, but it was certainly interesting. The bit this guy took us around was a large hanger containing a fighter plane training simulator. Not the modern sort you see on TV, with a cockpit and a video screen. It was a thirty-foot diameter canvas balloon including an air lock and all, with a cockpit out of a fighter plane in the centre suspended on jacks that must have moved it up and down and around. There were a lot of projectors that simulated the sky and the ground on the inside of the balloon and a little model plane that moved around on a rod that the pilot had to shoot down. It was an amazing mechanical version of the modern computer video games. I really fancied the canvas balloon; I could see it making a rather fine planetarium! Yes perhaps a little grand for your average back garden, slightly less ambitious than a Vulcan bomber but no more practical I'm afraid. Luckily it wasn't for sale as planning permission might also have been a problem. Well John eventually got his helicopter gyroscope and I had another grand day out.

— 13 —

DERRING-DO'S

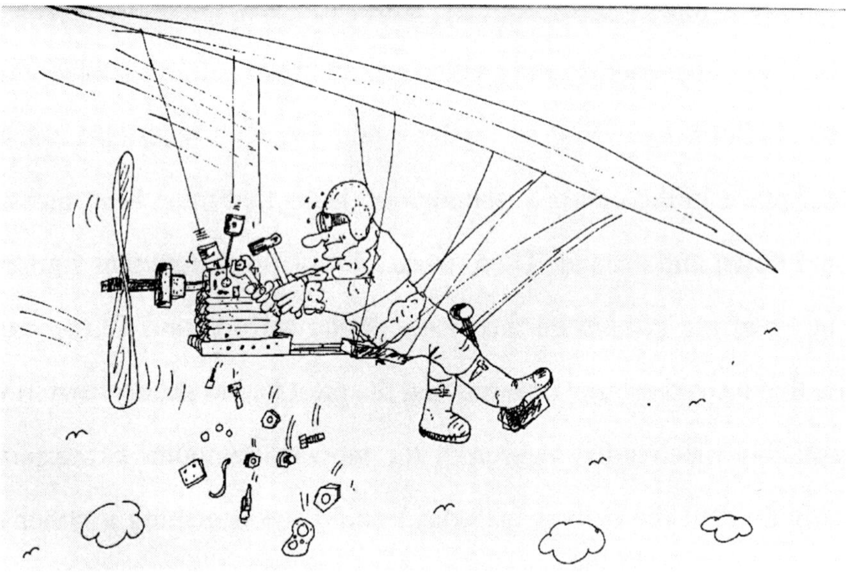

THE NUMBER OF this chapter is purely coincidental but not inappropriate as I always believe that no matter how stupid the things that I do, I'm extremely lucky. That's not to say I recommend that if you feel lucky, go and do something stupid. I don't think of myself as particularly adventurous or daring, but I suppose I've done a few things that some, who are more imaginative of the potential dangers, might think racy and foolhardy. Considering the chapter number, it would appear that I'm not superstitious either. Mind you is believing in luck a kind of superstition? I'm getting too deep now!

I did a parachute jump for charity once. Well, twice actually. Why twice? Did I like it so much? Could I not believe I did it the first time? Have I a death wish? No none of these, it was wind! Read on.

It all started as a charity raising event, you know one of these things where your friends sponsor you for fifty pence to do daft stuff, like seriously damage your health or maim you for life. Anyway I chose a parachute jump for my sins.

Again this was pre-Health and Safety whereby you don't jump out of a plane unless strapped to an experienced sky diver, after only three hours of training, you jump on your own. Having said that, it's not strictly true, not being left totally to your own devices. You are looped to what they call a static line that deploys your chute. So that forgetting to pull your rip cord and not employing your parachute in the trauma of falling at terminal velocity from two and half thousand feet out of the plane is not a life threatening experience.

Anyway, I must say our instructor for the training was excellent and did inspire confidence despite his macabre sense of humour of interspersing the session with horror stories of things that have gone wrong with parachute jumps in the past. But he never discussed fatalities, so as not to totally put us off the jump.

The first lesson was to strap us into a real parachute, and show us how to check if all the buckles were fastened properly. He pointed out, perhaps rather unnecessarily, that if one came undone it rendered the parachute useless as the thing would come down without you, only much slower.

Next we learnt how to jump off a table onto a mat; this gave us an idea of the force we would encounter on landing from two and a half thousand feet! Really? He reckoned it was about the same force we would land with, being appropriately slowed down by the chute. I was not sure whether or not I found that reassuring. It seemed a little underestimated to me and it was just a ruse to give us confidence. We also learned to keep our feet together as we land and roll, otherwise you can break a leg our jocular instructor informed us. (Although not breaking a leg per se, it's a lesson I should have taken more notice of at the time. It would have saved me some significant embarrassment during the actual jump)

Then there was the theory. It started innocuously enough about controlling your parachute during descent, and how to gather your chute after landing. Then he went and spoilt it by telling us what could go wrong! Like landing on a busy road or getting blown into a tree or being dragged along the ground by the wind.

Next he went into graphic detail what would happen if your parachute were to accidentally open in the plane. Again with a smile on his face, he described how, if we all did not immediately jump on it and hold it down, it would most likely fly out the open door taking the person attached to it out with it. This would not be so bad except that he or she would not go out the same way as the chute. He explained the slip stream would drag a person attached to the canopy towards the rear of the aircraft, making a new door way as that person exited, and ripping off the plane's tail for good measure. The whole class of eight, as one, took in a sharp intake of breath. Then the instructor tried to make light of the consequences by saying that the pilot would get really pissed off at this point as his plane just doesn't fly with out its tail.

The instructor then immediately launched into what could go wrong with the static line that opens your parachute when you are about twenty foot from the plane. He said it had been known for the line to get tangled around the parachutist and leave him dangling behind the plane. The instructor explained you could tell immediately if this happened to you by the fact that 'violent buffeting occurs', as described in the manual. Just visualise dangling on the end of a rope behind a plane doing two hundred miles an hour - 'violent buffeting' begins to make sense. At this point, he informed us, he would lean out the door and give us the thumbs up sign. Of course one of us had to ask the inevitable question, 'What the hell good would that do?'. With immaculate timing of a stand-up comic he replied, 'Well if you are still conscious and have absorbed my lessons, and are not in a catatonic state with fear, you will give me the thumbs up sign in reply. I will then cut the static line thereby releasing you from the plane. You can then pull the rip cord on your chute and float safely down to terra firma.' Then it was my turn to ask the inevitable question. 'What if we don't, can't, are distracted, or unconscious and don't give you the thumbs up?' This time with the precision and timing of a surgeon sewing the last stitch in a patient after a long and delicate operation, he answered the question, 'I simply attach this ring on my belt to your static line, slide down it to you, simultaneously cutting the static line and pulling your rip cord of your parachute and let you go.' Before we could enquire about the finer details of this manoeuvre, he added in a very serious voice, 'Now I've never had to do it, but a friend of mine had to do it once. But I'm quite prepared to attempt it.' Now we all had a lot of questions after that, but we were all kept quiet while we thought about the exact wording of his last phrase.

After a few more instructions about what to do if we got blown off course and landed in water, and, trivial things like, to look up when you are clear of the plane to see that your parachute had opened properly and if it hadn't, to un-buckle it and pull you reserve chute! Easy-peasy, no probs.

I'm sorry to say on the day all this was lost in the euphoria of leaping out of a plane at two and a half thousand feet. But needless to say I survived. Years later that came back to me when I was watching a programme about Richard Branson learning to skydive before attempting to do a balloon trip around the world, for part of his training was in the use of a parachute. The instructor, cameraman and Richard were hurtling towards the ground, when the instructor gave the hand signal for Branson to deploy his shoot. With the Branson classic cheesy grin he reached for the buckle that would release his entire harness. With a horrified look, the instructor slapped his hand away and signalled again.

Undeterred, Branson, still wearing the same cheesy grin, again reached for the harness buckle. The instructor had had enough; he mouthed a few rather ungentlemanly words which were bleeped out, (although I managed to decipher them despite the censor), 'Oh! BLEEP you,' and pulled Branson's rip cord. I would lay odds that Richard was not wearing his cheesy grin when the instructor had a debriefing of that day's first jump.

Then, after a few more horror stories from our trusted instructor we were given the date of our death ... sorry! the date of our jump. Then we all departed to fill in our sponsor form, and fight off our friends eager to pay money to see us ki ... No sorry that's unfair!

Finally the day arrived and bright and early I was at the airfield with my friends and fellow parachutists to be told that the wind was too strong at the moment, but it might calm down later so we could then go for it. In the meantime our instructor went over a few things, which was an excuse, I believe, to relate some more horror stories, sadistic sod! One in particular caught my imagination, that of a lady doing her first free fall parachute jump in Germany. A sudden storm had caused a massive up draught and instead of going down she went up, from five thousand feet to twenty thousand feet and started to experience breathing difficulties and lose consciousness. Luckily she had the presence of mind to release her main parachute, free fall over fifteen thousand feet then pull her reserve. At this point in the story our little group as one looked to the sky for storm clouds. None were in sight but it was still a little too breezy for the jump.

Time went on and still it was too windy. Finally by the middle of the afternoon my group of friends and fellow parachutists lost patience and went to the local town for a drink and a sandwich. Except me that is. Being a true Yorkshireman I'd brought my own sarnies, so I lay out on the grass and had a snooze. Not ten minutes after they had gone, our instructor turned up and said the wind had dropped sufficiently to go for it and to get ready. Seeing that my group had abandoned me, I had to join a group of relative strangers. Having gone over to the other group and introduced myself, the parachutes were brought over and placed in a pile. One of the lads bringing the chutes commented, as he contemptuously dropped the chute on the ground, 'I wouldn't use that one, it's knackered.' We all laughed but the lad who was at the toilet when it was said got that one. Hey, this is life or death stuff!

Finally we were bundled into the plane and seated on the floor with our instructor by the door, giving us last minute guidance. He explained that if we were having difficulty making the decision to jump when he said go, he would give us an 'assisted exit.' This would consist of him grabbing our legs, pulling us over to the door and pushing us out! But if we resisted he would leave us where we were, and we could stay in the plane and land with the pilot. Then went on to explain that this might be a bad idea as the pilot had this bet on that he could land the plane before the first parachute landed and the trip down would be a little hair-raising. Enough said, we all jumped, unassisted, I may add!

When we reached the desired height above the airfield, it was my turn. With the instructor's invitation I shuffled to the door and dangled my legs over the edge. In reality I had very little option. The person who was first out of the door was a sixty-year-old granny. From this height houses are an inch-square, grey matchboxes, cars are little moving insects, and people just dots, if you can see them at all. Just to put this in perspective, I'm not too good with heights, I'm not brilliant on ladders and get weak feelings in the legs in tall buildings. Even in high heels I get a little unstable, but that's in a later chapter. Funnily enough, as the instructor said at the training, it's not the same as being on the edge of a tall building. Bullshit. It's worse! Anyway I slid forward to the instructor, dangled my legs over the side of the plane, looked down and slid off the edge on command. Wow what a wonderful feeling! That is once your parachute has opened and you are floating instead of falling. An amazing experience that is too quickly over. I described it, waxing lyrically, to my female boss, perhaps mistakenly, as 'the next best thing to sex.' I don't think she got it. One reason, she had no sense of humour and two she really didn't get it ... never mind.

Now on landing we had had strict instructions to keep our legs together, thereby having both legs going in the same direction when you hit the ground, and, in theory, not breaking one or both legs. Well I must have had them wide apart for some reason for over the headphones we had been issued with, this voice yelled, 'Legs together, legs together.' Then, in exasperation, 'My God, that must be a woman.' Apparently first-time female parachutist tend to have their legs wide on descent, so I must have been showing my feminine side.

Anyway by this time reality was setting in and the ground was rushing up to meet me. I snapped my legs closed and landed reasonably well without breaking either leg, or both. Absolutely fabulous, but friends and fellow fundraisers were in the pub and missed it! So I just had to do it again.

Sadly by the time they all got back, the wind had got up again so that was it for the day. So they all booked for another try, and I booked in for a second one.

The next time we arrived the day was perfect and there was no sitting about at all. We went straight up with no horror stories. Although, we did have a bit of a drama. They split our group into two so half of us watched the other half land. When they were descending one of the parachutes didn't open properly and was drifting towards the concrete runway which would have been a hard landing at the best of time, but with only half a parachute it could have been quite nasty. The instructor was yelling into his radio microphone for the unlucky parachutist to pull the reserve chute, but the headphones must not have been working for there was no response. When she landed we realised who it was and to our great relief she stood up and waited for us. The instructor was even more uptight than we were, for he shook her gently by the shoulders and asked why she didn't deploy her reserve chute, to which she replied, 'I thought you would be cross with me if I did, for wasting your time having to pack it again.' Then she burst into tears. He just hugged her.

As far as my jump went, again it was just amazing, and I kept my legs together. It does appear that I have a thing about parachutes as I made one! Not may I add for jumping out of aeroplanes. Just par-ascending behind a speed boat. Much safer, well sort of. Water always seems more inviting to fall upon than the ground, although that's all relative to how high, and how fast you are travelling even parallel to it, as I found out falling off water skis at thirty miles an hour. It was almost like landing on concrete, almost!

I had a speed boat and as much as I found water skiing fun, I saw this advert for a parachute to drag behind a speed boat that lifted the skier out of the water. Alas my budget didn't run to one, so I made one, or at least I had my mother-in-law sew one together for me. One may question the sanity of this but I had great faith in her ability as a seamstress and she did like me really.

First the design, I took the advert for the parachute and measured the guy hanging underneath, calculating that the man was six feet, I had the rough dimensions of the chute diameter, curvature and all. The next problem was the material, it had to be light yet strong, and a surprising lot of it.

I'm a firm believer in the idea that if you want something strong enough it will come into your life, although not always how you would think. Sure enough within a few months of me having the idea, I was at an auction sale and one of the items was two rolls of anorak nylon material in red and green and, even better, as no-one else wanted it I got it at a knockdown price. It was superb as it had threads running through it that prevented it ripping, which is definitely priority for a parachute, even for only twenty feet above water. It was just wide enough to cut segments out to create the curved half-sphere when it was all sewn together.

I've got to say I do feel rather guilty about cajoling my mother-in-law into sewing this gigantic structure in her living room. What a mammoth task it turned out to be, apart from the responsibility of constructing something that your only daughter's husband's life depended on. However when it was completed she did point out that there was a small tag on one edge that had written on it, in indelible pen, 'The manufacturer of this parachute holds no responsibility for the death or injury of anyone foolish enough to use it.' I thought this was fair comment and I had no problem with that at all.

The next bit was easy, just knotting lots of nylon cord to the rim of the chute and down to two rings for the harness. The breaking strain of the cord was on the packet so by the time all twelve strings were attached it would have supported three of me. Now the harness was a bit of a problem. I had got some old car safety belts from a scrap yard, but my mother-in-law's sewing machine could not cope with the thick material. Eventually I had to go to a professional harness maker for mountain climbers, who, by the way, was very reluctant to make it for me when I told him what it was for. But he could see that I was serious and that I would have tried to bodge something together if he would not make it for me. So he eventually gave in and my parachute was complete. Now for the field trials.

Now I'm not quite sure why I decided to test the parachute over land rather than the softer option of water. I think it was because I would like an audience of friends rather than injuring and making a fool of myself in front of strangers. So rather than the launch taking place at Lake Windermere which was forty miles away, I let it be known the great day was at the farm. I must confess to some surprise at the number of friends who turned up to see me ki … make a foo...to ascend to the heights.

Well with all my friends assembled there was no turning back, so strapping myself into the harness, tying a rope to the back of my car and to the harness, the parachute spread out behind me, I gave a thumbs up to the driver and I was off.

It was difficult to say what exactly the problem was. The wind in the wrong direction, the car not getting up to speed or my inability to run fast enough but let it be sufficient to say I should have picked a field that had not had cows grazing in it that very morning! All I remember was tripping and being dragged face first through an awful lot of cow claps -'cow shit' to any one unaccustomed to the term - wet and some still warm! I have a strong suspicion the driver dragged me a few yards more than was necessary after I tripped and steered over just one or two patches of cow claps than was on the decided route, but it was fun, yuk.

Well it got a laugh anyway and by the time I got cleaned up the desire for the great blue yonder had passed. Actually I never did try the parachute behind the speed boat, the friends who were the driving force behind water skiing moved away soon after and a new kitchen took precedence over the boat so I sold it to pay for it. But all was not lost, the chute provided hours of fun on breezy days, for you could unfurl it in the field and see friends being dragged by the chute in the wind. Even my mate Mick who's a big strapping lad. His feet left the ground for yards at a time till he thankfully let go before he hit the wall at the end of the field. Albeit I picked a rather windy day as a special treat for him.

Before I sold the boat we did have lots of adventures in it. The speed boat was called Galadriel after the elf queen in Lord of the Rings that I was reading at the time. I'd bought it from my cousin whose friend had been given a kit for building a speed boat for a bad debt. My cousin had helped him build one and also built one for himself. So when his children had grown up he sold it to me. We usually went up to Lake Windermere. This was before the anti- speed boat lobby banned all motorised boats on the lake. Even then there were strict regulations. First you had to be licensed and there were speed restrictions in certain areas. Even with all the restrictions it was great fun. We were a bit green at first but soon got the hang of it. The launch area was a little crowded and you had to wait your turn and when it came you had to be quick so as not to hold the queue up.

This one particular time we launched the boat and were going to park the car when we realised we had not got petrol for the boat so we left the girls sitting on the front of the boat in the shallows, posing and sunning themselves while we went off to the garage for the fuel. On return to the boat the girls were still lounging on the front of the boat but the back end had sunk, as in our hurry we had forgotten to re-plug the holes that let the rain out when it's standing. It was very embarrassing having to bail out the boat even before it was launched. We didn't blame the girls and even helped them bail the water out! Well eventually, mainly because they were taking so long!

As we got more confident at skiing we tried stunts like two skiers at a time behind the boat and skiing on just one ski. This I found near impossible although the rest achieved some success. My lack of one-ski skiing made me all the more determined to prove I could when we had a week's holiday there. We parked our caravan and all, and I was determined that I was going to stay up on one ski for more than ten seconds as was my record so far.

That particular day, as the afternoon wore on, I had swallowed an awful lot of water due to falling off with my mouth open usually due to shouting, 'Bugger...glugg, glugg,' as I entered the water at speed and was feeling a little waterlogged if not decidedly queasy.

Inevitably that evening after dinner I had projectile vomiting, which is no joke in the confines of a caravan, that lasted three days in all, of which most were spent in Kendal General Infirmary after a blue light and siren ride in an ambulance. On arrival the doctor described my condition as 'Windermere tummy, the scourge of water skiers' and mumbled something about 'the lake's rife with duck muck.'

One of the rules in the little blue book we were issued with when we obtained a licence to use a speed boat on the lake towing a skier was that a minimum of two people must be in the boat. Obviously the driver but also an observer to watch the skier. In retrospect this is to prevent the driver turning around and watching the skier in case he falls off, and not watching where the boat is going. I say in retrospect because it took a potentially serious incident to get the message home.

The incident in question took place one sunny Sunday in August. Albeit we did have an observer in the boat dutifully watching me skiing. My mate, the driver, was also intent on watching me as he attempted acrobatic turns with the boat, trying to dislodge me from my determination to stay upright. In among negotiating the wake of the boat and navigating potentiality impossible turns, I noticed we seemed to be on a collision course with a rather large motor launch leisurely cruising along the edge of the lake. As we got close to a conjunction with the launch I realised that the driver was watching me and had not noticed the danger. A panicky wave from myself was only reciprocated with a jaunty wave back from the driver but no evasive action. At this point I gave up and let go of the tow rope and sunk below the waves, not being able to bear witness to the impending devastation, for if he didn't actually hit the launch, our boat was definitely heading straight for a crash with the shore. On surfacing I expected smouldering driftwood where the two boats had been. To my relief I found only a very irate and justifiably angry grey- haired man on an intact launch (I can't swear to the fact that he had dark hair on my previous observation). My ex-mate, the driver, was looking very sheepish, and on picking me up out of the water asked me if I was OK! I'm not sure my reply would be suitable for publication but it ended with the immortal words. 'Just get me to the shore so I can change these shorts.' Then we were able to laugh about it. On shore, over a mug of hot sweet tea, (I wonder if all this hot sweet tea could have been the cause of me becoming diabetic?) my driver sheepishly related the story. When he finally decided to look forward, all he could see was the side of the launch filling his entire field of vision, he swung the wheel and he said if he'd have had his fingers over the side they would have been trapped between the two boats.

We all had a go at severe steering, trying to dislodge skiers although we all kept our eyes forward. One of my friends, who was really good on skies, had seen a skier let go of the tow rope close to the shore and glide to the bank and walk casually up the beach, so he wanted to try it.

He requested that I should drive the boat. In retrospect that might have been a slight misjudgment for, in my usual lack of restraint in matters of trying new stunts, I have been accused of being a little reckless. Anyway I pulled him out to the centre of the lake and then headed back to the bank. About a hundred yards from the edge of the lake I swung back into the middle. Now you've seen ice skaters in a long line and a big guy at the end swings the chain of skaters round at the end of the rink, with the little guy at the other end of the chain doing about a hundred miles an hour as the chain swings round. Well my mate was at the end of a long rope being swung towards the bank at about two hundred miles an hour (well ten at least). I had this vision of his skis digging in and he being catapulted twenty feet up the bank, I could hardly look! Now my mate was a bit of a poser but he was very athletic and did have quite a chunk of talent (and a lot of luck) for his skis hit the bank and instead of being flung up the bank and falling flat on his face, as I'm sure I would have done, in one fluid motion he stepped out of his skies, ran up the bank to where the rest of our party was having a picnic. Managing to come to a dignified stop, he picked up a glass of wine and took a sip. There was a moment's silence followed by a monumental cheer from groups all along the side of the lake in appreciation of his skill. To give him his due, he did have the humility to say in a quiet voice to our small group, as he raised his glass to his appreciative audience, 'I won't be trying that again in a hurry, and oh, I need to change my shorts.'

One of the less momentous episodes but with a fair amount of embarrassment was the time we decided to take a leisurely trip up to the far end of the lake. We'd been skiing most of the day so we thought we'd do a bit of sightseeing. It was rather fine compared with the hurley and burly of the skiing area. We waved at the sail boats rather than apologise for not giving way to sail, and they actually waved back instead of waving a fist.

We had no sooner got to the top of the lake and turned round when the outboard motor revved up and we drifted to a stop. We all looked at one another then looked over the back of the boat to see the propeller lying on the bottom of the lake, luckily in only five feet of water. I think we must have stayed like that for five minutes just gazing at the sunken prop before I said 'bugger.' Well, I fished out the propeller with a quick dive and discovered that the rubber mount had split and there was no way it could be repaired. That left us with only one problem - how to get back to the other end of the lake to our launch site and boat trailer three miles away.

We must have obviously looked in distress as a sail boat pulled along side and asked us if we needed help. I replied, 'Not unless you can tow us the other end of the lake.' To which he answered, 'No problem' and threw us a rope. In true nautical tradition I thankfully grabbed the rope and then was nearly pulled overboard as the sail boat set off. I was quickly supported by my friend and the rope was secured to the front of the boat and then we were off. Just a bit embarrassing, a speed boat being towed by a sail boat, but we swallowed our pride and thanked our rescuer warmly when we reached our destination, loaded our boat onto the trailer and headed home for repairs.

We did once go water skiing in the sea with, our skiing friends, on a holiday in Wales. It was a sunny day and the sea was reasonably calm so we got permission from a local ski club to use their launch ramp and we set off down the coast to a little bay that the club had recommended for skiing.

Now skiing in the open sea can be a little daunting especially as you are zipping along behind the boat and some large fish of some kind are jumping out of the water alongside of you. Well they weren't as big as dolphins or even sharks for that matter but if there are fish that big swimming with you it's not beyond imagination that there could be much bigger ones, perhaps waiting for you to fall off and eat you! Or at least chew your toes off. This goes up a notch when you do fall off you skis and tread water till the boat comes to pick you up, especially when friends go to pick up the valuable skis first after they have drifted away. There is definitely a sensation of cold panic when the boat is a few hundred yards away and something big and cold touches your leg.

That apart, it was an exhilarating experience. We even went out a couple of miles to a small island. It was covered in seaweed and only a few feet above the water. In the middle there was this pile of what looked like scrap until you got up close and you realised is was the remains of a large ship that had been wrecked there. It was quite awesome to see those huge steel girders twisted by the power of the sea. Our little boat looked very vulnerable so we quickly got back to shore.

After about four hours of skiing we were ready for our picnic, so we beached the boat, walked up the sand and prepared lunch. A sandwich and a cup of tea later we realised, looking across to or boat, that the sea is tidal, 'duh'. Landlubbers that we were, we now had an immovable boat six feet up the shore out of the water. And six hours wait till we were re-floated again. In all fairness our usual venue of Windermere, being a lake, is not tidal and you can pull up to the shore without being marooned. Well it's my excuse and I'm sticking to it. Some time later as we sat on the beach contemplating the error of our ways a local just happened to saunter by and offered advice. 'You'll have to wait till tide comes in now look you.' The Welsh, eh, don't you just love them? Needless to say he wasn't offered a sandwich.

The boat was a lot of fun but things move on. Our skiing friends moved away and the boat was traded in for a new kitchen, boring eh? But soon I had another inspiration. I wanted to learn to fly, in 'a microlight aircraft!'

I must have been a bit flush at the time for I went to see this thing in a warehouse and bought it. The guy selling it said he acquired it as a bad debt, and that sums it up really, the bad debt must have been to the Wright brothers. But for about the price of an old car, it was superb!

Actually I've always had a bit of a yen to fly. I used to dream about it a lot but without a plane, and yes, I do know Freud's interpretation of that was.

Poor eyesight from my foray with a potato knife early on and not being born into money had frustrated my yearnings, until I clapped eyes on it. To be honest my heart was ruling my brain at the moment of purchase. I did mention the Wright brothers, well more accurately, remember those drawings by Da Vinci. It was definitely styled more on one of his foresighted scribblings. The engine was impressive, well not the engine that was fitted, exactly. That was an engine that would fit if it was a different design, although I was sure I could make it fit. The engine that was on was not impressive at all. Basically it was two lawnmower engines back to back feeding to a propeller by a rather frayed-looking belt. But that was by the by. It was going to be the better engine that was going to take me up into the great blue yonder and soar like a bird. The thought of flying made me rather poetic.

As soon as I got it home, I assembled it (did I mention it was in bits?) and set to fitting the new, different engine. It was a bit of a bodge job (no change there then) but it did look quite proper when I had finished.

Now for the big test. Not a test flight may I add (I'm not that stupid?), just a quick rev up in the backyard. This was a spectacle to be shared so I called my mate, John, who beat a path to my door in anticipation of a laugh.

After a little priming and coughing and spluttering and a lot of exhausting pulling on the starter cord, it roared into life. Wow, one quick rev and it blew my garden furniture, which was set out behind the plane, clean over a wall. Luckily the microlight stayed where it was as it was up against side of the house, but it did rather catch us by surprise and demonstrated its power. John with his usual wicked sense of humour, asked me what, if I ever crashed in it, would go through my mind. Pointing to the engine positioned directly behind the seat, he smirked, 'The engine.'

Undeterred by my mate's macabre sense of humour I was determined to actually fly the thing. I thought a spot of training might be in order so I borrowed a book.

CHAPTER THIRTEEN

Chapter one didn't really get down to flying. Chapter two didn't really grab my interest, and by chapter three I'd lost interest in the book but not flying so I decided to have a go anyway. You can get too deep into the theory if you are not careful.

The perfect opportunity arose when the school where I worked as a technician was running what they called a project week. This was a week at the end of the summer term when a lot of the kids had gone off with their parents on holiday. Instead of a normal timetable the children that were left were split into small groups and did projects like building models of Blackpool Tower out of matchsticks or cleaning up river banks and all sorts of different, exciting things. One of the projects just happened to be flying; history of, drawing planes, and such. I let it be known to the teachers in charge of the project that I had a parachute and a microlight aircraft. With a little prompting, they invited me to bring the parachute to show the kids what one looked like close up, then assemble my microlight on the playing field.

On the first day I duly brought the parachute in and spread it out on the playing field. It was quite breezy and much fun was had as pupils were dragged across the field as the chute caught the wind. None of the children were lost as the tennis courts fencing caught the lighter ones that could not stop themselves.

Then next day I brought in my microlight. It took me about an hour and an half to assemble it with an attentive audience of about twenty kids who kept asking questions I could not answer. Finally I was ready.

The pupils were herded well away to watch from a safe distance while I donned my gear. This consisted of a leather flying helmet, that I suspected might be a tank-driver's helmet, I had bought at a car boot sale, an old pair of motorcycle goggles, and a rather scruffy leather jacket. It had a fur collar that made it, with a little imagination, look like fighter pilot's jacket. With a nonchalant wave to my audience I climbed into the seat.

Can I clarify at this point that this was an inaugural flight and it might have been advisable not to have had an audience. But that would have taken the spontaneity out of the adventure, and I'm into spontaneity. I had nearly read chapter three of the manual so I wasn't all that unprepared, was I?

The engine spluttered into life and with a few revs to warm her up, I floored the accelerator. Amazingly enough, the microlight began to pick up speed across the grass, as did my pulse rate.

The school playing field is quite large but some inappropriately sited electricity pylons loomed just as I was achieving lift off by a few feet. I could not hear the cheers from my audience over the magnificent noise of the engine but I just glimpsed a lot of excited children and teachers waving and jumping up and down. I took this to be encouragement but in retrospect it may well have been a warning. Nevertheless, discretion got the better part of valour, and I cut the engine. Now I'm sure I could have flown under the high tension electricity wires, maybe not over but definitely under, but I didn't want to unduly alarm my audience. It was only slightly humiliating having to pull my plane back by hand across the field, but as soon as I switched off the engine the pupils were released to help me drag it back. The encouragement I received from the kids like 'awesome', 'mega sir', and 'can you do it again?' convinced me to have another go. This time I was determined to get past the pylons one way or another and my engine was nicely warmed up now so I was convinced this was the big one.

With the audience at a safe distance again and a quick rev of the engine, I was off across the field again. I did better this time and was soon airborne, and then disaster struck! One of my carburettors fell off! The engine lost rather a disproportionate amount of power as I still had one carb left, but my ambition to get over the pylons was thwarted.

This came as only a slight surprise as I had had trouble before, although not in flight as then. As I was building up the engine for the first time the offending carb was rather loose. It was rubber mounted and the rubber had come away from the metal, so I glued it back on. Again hindsight or perhaps a little more technical knowledge would have warned me that the glue I used would dissolve in petrol, and seeing that the carbs are bathed in petrol it is little wonder that my repair failed.

I have since glued the carb back on with glue that is immune to the effects of petroleum but I've never got around to reading chapter four or for that matter fulfilling my aeronautic ambition.

I did manage a trip in a two-seater plane. The short flight was a birthday present from my partner who knows my passion for flying. It was from Yeadon as there is a light aircraft club next to the main

Leeds-Bradford Airport. The pilot asked me were I lived and we could fly over my house which was only about ten miles away. It was amazing to approach the farm from the air then fly around it and then across the Aire valley. At that point he let me take the controls and fly towards Skipton, up the valley. A message came over the radio to say there was another plane coming down the valley so we had to keep to the left. As I was still in control of the plane. He instructed me to turn the control to the left. I had seen on TV that if you turned the control too fast and too much the plane went upside down, and as much as my slight airsickness was under control it would not have stood up to a flying upside down. With my minimal steering the pilot took over and moved us to side of the valley and then headed back to the airport. All this excitement had weakened my control of my airsickness and I was feeling a little queasy. With a little Zen meditation which involved shutting my eyes and thinking of walking through a cornfield on a summer's day with my feet firmly on the ground, I came round a little. Well enough at least to open my eyes and reply to the pilot when he enquired if I was all right as he had noticed I was a little pale With my meditation disturbed I decided to try taking my mind off my distress by talking to the pilot about the plane. I could see the airport approaching so I was confident I would make it. Then I had to ask the stupid question of 'what's a stall like' without hesitation he just reached for the dash board and switched of the ignition, and said 'like this' as the dashboard lit up with flashing lights and at least two piercing alarms went off. I'm almost sure he did not intend to frighten me but he certainly took my mind of my stomach.

The plane's nose began to drop alarmingly and the propeller was just turning gently in the wind. My next question was spontaneous and blunt, 'yes but how do you start it?' I had visions of having to climb out on the wing and lean over and give the propeller a quick twist, like you see in old films but with the guy standing on the ground. I had forgotten that when we set off the pilot just pressed a button on the dash and the engine burst into life, as he did at that moment and we just carried on as if nothing had happened. When we landed and were having a coffee in the club house I thanked him for the experience and especially for the instant cure for my airsickness. Although he swore it wasn't intentional.

That reminds of a story that appeals to my sense of humour of a TV interview of Ian McKellen the Shakespearian actor who played Gandalf in the film 'Lord Of The Rings'. He was telling how he owned a small plane and offered to take a friend up for a ride as he was frightened of flying and had to take a business trip to America, and he thought it would help him cope with his imminent trip. He related how they had been flying for about half an hour and McKellen was a little bored as his passenger just sat next to him not talking or even replying to conversation. Just to liven things up McKellen slumped over the controls and pretended to pass out. After about a couple of minutes with no response from his passenger, he looked up and carried on flying the plane. Glancing across to his passenger he saw that his friend was catatonic. He was drawing blood from his clenched fists as his nails dug into his palms, his face was white and his eyes bulged staring into space. McKellen headed back to the airport and after quickly landing had to get help to lift his passenger out of the plane. McKellen told the interviewer how he did not know if his friend made the business trip to America as his friend has not spoken to him since or replied to his messages. Some people have no sense of humour. I did offer to take my ex-wife up in my microlight to cure her of her fear of flying but she declined. I think she must have seen the interview.

As you get older you do less daft things. It's nothing to do with learning from experience, or losing that adventurous spirit. It's the fear of pain, broken bones that heal slowly, with long stays in hospital. All this becomes a reality as your body loses its ability to bounce.

Then there was my brush with Acapulco diving. To set the scene, we have a group of teenage lads off to Cornwall, camping for a fortnight by the sea. The fleshpots of Costa Del Sol were in the future and Butlins with mummy and daddy well in the past. We were young, fit and out to enjoy ourselves and maybe impress a few lasses with our inherent Yorkshire charm, prowess, and charisma. I cannot honestly remember that it was showing off to the fairer sex that made me do what I did but the deed is the thing. Acapulco diving! I'd seen them do it on TV and it really appealed.

I was a regular at the local swimming baths and was quite proficient at swimming and diving. Our local pool had a half decent diving board that was great for doing bomb dives off the top box. This is the art of diving straight down as near the side as you dare and curling up as you hit the water. This creates a fountain of water that if done just right will wet any unwary attendant who is in range, or better still little old ladies sat in the spectators' gallery next to the pool. No not really! But girls were always fair game as their screams when they were drenched were rather gratifying.

Anyway back to Cornwall, there were these local lads diving off the cliffs into the sea and it looked really superb, so I thought I'd have a go. The locals made it look so easy and they had obviously sussed out the best spot. I climbed the cliffs that were about a good twenty to thirty feet above the sea to where they were diving off. It didn't seem all that straightforward. For a start the sea began a good six feet out from where we were stood as the cliff didn't go straight down, so a big push off from the cliff was essential to prevent you from hitting the face on the way down. Secondly, the sea was rather rough, advancing and receding thereby altering in depth, and depth is rather essential to prevent you from hitting the rocks on the bottom when entering the water from this height.

But not to be deterred I did a quick risk assessment on my not sustaining serious injury and went for it. Apart from the necessity for a good push off from the cliff to avoid catching the protruding base, a swallow dive with your arm outstretched gives you a little extra feet and always looks impressive. I had done this many times at the swimming pool, so was reasonably confident I was not going to hit the water in a belly flop. It was a long way down and the water was hard but I entered it with style and surfaced to cheers as I swam to the beach.

Back on the cliffs I asked my mates, who were equally good divers as I was, who was next. Not one was up for it, would you believe, so I just had to do it again to show them how easy it was. My next dive was technically superb but a little ill-timed, or I was lucky the first time, I'm not sure. All I know was that on my way down the water receded from about eight foot to about five as the waves hit the cliff base and went away again. Eight foot is just about adequate for a dive from that height but five ain't. I still have a slight scar above my right eye where I met the rock at the bottom of that five foot of water. It was lucky in a way that there wasn't any sharks in about five miles of the spot as the amount of blood would have caused a feeding frenzy. Mothers gathered up their children and turned their backs as I passed, staggering up the beach. Can't say that I blame them. I did look a little scary emerging from the waves, blood streaming down my face and body.

Having said that, with a reasonably clean hanky pressed on it for half an hour and a band aid stuck on the gash, I survived without an embarrassing trip to A&E and being told by a petulant nurse that I had been an idiot. You just don't need it, do you?

Apart from luck I do heal well, perhaps a good job I reckon.

We all went to the cliff the next day to see what it looked like when the tide was out. I've got to say that was really scary. There were jagged rocks down there with just a small patch of sand. Even with ten foot of water never mind five, if I'd landed in the wrong place I would have broken my silly neck.

I'm rather addicted to those camcorder-filmed stunts you see on TV filmed by kids skate boarding off roofs and riding their bicycles off mountainsides. It's really strange I do not relate to them in any way, I just think they are stupid. What do you make of that?

Well you would think at sixty-odd I would be getting a little less intrepid, if that's the right word or is it just that I should grow up. What set me off was a rather prolonged winter just like the ones when I was a lot younger that gave me a yen to go sledging. At some stage because of the poor sledging winters or deciding I was past such childish pursuits, I had sold, at some car boot or other, my childhood sledges. No big loss as they were at best only big enough for two people and I was thinking big.

Tucked away in one of my sheds I had a pair of old wooden snow skis that were ideal and of the dimensions I had in mind. Next I needed a body and quick survey of another shed produced a rather fine, large, sturdy, square coffee table. It was relatively easy to marry the two together, just a few screws through the skis into the base of the table and the result was superb. In the final finishing stages in my workshop the neighbour popped his head round the door to see what was going on, took one look and started reminiscing about his childhood fun of sledging. So what with his wife and my ever-give-it-a-try partner, my grandiose design was justified as a four-seater

You would think that there was loads of ideal sledging spots around the farm but none was suitable as the only field that I sledged in as a kid I had planted trees in. Then walking through the local park the ideal spot presented itself. The local kids had already given it a go but only on bits of cardboard and tin trays. It was crying out for a proper sledge. There was one little drawback, it was very steep. Not that that was a drawback as such, just a bit of a challenge. Well it might not have been a challenge for a bit of cardboard or a tin tray but for a sledge that would not have been out of place on the Cresta Run, it was going to be a little hairy. Another minor point that was pointed out to me by my fellow-sledgers, was that at the base of the slope were trees and a wall. Have you noticed how some people just look for problems. Surely that would have to be sorted when we reached that point. Word had got out that we were attempting the world down-hill sledging speed record as two more friends showed up to watch us kil... have fun. We could have managed six on the sledge with a little close contact but sadly they declined. . The latecomers retreated to a good viewing spot whispering to one another and shaking their heads. We now had the venue, audience, reasonably eager participants and a superb sledge. What more could one ask for. Apart perhaps for an ambulance in attendance.

Strategically placing the sledge at the top of the hill, pointing roughly at what we decided would give us the best chance of stopping before the obstructions, I briefed everyone, as we all sat aboard, for everyone to drag their feet when nearing the bottom.

Did I mention I had waxed the skis in the workshop as I remembered my dad showing me how to rub a candle on the runners to make it go faster? It just did not need the extra speed! We set off down that hill fast enough to make you nose bleed with the acceleration, probably only doing about twenty miles an hour, but just six inches off the ground on a coffee table it felt more like two hundred.

I have to admit to screaming but I was in good company, all four of us did. Luckily regardless of the fear or perhaps because of it we all dragged our feet in plenty of time. In fact we were all dragging our feet well before half way down the bloody slope.

'Well that was exhilarating wasn't it, shall we do it again?' I asked my fellow passengers as we all lay in the snow recovering. I didn't get a particularly positive response but we took the sledge back to the top anyway. While my fellow tobogganists were recovering I decided to go it alone. A physics problem here. Does a sledge go downhill faster with more people i.e. weight or slower with one. Newton with his laws of motion may have come up with, I can tell you, it goes a bloody sight faster with one. Forget dragging your feet at the bottom or half way down for that matter, I was wearing out my boots after ten feet down that slope. Even then with the brakes full on from the top it was touch and go whether I was going to make the trees.

At the last second I bailed out, still clinging to the steering rope and slid to an undignified stop on my arse inches from the trees. Just for effect I did lie prone for a minute just to see if anyone would rush down the hill to see if I was OK. No-one did. I suppose it was a long way down just to see if I had lived, so I got up and pulled the sledge back up to the top.

My solo run had inspired a competitive spirit in my friend so he wanted to do a solo run and, not to be outdone, he was going head first lying on his stomach. Never one to stifle foolhardiness I let him go. Whether dragging you feet as opposed to digging your heels in as I did made was a less efficient braking system or he didn't brake soon enough, he was still going strong when he reached the trees but managed to only skim two of them which actually slowed him down a bit. Whether it was luck or design he approached the wall at a gap, but not so lucky as there was a six foot drop at the other side. He shot through the gap, teetered on the edge and toppled out of sight.

We just stood there and looked at one another, and then his wife asked the question, 'How high is the drop?' I tried to make it sound trivial at six feet but I was rather unconvincing for inasmuch as six feet isn't much, it's not to be shrugged off, head first on a sledge. We were all just about to run down the hill, mobile phones at the ready to call an ambulance when a little head popped up through the gap and waved, he was OK and the sledge was fine too. After that we were a little more cautious and set off from half way up the slope which was still great fun, but humping that big sledge back up the hill every time took it's toll, even going only half way up. So after half a dozen more runs we all retired back home for a cup of hot tea. I just don't have the stamina any more, just the imagination.

— 14 —

SPORTING ACTIVITIES (NOT!)

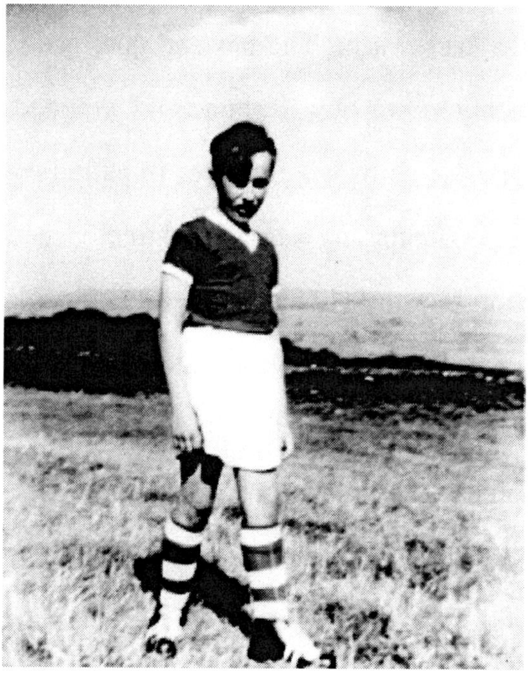

I NEVER WAS one for sports especially football. That was killed off early at school by our PE teacher, an ex-sergeant major, a lot like the gym teacher in '*Kes*,' if you ever saw the film. He would send us out onto the playing field in shorts and tee-shirt, even when snow was on the ground and not only on the ground, it could be a blizzard with snow and ice crystals being whipped up off the field and drifting across the pitch (get the picture?) while our beloved gym teacher would be snug in his track suit, no doubt with thermal underwear.

For some reason, perhaps because of my lack of enthusiasm and my inability to kick the ball, I would be the last one to be picked for the team by the team captains, me and the fat guy and the anorexic, thin, tall, specky one. Guess what, I would end up in goal where I couldn't even run about to keep warm. The net and goal posts gave no shelter whatsoever. The only source of warmth was if I wrapped my arms around my body under my tee shirt, which rather impaired my meagre ability as a goalkeeper to intercept any unexpected approaches of the ball even further. The driving blizzard always seemed to coincide and persist just for the four sports periods per week. If this seems to be plagiarising the film 'Kes', believe me I was there first. I was twelve and it was nineteen sixty. Captains on each team would pick which professional team they pretended to be. I used to say I supported Manchester to be one of the lads but I don't think anyone was impressed.

Probably I could qualify that slightly by saying I am just not a team player. I did master some sports. Ice skating for one. For just on the road from the farm was a fair sized lake or as it was affectionately known locally 'as 'Keighley Tarn' which, long before global warming, seemed to freeze over on a regular basis in winter and even stay frozen for months. So for Christmas one year I was given a pair of ice skates. The Tarn was relatively safe as its deepest point couldn't have been more than three feet. So I was allowed to go on my own after I had finished all my chores around the farm.

There were always lots of people skating and I soon got the hang of staying upright. Nothing fancy mind you but I liked going fast, weaving in and out of the wobbly ones and making them wobble even more. I also used to pull other kids who couldn't afford skates around on their sledges on the ice. Even at night after it got dark you could still skate as people would drive their cars to the edge of the lake and illuminate the ice with their headlights and later we would help them push start their cars because of flat batteries.

It was pretty exposed up there as it was on top of a hill. This, by the way, was always a controversial point as no-one seemed to know how it filled up with water. Anyway the ice would be quite rough in places due to the wind and one of the games we played was skating fast over the bumps without ending up on your backside. When the ice went slushy and was about to melt it was always fun and an extra incentive to stay on your feet with it being a long walk back home in the icy wind with wet pants. There was also the added excitement of the possibility of going through the ice. I have only gone through twice. Once for a dare to see how far you can tread when the ice all around is creaking, cracking, and groaning. And sure enough I went through up to my crotch, a rather chilling experience and one can imagine how easy it would be to drown. As you try to pull yourself out onto the ice it breaks away, and with the cold you soon get exhausted. Luckily I was close to the side and did not have much trouble but further out in deeper water it could easily be fatal. Be warned!

The other time I went through the ice I was doing my hero bit and went to pull a young lady out of a hole in the ice. The adults could not get near her so I went in where angels fear to tread. I was not too worried about breaking through the ice as from my previous experience I knew I could stand up; sure enough I ended up stood next to her in the water in the hole in the ice. I soon bundled her out and, with a little more effort this time, managed to get out myself. My reward was a lift home in a car so I was well pleased.

I'm rather a good swimmer and diver if I do say it myself. This again was due to the local amenities. No not the local swimming pool, although I was a regular there, but the local reservoir! It had large signs up saying 'NO SWIMMING. WATER USED FOR PUBLIC WATER SUPPLY'. This was a direct lie for we knew our local history, and this particular reservoir was built to supply the woollen mill in the village. Not that it would have made much difference if it was drinking water anyway, it was too much of an ideal spot to be put off by official notices. It was lovely clear water straight off the moors with an earthy peat smell that I still find brings back memories of summer days larking about in the water with my mates.

Its only drawback was some keen fisherman had stocked it with pike, and if you swam by the reed beds you stood a chance of having a toe bitten by a hungry pike, as I did on a few occasions.

Apart from honing my swimming skills, diving off a three-foot high banking into two foot of water could also be enjoyed as long as it was a rather shallow dive and with a run to get you sufficiently far enough out achieve the minimum depth and prevent the sandy, gritty bottom taking significant amounts of skin off nose, chest, and knees.

My father even scrounged a two-seater canoe for me which we used to manhandle across fields and walls to sail on the 'res'. We used to copy doing death rolls we'd seen canoeists do on TV, the only problem being the canoes on TV were sealed so they didn't let water in. Ours inevitably sank. We never managed to turn it back with us still sitting in it so it was a swimming matter anyway and dragging the canoe to the side before it sank completely. It was a time of simple pleasures.

As much as I was not into sports I did organise a few. Well kind of. It was a time when 'It's a Knock-out' was all the rage on TV so I had the idea to run one in the back field between the two local rival amateur dramatic groups both of which I was a member.

I was amazed at the enthusiasm both for the idea and the daft games I had constructed. They tackled the assault courses and games that I devised with exuberance to the point of abandon. In fact it became such a muck or nettles competition by the second one I ran, we had St Johns ambulance in attendance as sprains, cuts, and bruises were rife.

The main event was the assault course which consisted of suspended poles you either had to climb over or run along, with just a hint of grease to make it interesting.

I laid out an old carpet pinned down on two edges, which the contestants had to crawl under. It was pure coincidence that it was placed over a few cow claps. There was some choice language coming out from under that carpet at times, but all in good fun.

There was the inevitable tug-o-war with one of my dad's old tow ropes. This was always situated in a muddy part of the field as less traction inevitably led to at least one team falling over and I thought it would be a softer landing. I'm so thoughtful I surprise myself!

Of course there just had to be water, it would not be 'It's a Knock-out' without it. Not having a swimming pool like on TV we had to manage with buckets of the stuff. But we still managed to get everybody suitably wet. The water game involved caring a bucket of water over the assault course. Well at least most of it as even I thought getting the bucket of water under the carpet a little excessive. The winning team was the one who got the most water in the milk churn at the end of the course.

I was quite surprised and gratified how wet the competitors had gotten carrying the water over the course. You can't beat a person getting wet to spice up the entertainment factor for we did have a substantial number of spectators. One incident on the assault course I found particularly entertaining was when Sheila, my wife, who was one of the competitors was climbing through a suspended car tyre and lost her shorts. Luckily her knickers stayed secure. We did manage to catch it on video, but resisted the impulse to send the tape to 'You've Been Framed'. There are limits, and castration was mentioned if I posted it off.

There were lots of minor events like 'welly wanging' which was quite a laugh although my favourite was 'cow clap slinging'. This was achieved by collecting sun-dried cow shi ... dung turning it over to dry both sides, and then you end up with a throw-able projectile, very similar to a Frisbee only organic and smelly. I was very impressed that even the women contestants participated albeit with a wrinkled nose.

All really great fun, sport at its best as far as I am concerned. The competition went on for a number of years and became an annual event, but I decided to call it a day when one year we had quite a nasty accident and someone fell off the greasy pole head first, mildly compressing his spine. He was OK but it was a bit of a wake-up call with Elf and Safety rearing its ugly head. Another problem was that we invited the next village's theatre group to take part in a three sided competition. Mistakenly as it happened, as quite a few of their members were also members of the local harriers cross country running club and showed us up something shocking by trouncing the other two teams.

In my late twenties I did take up judo, but only for four weeks! I found that the bruises on bruises and sprains took longer than a week to lose at least some of their tenderness, so I was attending the next weekly session still rather sensitive to further abuse, and the torture would start all over again. Needless to say I never achieved a coloured belt and was constantly being thrown about by black belts half my size and under ten years of age.

Our enthusiastic instructor was an ex-SAS commando, and was always keen to demonstrate some of the killing methods they were taught. As a break from our official judo routines, he would sit us all around in a large circle and call for a volunteer. I can not truly remember if in my innocence I volunteered or, being new to his demonstrations, I was the only one that did not look at my feet, but looked him in the eye, which was sufficient for him to gesture for me to stand up and join him in the arena. After a brief lecture on the etiquette of hand-to-hand fighting methods of war, which basically involved killing or at least severally disabling your opponent before he kills you, he told me to come at him as if wielding a knife as if I was about to stab him.

When I was about an arm's length away with my imaginary knife raised in the air poised for the kill he moved in for the slaughter. First he chopped my knife arm with both hands, one from above and one from underneath, pausing only briefly to explain that he had now disarmed me and broken my arm in two places, possibly three. He them almost gently brought his elbow down into my ribs again explaining to his now enthralled audience that he had now broken four of my ribs and his opponent would have severe breathing problems.

At this stage even though this was done in slow motion and with little force, I was already fast losing the will to live.

His next disabling move involved bringing his knee smashing into my thigh bone. Explaining to his audience that a knee to the genitals can be very ineffective, your opponent could possibly be wearing a jock strap so a broken thigh bone was just as effective. I was thankful for this as I was not wearing a jock strap and even considering the slow motion and reasonably gentle force applied I could well have been in a lot of pain. His next disabling move involved bringing his foot down the front of my shin, painfully removing large quantities of skin and, with a coup de grace, smashing down on his opponent's foot breaking several bones. Explaining that heavy army boots were very effective for this last manoeuvre, again my luck was in as the instructor was in bare feet. Slightly less luckily I was also, and he managed to catch, purely by accident, my big toe. All in all, the whole thing was an experience and the bruises and sprains healed and I feel slightly more confident to defend myself if I was attacked although I don't think I would go for the commando killer option.

So that's about the limit of my sporting interest, with no regrets.

— 15 —

THE GORILLA

WELL I WAS just driving through Bradford and I saw this gorilla. It was big and fierce looking, about twenty foot tall clinging to the side of a tall building, King Kong like. I stopped my car in the middle of traffic and uttered the magic words, 'I want it.' Now I'm a firm believer in the phrase 'be careful what you wish for' for what you want will arrive on your doorstep in one form or another and not always in a welcome form.

But I just could not see the problem with having a twenty foot gorilla in your garden. Then the honking of impatient motorists moved me on.

I suppose its time I explained my vision before you assume I'm on LSD or something. The gorilla was an advertisement for a film and although it appeared to be three dimensional it was just painted on a six-ply board cut out, but painted so superbly that it looked real.

I have quite a large garden with mature trees overlooking the Aire Valley, an ideal place for a gorilla to swing about in to the entertainment of passers-by. OK a little eccentric with a dash of vivid imagination but I hate being boring.

As much as I believe that what you want will come to you, a little work and planning is essential. Now it just so happens that the gorilla was climbing up the building where my very good, long-suffering friend John works. Just for the record, I don't believe in coincidences, as I said if you want something enough it will come, albeit in roundabout ways.

So a quick phone call to my pal established that the advert would be up there for about another year then the building was to be altered and the gorilla removed. That was no problem, I could wait. Meanwhile occasional trips to Bradford established that 'my gorilla' was being looked after and being fed and watered properly. Notice how it is 'My Gorilla'. This is all part of the process of achieving what you want. Also progress reports were received from my friend, and we established that the time was getting close and to be on stand-by. Then it came, one Monday morning, the phone call that I had been waiting for, for the past eighteen months.

Panic! No car or till at least a week on Tuesday when the garage could get the part, and that would be too late! Plus the fact I had work, but a quick phone call to work explaining I had an upset stomach got me the day off. Well, I was very excited!

I'm not quite sure if it's the type of good friends I have, or my good friends are well used to my mad ways. Probably both, but a quick phone call to another long-suffering friend with the request to help me to 'Pick up a gorilla from the centre of Bradford' only evoked a simple 'OK I'll be with you in half an hour'. I like friends that don't question my eccentricity, a sign of a true friend!

As good as his word, Phil was on time. We hitched up my trailer to his car and we were off. There was a sinking moment when we turned a corner to gaze on a bare building with no primate in attendance. But I had been assured that the gorilla had only been taken down that morning so hopefully it hadn't escaped. Now came the tricky part. As much as my mate had told me when it was coming down, he could not negotiate with the contractors who were doing the work on the building, so it was up to me to scrounge 'My Gorilla' off the work men.

As I approached the foreman my mind was a blank, then as I saw 'My Gorilla' propped up against a wall, I had an inspiration. Lie! I looked the foreman straight in the eye, pointed to the gorilla and said, 'I painted that, can I have it?' He shrugged, said 'Yeh take it away', and walked off. In retrospect the foreman hadn't the same perspective as I did for a twenty-foot gorilla, to me it was a desirable object that I had waited eighteen months for. To him, it was in the way. I do feel slightly bad about lying and could probably have achieved the same results by being honest (there's a moral for you. This book has everything!). But I was now the proud owner of a twenty-foot gorilla.

I have found that 'Now what are you going to do with it?' and 'Why?' are usually asked by the female of the species, and true to form neither John nor Phil did, but the same cannot be said for the wife. It was definitely a touch of the Vulcan bombers and Jeremy Clarkson. Anyway I already had plans.

First I coerced another friend to help me construct a twenty-foot scaffolding tower. Coerced is not really correct as he was willing and I think he actually volunteered when I was talking about it. Again I have a great set of friends that rarely question my motives, or sanity for that matter, and often suggest greater eccentricities to add to my own.

Twenty foot is higher than I had envisaged and I'm not too good on heights but the scaffolding tower was well constructed so felt reasonably safe even when lifting large heavy pieces of plywood to the top and securing them with thick wire. The gorilla was in six parts so it was like a simple jigsaw with large heavy pieces.

The end result was spectacular! I had positioned it so it looked like it was climbing up a tree. Standing back was insufficient to appreciate the magnificence of it, so we climbed into my car and drove to the other side of the valley, a good two and a half miles as the crow flies, and it was still discernible as a gorilla peering around a tree. WOW!

But it needed just a little something else. Gazing at it, the inspiration came to me. It needed Fay Wray. Now where was I going to find a fair damsel, prepared to be carried off by a twenty-foot gorilla? It so happened that I coincidentally had a female shop dummy in my shed. (Doesn't everyone?) Unscrewing her bottom and legs left me with the perfect handful for Kong. So that was duly wired in place, appearing to be held in Kong's giant fist. Perfect.

Soon after that the fun really started. There was definitely increased traffic on the road being overlooked by Kong and Fay. Quite a number would stop and get out of their cars and stare and point. Then people would ask if they could take pictures of their children with the gorilla. Just a week later the local rag arrived and asked if they could do an article. Just for a laugh I agreed, one of the first questions they asked was my age. When I explained that I thought their habit of printing my name then my age was a little old hat, the reporter pulled a bit of a face and agreed he would try something different. This should have rung a few alarm bells for when it was published the next week the headline was 'John Leaver the local eccentric' Well I've been called worse so I settled for that. After a quick photo session with me and my gorilla the reporter left, promising it would be in next week's paper, and as good as his word I was in print. (I have noticed that age rarely appears now after the name in articles unless it's relevant. An eccentric with influence!)

Within another week after the local rag covered me, I was in the nationals with varying twists on the local eccentric theme. First the Mirror, then the Star, and best of all, page three of the Sun, next to a rather pretty young lady with pert bare breasts. Fame or infamy?

I did receive a few strange telephone calls. One was from a woman from a TV company in London inquiring about the gorilla in the garden and could they do a programme on me. She was a little evasive about the nature of the programme and begun to ask more questions, one of them being if I had had any complaints from my neighbours. I thought that was a strange question especially when she was disappointed to hear that all my neighbours thought it was great and brought their children to be photographed with the Kong. Then it dawned on me, the programme was the 'Neighbours From Hell.' We mutually agreed to go no further with the programme!

Another call was from a man from a charity wanting to borrow the gorilla for a charity event for he had seen it in the newspapers and thought if it could be inflated easily it would be a great attraction at his charity event. Now as much as I'm all for charity events, I had to disappoint him by telling him that it was about four hundredweight of half-inch ply which needed scaffolding to support it and a day to erect. It just goes to show how well it was painted to give the perfect impression it was 3D.

I was driving home one night and looking up at Kong. It lacked a certain splendour in the dark that it achieved in daylight, even with a full moon, so the next logical step was obvious, flood lighting! No problem, two old street lights that I just happened to have in my shed fitted the bill (one needs to see my sheds to appreciate that I'm an obsessive collector of junk that will 'always come in handy sometime' and it usually does.) Immediately after dark on the evening of the installation and inaugural switch on of the flood lighting, a quick drive over to the other side of the valley exceeded all expectations. Mega, Fantastic!

All went relatively quiet for a month or so apart from a visit from the local planning officer checking that the gorilla was only a temporary structure, as they had had complaints I had erected a permanent gorilla in my garden (what was that about?). Anyway it passed the temporary structure test and I was allowed to keep it (Temporary). No problem as I had all intention of setting it free eventually (possible title for a film there, 'Free Kong?' I'm open to offers, Mr Spielberg).

Always seeking perfection, my next innovation to enhance the impact for the sightseers was to add sound effects. I needed a gorilla roar, not so easy to come by as you might think. Then inspiration! I had an electronic organ that I bought for a couple of quid at a car boot sale (absolutely wonderful inventions are car boot sales. Don't get me started). As I remember it had a small set of keys for sound effects. Sure enough when I dug it out of my workshop, it had a whole section of animal noises. Sadly there wasn't a gorilla roar but there was a lion and with modification of a little added distortion I found that surprisingly realistic, few people complained that it didn't sound just like a gorilla. Enhanced with an old amplifier and a couple of PA speakers the sound was a little distorted but unmistakable as a lio … gorilla. When I pressed the button the sound made small children run to their mothers and even a few grown men flinch

'The Gorilla' was now complete and was a talking point for some years till I finally gave it its freedom and let it loose in the wilds of Yorkshire.

Years later people still ask if I was that person who had a twenty-foot gorilla in my garden, I look nonchalant and confirm it did reside with me a while.

I do seem to attract the species Hominoidea. That's Latin for apes if you weren't aware. What with wearing gorilla suits on stage, gorillas carrying me in a cage, and a twenty-foot one in my garden, and of course my grandmother actually owning a live one. Now damn me if someone hasn't given me a stuffed one. Well not exactly stuffed, it's a prop off a film set and it's got wires sticking out of its bum to move its eyes, nose, and mouth, in fact its all face can change its expression by pulling a few strings, it's amazing! What am I going to do with it you may ask, my partner certainly did, in a rather exasperated voice actually. I'm first going to make its facial movements work with electric and so it will constantly change its expression, then the skies the limit. I think I will install it in my car on the back seat for starters. That should turn a few heads, although it will have to be easily removed as I have been informed by my better half she's 'not riding around with that in the car!' Actually the possibilities are endless, so keep a look out! It could be in a car near you.

— 16 —

A BIT OF A PASH FOR OLD CARS

FROM THE FIRST, having passed my driving test I've had a car of one form or another, from an old van inherited from my parents, who used it on the farm, when they bought a bit better one, to a fifty-year-old Humber. From the iconic butt-rotting, rusty Beetle to an equally iconic Morris Minor but this one having wooden wings.

The driving test! Well it didn't go straightforward, as is usual in my life. I was proficient enough even though I had not had any formal lessons with a driving instructor. I had plenty of practice driving a tractor around the farm, and my dad took me out once for practice in his car, but we seemed to be in a little disagreement as to a few minor points of driving skills. It never works, parents taking their offspring for driving lessons, and after two or three little incidents and tiffs we abandoned the instructions. I had enough sense not to engage my mother as an instructor, for as much as my father could be a touch opinionated about my driving skills and a little unsubtle as to how this was communicated, he paled into insignificance compared to my mother. Even when I eventually passed my test my father would give me a sharp kick on the ankle bone if he caught me driving with my foot resting on the clutch pedal, as he informed me, quite rightly, it tended to burn out the clutch. A friend of mine said when he drove my dad somewhere he also got a sore ankle bone for the same offence.

Luckily the firm I was apprentice to at the time wanted me as a go-for in one of the vans so I would drive about with one of the other lads who had a driving licence. I actually took my test in that van so I was well used to it and my boss paid for it as he was desperate to get me on the road, so it wasn't charity for he wasn't exactly renowned for his generosity.

On the day of the test I was really nervous, there seemed to be a lot of pressure to pass, from work, home and socially, as all my mates had failed first time and I wanted to be one better, as I had ribbed them no end about their failure.

The test examiner was a little non-communicative but I suppose it was his job to be aloof. I have this thing about left and right and, with all the stress, I was worried I was going to turn right when the examiner told me to go left, so I had biro'd ‘R’ and ‘L’ on the back of my hand, subtly may I add. But I bet the examiner saw, as he tended to gesture with his hand when giving directions, which I thought was a kind touch.

My biro'd hand didn't do me much good at one particular right hand turn for it was the time of hand signals. Even though the van and most cars for that matter had indicators, you were required for the test to drive with your window open and stick your arm out and give the appropriate gesture for right turn, left turn and slowing down. Medieval or what? Anyway at this particular right turn I duly stuck my arm out of the window, pulled to the centre of the road and changed gear. Oops, no hands on the steering wheel! Such a minor point, we all do it from time to time, but not while your test examiner is sat in the passenger seat. I knew I had made a mistake and with lightning dexterity replaced my hand on the wheel. Out of my the corner of my eye I saw the examiner do a double take but I was quicker, and as much as he knew I had done it, I don't think he actually saw it.

The rest of the test was fairly uneventful, apart from going on the kerb reversing around a corner and hitting the kerb on the three point turn. I think the emergency stop impressed him as it was before seat belts and I was so enthusiastic with the brake pedal his for head was only inches from the windscreen, even though he should have been ready for it.

When eventually I pulled up outside the testing station and managed to park without hitting the kerb the examiner gave a deep sigh, hesitated for effect and announced I had passed, handed me the paperwork, got out of the car and walked away. I was gob-smacked. I was still sat there when the lad from work got into the van and said, ‘Well?’ I answered in a weak voice quizzically, ' I've passed.' All business-like he said, 'Good. Drive me back to the shop and there's a stack of deliveries waiting for you.' I just got out of the driving seat, went round to the passenger side, opened the door and told him to drive me back to the shop and there he could make me a cup of hot sweet tea before I passed out. He didn't argue as he could tell I was a little nerved up and he reckoned I might have an accident.

How I passed I will never know, my only suspicion was that my boss was very influential in the town and the word was out he needed me on the road.

In the beginning was the green Ford van. It wasn't new when my parents bought it and it had a hard life on the farm but it was wheels! This made me unique among my friends so I became quite popular as transport to out-of-town venues like the Cow and Calf disco which was 'The' in place at the time. It was hardly a passion wagon, even with a hand-painted yellow go faster strip down the side, but it did participate in my first sexual encounter by providing the venue. (For all sexual explicit stories, see my next book!)

Eventually the van started to pour out vast quantities of white smoke and the oil usage rose above the petrol consumption. Finally the bank of daddy stepped in and subbed me for a new car, new to me that is. I did contemplate keeping the van as a monument to my lost virginity, but was persuaded to trade it in for the new one (the van not my virginity!). The van had one last say in the matter by almost seizing up completely on the way to the trade-in garage. My dad had to tow it to a few hundred yards up the road from the garage. Then I started the van and carefully drove the rest of the way, parking upon the forecourt before it packed up all together. With slightly unseemly haste I drove away my Singer-Chamois, feeling only slightly guilty as used-car salesmen are, in my opinion, on a par with solicitors and estate agents and are fair game for any little dodgy deals you can bestow them with.

The Singer was superb, small but beautifully formed. It was a rear aluminium engine, 1200cc, nippy little beast that could make your nose bleed taking fast corners.

Two days later, I was driving to college in my new car, through Bradford with two friends, when I had the most horrendous accident. An elderly gentleman stepped off the kerb right in front of me, he bounced up on the bonnet, hit the windscreen and ricocheted six feet on to the road and lay still. It is the most devastating experience one can imagine, for the first thought is, 'I've killed him'.

By the time I had leaped out of the car and got to the gentleman he was conscious and, would you believe, apologizing for stepping out in front of me. It seemed little consolation at the time as he lay in the road with a broken leg, but as the police and ambulance arrived, he repeated his apology for stepping out on the road without looking as he was blind! Which was a bit of a shock. His explanation of how it happened to the police saved me a prolonged interview at the police station and a possible prosecution. A great relief but I never did get the chance to thank him for his honesty in pain and adversity.

When finally the Singer developed serious engine problems a few years later I bought a friend's Beetle which was a bit dilapidated but a good runner. The main problem with the bodywork were strange grooves from front to back where it had been driven under a chain link fence. This occurred, explained my friend, when he had a puncture. After changing the tyre he found that the spare wheel was a little under-inflated. So he drove to the nearest garage to blow it up, only to find it apparently closed. Undeterred and desperate to inflate his soggy tyre, seeing the air pump machine, he drove straight into the forecourt. He was completely focused on the air pump, not noticing a rather conspicuous chain across the entrance.

Now in most cars this would have had serious consequences. Not so in a VW Beetle, with the curved front and sufficient speed the chain slid up the sloping bonnet up and over the windscreen and down the sloping engine compartment and off the car, not, may I add, without a certain amount of damage, like ripping the windscreen wipers off and creating those rather distinctive grooves from bonnet to boot. This was not all in vain as he managed to inflate his tyre, only leaving him with the problem of getting out again. He decided to take the same route except this time the chain was a bit longer than it was when he entered the garage having been stretched over the car, not long enough to drive over, but a touch low to drive under. Enter long-suffering girlfriend. With a little persuasion the young lady was instructed to hold the chain up while he drove under it. This was done at a rather more sedate speed than his entry. Even so the danger to his girlfriend was not insubstantial. Her faith (or naivety) paid off as he exited the garage forecourt with a fully inflated tyre, an extra set of grooves, and without injury to his girl friend, whom he finally married, and, I got a cheap car.

The Beetle lasted me some years with the gouges over the car being quite a conversation piece, until I took some friends on a trip to Morecambe Bay, driving it on the beach for a picnic by the sea. That in itself would not have been a problem except I got carried away with the ambiance, and drove the Beetle though the incoming shallow tide, as you see on the films. This was rather spectacular and we all had a great day.

The problems started about a month or so later when massive rust patches appeared all over the car, and when the M.O.T. came up and the mechanic put the car on the hydraulic lift, he took one look and ran out from underneath and said it was to dangerous to be under there. The mechanic had aspirations to be a stand-up comic. Failed! But when I looked I had to admit that while it may not be a real danger to stand underneath, it would be a definite life threat to drive. The salt water had completely eaten away at the structural parts of the chassis. This instigated a quick journey to the scrap yard, and the end of the Beetle era.

The demise of the Beetle was not too much of a disaster as I had had my eye on a cheap Morris Minor from another friend, and was soon the proud owner of another classic.

This was the late seventies and cars were total rot boxes. I once read an article that cars left the factory rusty, as the steel was stored outside and was poorly treated, if at all. It was the time that the M.O.T. came in, and the joke doing the rounds was that the test started at five-year-old cars, then progressing down to four, then to three as it is today, and rumour was that it would even go down to one–year-old cars. The joke was that new cars were so poor they were even going to test them before they left the factory!

Salt spread on the roads was also a killer for untreated cars and, with a few bad winters, the councils were spreading it on the roads like it was going out of fashion.

The Morris Minor was a good runner but soon the wings and sills began to show similarity to lace curtains. Again thanks to the dreaded salt and its liberal use on the roads. To put it in a garage to have the work done was a little beyond my means at the time and I liked my little Minor, so my mate who was a carpenter suggested fitting solid wood sills. This was perhaps not as impractical as it sounds. Wood is light, structural, and cheap, and with a bit of sawing, planing, and sanding, they were ace. A quick spray with a can of paint you could not tell they were not the originals, and they sounded really impressive when you tap them, not tinny and hollow like the originals and absolutely rust free.

My next problems were the wings. Having had so much success with the sills, the obvious answer was again wood. The problem was my woodworking skills weren't up to it at the time (not that they have improved all that much). So scouting around in my shed, an old sideboard caught my eye. If I carefully cut it into quarters all the joints were made and it had a lovely veneer finish and of course they matched perfectly as they were opposite ends of the same piece of furniture. With the wings securely fixed with wood screws from under the bonnet and a coat of exterior varnish the finish was impeccable and sound. All it required now were headlights as the sideboard was not originally equipped with them. I did think a pair of table lamps would have looked rather fine but I decided a couple of spotlights were a little more practical. The comic mechanic who did my M.O.T. surprisingly passed them with only minor rude comments.

I drove it around for about a week before the inevitable blue light pulled me over. The pair of policemen were not impressed with the quality of the veneer but could not fault it for its solid structure. Even the tubby one couldn't detach them when he sat on one, although I was a little disappointed he didn't get splinters. They said I couldn't have spotlights for headlights as they didn't dip, and were really pissed off, when I pointed out that they had proper headlight bulbs and dipped from the original dip switch. They finally got back in their patrol car and drove off with a curt 'we'll find something'. Funnily enough I was never stopped again, whether word had got around I was a smart-ass and knew all the answers or they treated me as a harmless eccentric, who knows? Eventually after about a year the veneer became very tatty and started to peel but it was fun while it lasted.

While the Minor with wooden bits was still running I had a project on the go. A friend had told me about two old Humbers rusting away on an allotment so I went to investigate and found two 1935 Humber saloons. One was definitely past redemption but the other one was a possible runner.

With a little detective work I found the owner and bought them both for a very reasonable sum as he wanted to see at least one restored but he was getting too old to tackle the project. Getting the good one home to my dad's farm proved a bit of a problem as I didn't want to start it till I could check it out, and anyway the brakes were rather rusty and looked a tad unsafe for the journey home.

Enter my long-suffering father, and his Austin Cambridge as the tow truck. With me behind the wheel of the Humber and my dad in his car we set off. He wasn't all that happy about the size and weight of the tow, especially when there was a strong smell of burning clutch just towing it out of the allotments, mainly due to the fact that the brakes were seized on and only released properly twenty yards down the road. Anyway when we got going the wheels began to turn more freely, and everything was going well till we started to go up the hill.

Now as I've explained before we lived on the top of a rather steep hill, and it was definitely too much for the Austin. With an even stronger smell of burning clutch and the engine overheating, the tow came to a shuddering halt. As the brakes were nonexistent, this left me in the middle of the hill with stones quickly jammed under the back wheels to stop me rolling down the hill backwards, . Dad unhitched his car, mumbled something about 'I'll have to fetch the bloody tractor then', and drove off.

He was a treasure, my dad, no matter how mad and sometimes crazy my projects he tried his best to support me, he might not have approved, but he went along. I suppose he was quite proud of me really, I don't think I always deserved it.

Even the tractor struggled to tow me home, as I think the brakes were still binding, but once snugly parked in one of my dad's sheds, that I had commandeered as a work shop, the renovation began.

I really did not appreciate what I had taken on. For a start the brakes were knackered. They weren't hydraulic as in modern cars but cable as in a bicycle, and the cables were seized. The brake shoes were badly worn, but the good news was the shoes were the same as Land Rover, would you believe, so they were easy enough to replace. The big one was the roof, it had a sun roof that had got water in the seal and was badly corroded. Now I'd always had a desire for a convertible so the obvious answer was to cut off the roof and add a soft top. Just like that! Have I mentioned my motto of where angles fear to tread? I jump in feet first!

In retrospect I suppose it was a bit of a mistake but I have a tendency for the bull in a china shop syndrome, perhaps it the Taurus in me, anyway I did it, not without its problems may I add, surprise, surprise.

Cars with a chassis don’t need the roof for structural rigidity as mine had, so that wasn’t the problem. But the door pillars did, hence the fact the back doors opened when you opened the front doors. Minor problem really for with a bit of strengthening they only opened occasionally, all be it at inopportune moments.

A trip to the scrap yard secured me a frame work for the soft top off a similar sized car body. A roll of black leatherette from a closing down warehouse, a pot of glue and a fair amount of time later, I had constructed a reasonable soft top. The seal around the side windows was difficult and I ended up using bulldog clips! When clipped onto the soft top the windows rolled up through the clip handles. Not ideal but I had all intentions of improving the design at a future date.

The restoration work went up apace when a friend of mine got interested in helping me and we decided to all go on holiday down to Wales the following month, in the Humber with our respective wives, , they oblivious of the fact the car had not even run and had no M.O.T. Just what we needed to spur us on. Panic!

It’s new paintwork of yellow and black was dry and looking spectacular. It was about a fortnight before we were due to set off for Wales and it still wasn't running, and it was booked in for its M.O.T. so we decided to take it for its maiden voyage.

It was a little reticent to start and we had flattened two batteries before we decided to run it down the hill to jump start it. My father was not too keen on the idea (understandable in retrospect) but we set off anyway. Well it's a very long and steep hill and really scary as the brakes were a bit poor, but at the bottom of the hill it still refused to start! Good old dad wasn't psychic but that day he had a premonition that it was a non-starter. So as we sat there at the bottom of the hill discussing the possible reasons for the failed lift-off, he turned up on his tractor to tow us home. To give him his due he never said I told you so, but after a long meaningful look at the Humber he uttered the memorable words, 'Just take my car on your holiday otherwise it will be four holidays ruined.'

Needless to say we took the Humber, for with a little tinkering with the carburettor and after two freshly charged batteries it started. One of its quirks we found once we got it running was a device that automatically started the engine when you switch on the ignition or if you stalled it. After a few near accidents where it started when you weren't ready for it, we decided to disconnect the ingenious innovative device.

Miraculously enough it only failed its M.O.T. on one thing, much to our surprise and also the garage-owner's for that matter. Not that it would pass nowadays. This was in the seventies and the M.O.T. had been running for just over ten years. Things were a little less strict then. The one thing it failed on was not exactly minor. The mechanic said that the back axle had too much play in the differential, (that's the little gearbox in the middle of the back axle), and with a bit of a smirk said, 'You won't be getting new one of those in a hurry.'

Well there was still the old wreck on the allotment, so armed with jacks and a couple of tool boxes, we went to see if the back axle was in better shape than our holiday car. This involved hacking through a large patch of nettles that were growing up around the old car. Once it was jacked up climbing underneath was rather uncomfortable with a carpet of stinging nettles for a pillow. We had no way of telling if the axle was any better till we removed it, for the space was a little restricted for a detailed examination. So with a bit of tenacity and a lot of bad language we got it off, and miraculously it seemed sound.

With a slightly longer time than it is to say it, we swapped the axle, filled it up with new oil and took it in for its retest.

The mechanic who had smirked at the initial test looked with total disbelief, after he put the car on the ramp, walked under it and started heaving about on the back wheels. He mumbled, 'I don't know how the bloody hell you did it but I will have to pass it.' Then giving us a sly look, 'I bet you put sawdust in the oil in the axle to take up the slack didn't you?' We looked really hurt and answered in unison, 'Most certainly not.' Then with feeling, he said. 'Well if you have it'll only pack up in a couple of weeks so you've wasted your time.' We never did tell him how we did it but I made a point of regularly driving past his garage in the car and waving, with a cheeky grin and a toot of the horn.

Well we did go on holiday to Wales in it with only a few hiccups. Just minor things you understand, like when our soft top roof flew off at eleven o'clock at night on the M4 Motorway and we had to do a quick reccy along the hard shoulder for the bulldog clips to refasten the roof back on. Luckily in those days, at that time of night the motorway was completely empty. Nowadays we would never attempt it, as explaining to the motorway police that we were wandering up and down looking for bulldog clips would have had us arrested, and not just for stopping on a motorway. The problem was solved by finding two out of four clips and driving below forty miles an hour for the rest of the motorway so the thing didn't blow of again.

Later still we started to lose power which was a bit scary, until we lifted the bonnet to find two out the four spark plugs had fallen out and the third was loose. We were again fortunate as the engine was what they call a side valve engine. And for the non-mechanically minded who might be unfortunate enough to be reading this book that means that the spark plugs are on top of the engine not down the side and were conveniently lying out ready for us to refit, and not lying at the side of the road randomly spaced over the past twenty miles.

With a quick twist of the spanner we were again on our way with no further problems, except we vowed to fit a heater as the hardy motorists of the day seemed not to specify to the designers that it should be an essential extra.

I did run the old Humber as an everyday car for a couple of years, but finally the maintenance became too daunting and I moved on to a boring but practical Ford Fiesta.

The only other old car I owned was a 1948 Triumph Renown which I had great affection for, not just because of its classic lines or its head turning ability, but because it was manufactured the same year I was born.

When I bought it the front suspension was knackered and while the engine had only done about sixty-thousand miles, it appeared never to have had an oil change in that time. So, as you do, you go get a fairly modern Triumph and swap front suspension and engine! The only trouble with that is about ten models and forty years in between!

Anyway to cut a long story short, I managed it, reasonably successfully, like having to shorten the prop shaft, that's the shaft from the engine to the back wheels. Really it should have been done professionally but I reckoned I could do it. First I sawed it in the appropriate place then I tried to weld the two parts back together. This had to be done very precisely as it revolves quite fast and if it's not perfect it will vibrate. Violently! I tried to clamp it in various ways and finally settled on just laying it in a gutter which ran down the middle of the workshop. Crude but effective. When it was installed there was not a hint of vibration, well at least from the prop shaft. Another little glitch was I mounted the engine a little too close to the radiator. For when I took it out on the road for the first time and braked, the engine shifted on its mountings and pushed the fan into the radiator, hacking a rather neat circular hole amid a lot of steam and boiling water. But everything can be fixed with time.

Perhaps it was a mistake to take it to the same garage as I took the Humber to have the M.O.T. done. I vividly recall his words as I drove it into the forecourt of the garage, 'Oh no, not you again, and what the bloody hell have you done to this one?' Not one to mince his words, our true Yorkshire car mechanic. To give him his due he did pass it although it was an hour-long trashing of my welding and mechanical skills before I received my certificate. He likened my welding to butchering meat, my mechanical skills taken from a child's Meccano manual, and my taste in renovation to the crassest bodge he had ever witnessed in thirty years as a car mechanic. Don't you just love an honest car mechanic? (If that isn't a contradiction in terms). But he reluctantly passed it! So it couldn't have been that bad, could it?

I added a few refinements to the Triumph that true enthusiasts would definitely not approve of but I thought at the time enhanced its intrinsic beauty, and should have been incorporated in the original design. Just minor things. For example the indicators were the ones that popped out of the door pillars and lit up. Apart from being a bit boring if you forgot to switch them off and got out of the car they could poke you in the eye or you would break them off all together. My modification was a relay that made them pop in and out and flash like modern indicators. Rather stylish I thought.

The other mod was, instead of fitting a spotlight on the front bumper that was all the rage on young men’s cars at the time, I fitted full-sized headlights I took off an old car at the scrap yard. They looked really impressive mounted on the wings and vaguely as if they were a standard fit, well almost!

The Triumph was the transport for two trips to France and was everyday transport for a good three years with few mechanical problems and it was a sad day when it had to be retired for something a little more practical.

Desiring practicality must be an age thing, so at the decrepit age of thirty-five most of my later cars have been relatively ordinary, although I did have a Triumph GT6 which was a poor man's E-type Jaguar. Poor man's because it certainly wasn't as fast, and it had a nasty habit of the back wheels tucking under if you went around a corner a little fast, reducing the tread on the road to the area of a bicycle tyre, and corners are when you need traction most, if you think about it.

I speak from experience as I once did a rather snazzy unintentional 360 degrees spin on a bad bend which really impressed the two cars following me in a bit of a race we were having on the public highway, I'm embarrassed to say. By more luck than management I kept on the road, ending up facing the right way and as I was then around the corner, had no option, to just keep going, albeit a little slower. The following cars passed me, giving me the thumb up sign, with impressed expressions. Regardless, that was the end to my road racing aspirations (with a trip home to change the underwear).

Apart from a desire for practicality there is a strong feeling that there is more to life than spending your weekends up to your armpits in grease and oil, laid on cold damp concrete under an old car. Sadly an age thing.

I was once clamped. Anyone who has experienced this legalised hijacking will sympathise with my horror at being mugged for fifty quid especially when money at the best of times is tight. I was in good company as a number of other cars had been shackled in a similar manner. We all stood at the side of our vehicles commiserating with each other. Now I wasn't going to take this lying down. Driving old cars necessitates carrying a decent set of tools in the boot. Selecting an appropriate spanner, I set about jacking up the car and removing the wheel and clamp in one. As I was removing the final wheel nut I felt a presence behind me. Turning, I first saw a pair of size twelve boots. My gaze ascending up the ample blue serge trousers, I then came across a gorilla in a blue uniform. Gulp! Luckily, or maybe not, it wasn't a copper, it was the clamper, so I gave him one of my winning smiles which wasn't reciprocated. He just stood there, so I just shrugged and carried on with removal of the wheel and clamp, half expecting to be stopped physically or at least to be warned. At that stage I had completely removed the wheel and clamp and proceeded to separate the two. With a bit of a struggle they parted company without either suffering any damage. I carefully laid the clamp on the pavement and replaced my wheel. Still no reaction from the gorilla. Then he made a move. He bent down, picked up the clamp and sauntered back to his van, knuckles dragging on the pavement. I could not believe I had got away with it. Then suddenly I was accosted by a gaggle of impressed 'clampees' who wanted me to release their cars at twenty quid a time. I glanced over to the gorilla who was now leaning against his van, watching the proceedings. Our eyes met, he raised his eyebrows in a manner that said 'don't even think about it, sunshine'. So discretion being the better part of valour I apologized to the disappointed clamped crowd, got in my car and drove away. I lived in fear of a summons in the post but nothing turned up. Charmed life or what?

I now drive a boring Nissan but it's reliable and I don't have to bribe the mechanic to get it through its M.O.T. every year. My uncle was a little incensed at my choice of vehicle as he fought the Japanese in the war and it has left some bad memories. Although he did concede it felt very comfortable to ride in.

— 17 —

HORSEY HORSEY KEEP YOUR TAIL UP

I'VE BEEN TOLD I have a good seat! This does not mean I have a box at the theatre or a nice comfy chair in the living room in front of the telly, although I have one of those as well, it's an age thing. No it's a horsey term for I sit well on a horse. I've never actually owned a horse but we rented grazing land for one on the farm when I was about twelve and I was allowed to ride him. He was a great horse, part Arab we were told, and was all white, although they call all white horses greys but to me he was white, and quite rightly he was called Snowy.

I would ride him in the fields, open all the gates across the farm and gallop full tilt from one end to the other, and back again. I think that was where I got my good seat from, because without one I would have fallen off a lot more. That's one of the most important lessons in horse riding is falling off, or at least how and where to fall off. It happens to all horse riders from one time or another; I've even seen pictures of Princes Anne come a cropper.

This lesson came in handy quite a few times over the years not least of all was when I was confronted by Vikings!

It was a beautiful spring morning. I had borrowed a friend's horse and I went for a ride on Baildon Moor. It's perfect for a gentle trot, an undulating grassy stretch of public land, and on that particular morning there was a picturesque mist lying in the hollows. I'd been riding for about twenty minutes breathing in the fresh spring air and thoroughly relaxed, when I heard this strange noise. It was the kind of noise that makes the hair stand up on the back of your neck, a sort of rhythmic beat you used to hear in old jungle films where the guide turns to the hero and quotes the immortal line, 'The natives are restless today'. But it wasn't quite like a drum beat more flat and ragged beat, with a guttural chanting in the background.

The horse had heard it too, as its ears shot forward and it came to a stop and just froze. Then out of the mist in this hollow a pillage of Vikings emerged, beating their shields with their spears and bellowing war chants. As far as I knew there are no ancient stone monoliths on Baildon Moor especially one that acts as a time portal, that cast hapless heroes back in time and space, but the thought did pass through my mind fleetingly, that I had been cast by some ancient magic into another time dimension, because you do hear of things like that, don't you? All of these buggers looked genuine. No horned helmets, yet another Hollywood myth created by an over- imaginative costume designer. They had animal skins jackets, leather breeches with axes in their belts, big beards and faces with a look of rape and pillage in their eyes.

The other alternative was, I was having a hallucination? Well if I was, the horse seemed to be having a very similar one! It whinnied, reared up, turned, and bolted. I must confess to being of a like mind as the murderous looking brigade were still advancing, so I was with the horse.

After about twenty yards sanity took over, realising time portals definitely did not exist, well not on Baildon Moor anyway and I wasn't into LSD, so I tried to reel in Ned. There's only one thing more dangerous than riding a runaway horse, that's pulling too hard on the reins of a panicked horse. Having tried the runaway bit, I went for the other one. The horse duly reared up so far that it almost fell backwards. Having a horse fall on you is not recommended so I decided that it was time to bail out so I chose my patch of nice bouncy, soft heather and went for it.

Once free of my pulling on the reins the horse didn't hesitate and was off across the moor, not having worked out the logic of the improbability of a time portal, leaving me laid on my comfortable patch of heather at the mercy of the Vikings, out of time or whenever. To my surprise I was gently helped up by the aforesaid Vikings who were quite pleasant fellows really and apologised for scaring my horse (I didn't like to mention they scared the shit out of me too).

They later explained that they were Sealed Knot and liked nothing better than dressing up as Vikings on a sunny morning, banging their shields and chanting war songs. What a set of wankers.

After a long walk back to the stables the horse was waiting for me with a quizzical look on his face. I explained that they weren’t real Vikings and he seemed quite happy about the explanation, but refused to go back on the moor. Unfortunately I had to as I had dropped my car keys out of my pocket on my fall. Walking back to the spot, I eventually found them, but the Vikings had disappeared, and I’ve never seen any since.

My next equestrian adventure was in Wales. We were on holiday with friends and decided that it would be great to go horse riding. We found stables that offered hacking. That's stables which hire out horses by the hour and then you go out trekking on bridle ways in the area. We duly arrived at the stables, and made our arrangements while the young lady who run the stables saddled up our horses.

When we were ready to set off she told us where we should ride, then she casually asked who the most experienced rider was? And without consulting my little voice that whispers in my ear ‘Keep quiet’,

I confidently answered, 'Well I am.' She gave a little quizzical look instantly appraising my survival skills and replied, 'Well you had better ride this one then.' At this point I completely ignored the little voice of my Guardian Angel actually shouting 'NOOOO!'

Let me at this point explain about my little voice. I know that most people have something similar they should listen to, apart from those with schizophrenia that is, but I know mine's always all too accurate because I tend to ignore it, and it always causes me pain one way or another when the voice proves to have been spot on. Well actually I have two, one that says 'don't do it' and one that eggs me on to go for it. But in this case he just kept quiet as he knew I felt confident on a horse and would go for it without his whispered advice.

True to form, once I was sat on the horse I had been given, it took off at a gallop (I was told later that the stable owner asked my fellow hackers if I would be okay, to a reply from my friends of 'yes he has a good seat'). As I shot off just managing to slow it down to get through the farm gate, but it speeded up brushing my hair on the hedge at the side of the road as I leant over to negotiate around a bend in the track. When it reached the main road that we had to go along till we reached the bridle path, it just shot onto the road and was going full gallop, weaving in and out of the traffic. This was a busy main road mind you and it did have the sense to gallop on the grass verge, most of the time anyway! I say it had the sense, for I had no control over its destination. At this point can I explain that some horses from riding schools get what is called a hard mouth. This enables them to literally get the bit between their teeth and go where they want to go and at whatever speed, regardless how hard you pull on the reins. This horse which I had been presented with was a classic example, and the stable owner had obviously not been able to palm it off onto any unsuspecting client for some time, as it was overdue for a bit of exercise.

For what seemed like hours but probably was only seconds the horse demonstrated its ability to avoid oblivion on the main road when it veered off onto the bridle way, and up a Welsh mountain. At this point I decided to take charge.

While galloping up this Welsh mountain I tried to rein in my wayward steed. Having established it obviously could only understand Welsh and 'Whoa, you bloody pillock' did not have the desired affect, I tried pulling hard on the reins. This had the effect of turning the horse's head around so I could look directly into at least one of its rather wild, bloodshot eyes with no reduction in its headlong gallop. At this I made a decision that could well have saved both our lives, I let it look where it was going and I just hung on for dear life.

With the increased incline my un-trusty steed did at least slow down to a reasonable gallop and I nearly started to enjoy myself. That is until a closed gate loomed. Now as much as I was quite an experienced rider I had never done steeple chasing, but I had this sinking feeling the horse had.

We approached the gate at a steady gallop and I prepared myself for the initiation into show jumping. Whether I didn't give the horse the proper signals for the jump or it was just trying to scare me, it skidded to a stop, majestically unseating me and I slithered over the horse's head to land in a heap at the other side of the gate. Rather shaken, but miraculously unhurt.

The horse snorted, looked me in the eye and I will swear it said 'well then open the gate'. This could be the consequences of the onset of concussion, but rather than argue with the horse which would have confirmed my demise into total unreality, I opened the gate.

Once through the gate, surprisingly the horse waited patiently for me to remount, only to set off again with me having only one foot in the stirrups. With no further obstacles and an increasing incline the horse took a slower pace and now with both my feet in the stirrups after a little manipulation, the wind in my hair blowing away the concussion from the fall, I started to really enjoy the view. When we reached the summit the view was wonderful, just a green panorama of Welsh valleys spread out below us. The horse had seen it all before, and was obviously not into the wonders of nature, for before I could take in its full natural vista, we set off back down the way we had come.

Now as much as galloping at a reasonably steady pace uphill was just the right amount of adrenaline to create euphoria, galloping down a mountainside is probably the equivalent to riding the world's scariest big dipper with square wheels and a saddle for a seat and no safety belt. I think I may have screamed.

From absolute dread to that moment of pure panic when all my life passed in front of me as the gate loomed again, it turned to almost relief when I saw my friends opening the gate on their leisurely way up the mountain. I managed to glimpse their surprise and mild concern as I galloped past but I failed to wave to them as that would have involved letting go of the front of the saddle where my finger nails were digging deep into the hard leather.

This was the first time I had seen my friends since leaving the stables and they were not to be seen again till they rode into the stables an hour later. At the time this was of little concern as now the road was fast approaching and my nemesis with the traffic.

I honestly can't say for sure whether I actually closed my eyes or my mind went blank with fear. Either way it would have made little difference. The damned demented horse was in control, as it weaved recklessly through the traffic. I came out of my trance a little when my hair was again brushed by the hedge as the horse and I leaned over to take the corner half way down the narrow farm track, just as happened on my outward journey.

On entering the stable area the damned manic horse from hell skidded to a halt and I barely managed to stop myself going over its head again, but slithered off the saddle and sat down on the cold concrete, dazed and twitching with adrenaline overdose. The horse looked round at me and I'll swear it spoke, 'That was great, can we do that again?'

I was brought out of my trance by a voice behind me. 'You're back early. You have another half hour yet, you can go out again if you like.'

Luckily saving the young lady's blushes, words at that point failed me for all I could manage was a faint whisper to the effect that I would just sit in the car thank you, and perhaps change my underwear at the soonest opportunity. The experience didn't put me off horse riding but I now tend to keep clear of Welsh horses with wild eyes and Vikings who bang their shields chanting.

A slightly less dangerous aspect of horse riding, but only slightly less painful, happened to a friend of mine. We were out riding with a group of friends, being led by the rather horsey and upper-class female owner of the riding stable. My friend is a little outspoken especially about the Royal Family. I'm afraid I am of a similar opinion but err on the side of caution when in the company of potential Royalists. I confess to egging him on a little especially when he started slagging off Princes Anne. This apparently did not go down well with the stable owner, obviously a great fan of our Anne, as she leaned over and whacked my mate over the head with her riding crop to the great amusement of us all. Even wearing his riding hat for protection he certainly kept his opinion about the Royals to himself for the rest of the ride, as we all did for that matter.

I still have horses at the farm to this day as I built some stables and rent out the field which is suitable for two horses. This suits me well as I have horses in the field that I like to say hello to and feed the occasional carrot, and someone else pays the vets bills, cleans them out, and feeds them. I do occasionally ride one of them but most horse owners are very jealous of someone else riding their horses.

With one owner I played on this by telling her that I had seen two young girls riding her horse around the field. She was suitably incensed, especially when I explained that I thought they looked very pleasant young ladies so didn't stop them. The lady who owned the horse was furious! As I hoped she would be. There's nothing like a good wind-up. 'Why didn't you stop them, how could you let strangers ride my horse?'

I let her carry on for a while then handed her a photograph, explaining I even took a picture of them riding about. Now I'm a bit of a dab hand at manipulating photos on the computer, putting things and people where they don't exist. Having had lots of practice with my faeries, it wasn't too difficult to add a couple of young ladies on a picture of her horse that I had taken earlier. Just one little twist was that the girls were totally starkers! While she was digesting the first picture I handed her another saying, 'They were such grand lasses that I joined them..' This picture was of me and the two still-naked girls, all astride her horse. I would just like to add I was fully clothed! Anyway the penny dropped at that point and luckily she saw the funny side. Not everyone copes with my humour.

— 18 —

A SPOT OF DIY

PERHAPS DIY IS a little of an understatement, I gutted the place. When my parents retired from farming they sold off most of the land and I bought the farmhouse from them. I've always been a bit handy, and by the time I was forty had acquired a certain amount of skills. Although my woodwork has been likened to butchery, I can't plaster and I hate plumbing, I think I have a fair amount of imagination and I'm not one for sitting around talking about what I'm going to do, I get stuck in. My mother was always altering the place one way or another with a little help from my dad, so I was brought up among the occasional pile of rubble, the smell of fresh paint, and the occasional doorway installed where there didn't use to be one.

In the early nineties I decided to modernise the old place. This was a far cry from the occasional pile of rubble, I lived in what could only be described as a building site for ten years! Each year I would destroy another room and my living space became smaller and smaller. I remember with a shudder one winter night walking a plank across some exposed joists to go to bed, with snow blowing through a large hole in the wall that was about at least three months away from having a window installed, because finances were low.

One of the major renovations was knocking through to the barn to make it part of the house. The walls were two feet thick with squared off stone both sides and just loose rubble sandwiched between them. This sounds very unsatisfactory but a lot of old houses of that period were built like that. I would not think it would come up to modern insulation standards but it works, for it's cool in the summer and reasonably warm in the winter, as the loosely packed rubble holds air which acts as an insulator.

Just recently I received a phone call from a firm that was doing cavity wall insulation. I got the usual sales patter till I said that it wouldn't work for my house. Then the salesman went into overdrive quoting vastly inflated energy savings figures for his product. When I was able to get a word in edgeways, I explained that the house was around two hundred years old and as much as it has a cavity the ecology at the time it was built deemed that the cavity be filled with rubble, rendering any injection of insulation into my cavity, inappropriate. He apologised for wasting my time and hung up. What a polite young man!

Now the downside of this cavity phenomenon is that certain members of the rodent family find this an idyllic nest site and also find their way into underfloor spaces and lofts, and particularly from the barn where the odd hole in the stone work was ignored. By the way we aren't talking just mice here, there were rats and big ones at that.

All farms have rats and mice. Even if you are careful with animal feed and keep it in bins with lids, they will chew their way into everything. When the farm was a working farm we also had about half a dozen cats. These weren't your ‘laid out in front of the fire’ pet tabbies, these were killers. They were working cats whose job was pest control and damned good at it they were with a few songbirds, field mice and the occasional rabbit thrown in for the sheer joy of the kill. Even so the cats could not get everywhere and could only pounce on the unwary rat or mouse as it came out to feed.

The rats were not a problem by the time I started renovations as the rodents had moved out when there was no longer any animal feed for them and no hay in the barn for nests and shelter. There was only the occasional mouse, or so I kept telling myself.

When I broke through the first layer of stone to create a door into the barn from the house I found the rubble interior packed full of ancient rats' nests! You could well imagine that the plague or Black Death was still rife in this dusty, ratshit-laden infestation, so I donned a mask! This was perhaps a little late because I spent a week in bed after that with a rather bad cough and fever, which turned out not to be the plague or even the Black Death , my doctor was pleased to assure me. Mind you I even donned gloves eventually as I dug deeper into the fetid depths of the nest and found a rather gruesome mummified rat. Not a pretty sight!

The breaking through into the barn was perhaps a little premature as the only barrier to the outside were two a rather ill-fitting sliding barn doors. Stuffing the gaps with old sacking did not really keep out the draught for the two years it took me to build in front of the doors, seal it to the elements and nor did it prevent mice, for that matter, finding shelter in my house for the duration. It took me some time to eradicate the infestation after I had sealed the house for the final time.

Part of the house that used to be a hayloft and that I was going to make into a bathroom needed the roof redoing, so Mick, a builder friend, took on the task, as I'm not that brilliant with heights.

As I had a full time job I left him to it. When I came home one afternoon I could see that he had finished the repairs and was just about to make a hole to fit a roof light. As he did not see me arrive I thought I would give him a little surprise as he was always having a laugh at my expense. I found an old rubber Halloween mask, stood on a step ladder, and stuck my head through the hole he had just made in the roof. Well perhaps it was a little cruel and a tad dangerous in retrospect as he was perched twenty foot up on the roof, but he hadn't a heart condition as far as I knew and had a robust constitution. He also lacked the kind of imagination that would have had ghouls in loft spaces. So luckily he didn't fall and quickly recovered enough to call me a ''daft bugger', wallop me on the head with a lath of wood he had handy, and told me to go put the kettle on before he died of thirst.

Mick got his own back on many occasions as he had a habit of telling jokes at inopportune moments, usually when we were lifting something that was almost too heavy for us, or a piece of delicate manoeuvring requiring our uninterrupted concentration.

One particular time we were placing a rather large heavy stone lintel over a doorway. As it was eight foot up we were standing on ever higher planks as we gradually lifted it higher. Finally we ran out of planks and just used plastic milk crates. Now milk crates are just fine as long as they have planks on them. But without reinforcement they are a little prone to collapse. In retrospect we were asking a lot of two plastic milk crates to support our combined weight and the rather large, very heavy, lintel. True to expectations, at a crucial 'heave oh' and a silly joke from Mick, both our feet crashed through the plastic milk crates simultaneously. Our eyes met across a rather precariously balanced lintel and without any more jokes funny or otherwise, we carefully lowered the stone. After a cup of hot sweet tea and a more substantial support the stone lintel was installed. I often look up at it now and shudder for we could have done ourselves a lot of damage.

Part of the plans for the house involved building an extension in front of the barn doors with the grand name of The Barn Porch. It is rather a grand room with a large half round window in one wall that I scrounged out of a skip in Halifax where they were renovating an old mill. Actually I paid good money for it - twenty pound. Oh and a cast iron bath was thrown in, so it was a bargain for I used the bath with a little restoration in the en suite. The window was the best though. I asked a joiner friend how much he would charge me if he had to make one like it. He screwed his face up and in a typical tradesman-shocking-estimate fashion said it would be over a thousand pounds! In hindsight it might have been more because when I was fitting it, I broke one of the twenty panes of special glass that acts as a semi-mirror from one side and it cost me seventy pounds, like for like.

When Mick and I had nearly reached the construction of the roof he asked me if I had acquired the roof beams yet. I replied that we were going to collect them the next day and to bring his trusty chain saw. Mick was well used to my enigmatic replies so without a word the next day we set off down to the woods. I'd noticed a while back there were two wonderfully tall, straight oak trees growing in a deep gully. They had grown like this to reach the light and were ideal length for my roof beams. 'Yeh they'll do but how the hell do you expect to get them out of the gully once I've cut them down?' Mick said when he saw them.

'No problem,' I replied. 'You cut em down so they fall against the side of the gully and I'll go fetch a tractor to drag em out.' Half an hour later I was back with a big tractor with an impressive hydraulic lift on the front. I don't have a tractor of my own but I do know a man who does and with a mutual agreement for borrowing equipment and for doing bits of odd jobs for him the tractor was mine for the day. With big lifts and little lifts, bit by bit, retying the ropes, and shortening them each time, the logs finally emerged over the top. The next stage was to get them home before the owner of the wood realised I was taking a little more than a bit of fire wood as I had previously arranged with him (only a slight understatement!).

With one of the logs balanced on the tractor's forks I backed up to turn around and head for home. I must have reversed slightly uphill with one wheel, just enough to swing the log out to one side, unbalancing the tractor, and lifting one side up in the air. Now I reckon it went to forty five degrees before the log thankfully came loose from the forks and the tractor righted itself with my world becoming horizontal again, but Mick reckoned it was nowhere near going over, although he wasn't sitting in that tractor seat. A cup of hot sweet tea and a change of underwear later (I do seem to get through a lot of underwear in this book, verging on incontinence) I got back on the tractor and eventually got both logs home. I conveniently forgot to tell the owner of the tractor as I needed to borrow it again, for I got a feeling he would be reluctant to lend it if I had had to borrow his other tractor to put the first one back on its wheels. Back at the farm the logs had to be squared off, and not having a bench saw that would come anywhere close to doing the job, I set to with my chain saw. Rough as they were when finished they looked in keeping. When the house was first built the beams would have been hand sawn, a seemingly impossible task. Once they were squared off to my satisfaction, they needed to be dried out. As growing trees they were full of sap that has to be removed else they will warp and twist over time as the sap slowly comes out of the wood. Industrial scale beams are placed in an oven to dry them out. My kitchen oven being a little inadequate to take the sixteen foot beams I erected a polythene tent around them and set a dehumidifier going inside. It worked. Every day I took gallons of water out of the machine and within a week the beams had dried enough to be set into the wall to support the roof. I am pleased to say there's not a split or twist fifteen years later and hopefully for the next hundred years at least. When the roof was completed Mick was tidying up inside when he saw me gazing at a corner of the room with a certain wistful look in my eye. He groaned and asked me what I was plotting that would cause him problems. With a hurt look I explained I only wanted a minstrels' gallery seven foot up fastened to the wall. 'Oh that's all is it?' he said and went back to his work unimpressed, while I went away to look for appropriate materials.

There was a large pile of old oak that had fallen into the stream years ago and being oak had not rotted and that we had salvaged out of the wood when we were liberating the beams for the barn porch roof. I found a perfect bent piece that would fit across the corner from one wall to the other. It was duly cemented into the walls and with a rather rustic support, some old banister spindles and a further rustic rail on top it looked the bee's knees. The access to the small but perfectly formed gallery was by a parrot ladder I had bought from the next door farm. A parrot ladder for the uninformed is a large plank of wood with holes cut into it for feet and hands to cling onto. This forms a kind of crude ladder that's fastened permanently to the wall, usually to give access to lofts, where there is no room for stairs. It is safer and more convenient than having to prop a proper ladder up every time you needed to get up there. Years later when all the renovations were complete the structural integrity was tested when my partner's nieces and nephew all climbed up there together and pretended to play musical instruments. A finishing touch to the barn porch was a huge light-fitting in the centre, hanging from one of the beams. I saw it at an antique fair and knew it was just the thing for the big high room as anything else would be completely lost. It wasn't cheap at a hundred and twenty pounds, but I had beat the stall holder down from two hundred so it really was a bargain. I think the stall holder was fed up with carting it about as I don't think there would be many rooms it would fit into. The guy said it came out of a Scottish lodge; it certainly had that sort of grand look about it.

Fixing the thing was a major construction project on its own as it must have weighed about over half a hundredweight. Luckily the oak beam I bolted it to was well up to the job and it has not crashed down killing anybody yet.

I love oak especially old oak as it is almost indestructible. I bought, on impulse, a load of really old oak. Its history was that it had come from an old barn, probably over three hundred year old, that had been demolished . The surprising thing was it was as hard as steel and just as strong. The more amazing thing was that three hundred years ago it was against the law of the land at the time to use new oak to build barns. The only way oak could be used was to transport it from the coast where it would have come from old ships that were being dismantled. So my oak had probably done its duty as a ship before it became a barn. I have used it all over the house as decoration rather than structural but it definitely looks in keeping.

A true story concerning oak, involves York Minster. The story really starts a week before the roof caught fire. The Oakworth Village Morris Dancers were on a dancing trip to York that fateful week. My wife was a member of the women's dancers, which in itself is a sacrilege as traditionally only men were Morris dancers, but the main reputed sacrilege was that they were allowed to dance actually in the Minster. The official reason for the fire was of course lightning but it was obviously God sending a bolt down to punish the church for allowing pagan dancing in his house. I jokingly digress, anyway when it was being decided how the roof was to be rebuilt, the architects got together with the Minster's officials. The architects asked the Minster officials what criteria they had in mind for the restoration. They thought about it and replied that they required it to last at least five hundred years as the last one had done before it was destroyed by fire. An architect replied that to replace the roof with steel would last just over a hundred years, cast iron about two hundred years but to last at least five hundred years it had to be oak.

And so it was and some of that oak was taken from a wood in Bingley. If you visit an estate called St Ives there is a little plaque on an oak tree stump proclaiming that this tree was used in the reconstruction of York Minster roof.

For all my renovations on the house the plans were passed by Keighley council no problem but I still had regular visits from the planning office to make sure I was keeping to the plans and adhering to building regulations. The planning officer I dealt with was very good and was reasonably easy to please if any compromises were required.

I did have one close call I remember as I had put mullion windows in the extension to match one of the original ones. But one of the others was smaller, so when I ordered the windows I ordered an extra one and installed it, replacing the smaller one, so now they all matched, and looked much better I thought. But Planning don't always work like that, so when the planning officer came and I was showing him around he stopped, looking at the new window and back to the plans he was carrying. My heart missed a beat. Mick was just emerging from a door, saw the planning officer's perplexed stare, turned around and didn't emerge till the officer had gone. Thanks for the moral support, Mick! Finally the officer turned to me and said the obvious. 'That window is not on the plans like that, is it?' What could I say? But before I could get myself in deeper by blaming Mick the builder he just said, 'Well you seem to have made a good job of it and it looks right so we will leave it in.' I nearly collapsed with relief.

It did teach me a lesson though. When I was altering the back of the house the landing window was quite small and when I looked from the outside saw it had been a three mullion window that had been bricked up for some reason. I didn't think the house was built when the window tax was enforced (that taxed the number and size of windows) but checking on Wikipedia it probably was. Anyway when the officer came around again for his visit I asked him if I could open it up again. He gave me a shrewd look, obviously remembering his leniency on his last visit and said I would have to submit a plan. Bugger! Well I did, and it was passed no problem, although I added to my submission an extra mullion just for the hell of it. And by the time the officer came around again, where the old mullion were removed and the new ones installed there was no telling for he wouldn't have remembered how many mullions there was original, just that some were bricked up.

Mind you although the window was spectacular when it was finished, I had made a rod for my own back as a large section of the upstairs wall and roof had to be propped up, not a job for the faint hearted. I sometimes look at it now and wonder how I even dared think about doing it. Although Mick's a rock and not fazed by the seeming impossible. That's the window I mentioned earlier. All in all it was bad timing because I could not afford frames and glass for over winter and had snow blowing in. But it was all worth it!

Sometimes I could keep my imagination under control. I see something, want it, can't afford it, and have to make it. It was partly bad timing as I was just starting to install my en suite bathroom. I went into a rather expensive antique shop, just to see how the other half live, and there it was! A Victorian shower like you have never seen before. It consisted of four copper rings on three brass poles with the control all in brass and the shower head suspended above on a copper pipe. The copper rings had tiny holes and when the control was positioned in a certain way it would squirt water from all sides. I could just picture it in my bathroom until the proprietor told me the price, and I almost lost the vision. Four and a half grand was probably a fair price if you could afford it but not on my pittance of a wage. But with my usual entrepreneurial spirit, if that's what you may call it, I told the proprietor I was an inertia designer and I had a potential customer who might be interested and he let me take a picture of it.

I was hooked and a delay of about six months fitting my bathroom out resulted while I gathered the necessary bits and put it together. First I bought some lengths of copper pipe and had them bent into four foot diameter rings. The guy who bent them for me was dying to ask what they were for but I kept him guessing till I collected them a few days later when he just had to ask. I told him it was for a shower, he just nodded and you could see he was convinced I was a nut.

Next were the brass posts. Now those were a little bit more difficult until I was sat in this pub and had an Eureka moment. Around the base of the bar were ornate brass fittings, just what I required for my shower. I had the presence of mind not to ask the landlady if I could rip them out as I had a use for them because it was a nice local pub and I didn't want banning. This was pre-internet search engines or at least my use of them, but a quick search through the yellow pages revealed a bar fittings supplier. A quick phone call got me a catalogue in the post the next day and I was fit up with fittings. All the bits I needed to construct my shower were there and not too pricey., A week later they arrived in the post and I was away soldering joints and, with a few extra plumbing joints, I had had plenty of practice with the plumbing around the house and it soon took shape.

Just one problem! The shower had to stand in the centre of the bathroom for full effect so where was the water going to go. It wasn't a lack of planning just a slight oversight that cost me another few months while I shaped a hollow out a circle in the floor boards to act as a shower tray and made the entire bathroom a wet room with a sealed floor of non-slip resin, just another skill I have achieved that I will probably never need again in my lifetime, but it's all part of life's rich tapestry. Just to add the icing on the cake, at a car boot sale I bought four large brass fish that perch nicely on top of the brass posts, and with a little imagination and a lot of plumbing skill I got them to squirt cold water onto any one stood in the shower and inquisitive enough to turn a lever on one of the posts.

With the big switch on, it all works. It's one of my major achievements and it's also practical as I use it every day for my shower.

On doing some finishing touches with the bathroom I built two airing cupboards in a low part of the bathroom. After I had finished one I was sat in the other when I fancied a sauna! Well at least making one out of the unfinished airing cupboard it was easier than I thought, just insulated, lined with pine, a special heater, a bench and I have a sauna. It's not all that big but you can get three people in there at once, but they have to be good friends.

As I said I love horses so I decided to make use of the field at the back of the farm and rent it out for a couple of horses to graze. This required me to build a stable-block and tack room. I did look into buying a ready-made one, but the price was way beyond my means even if it was an investment. I wasn't sure if I would get my money back from the rent, so my only option was to build my own.

I look back sometimes to the projects I tackled, and just cannot believe I even contemplated them. I'm no joiner but my only saving grace is I get stuck in instead of thinking too much, as I've explained before. That's not to say I start without some planning. For a start it needed planning permission from the council, so I needed a drawing to submit to the council.

I nearly got a GCE in technical drawing, if only the teacher had put me in for it! (Are you reading this Sir?) but I did manage to produce a half-decent drawing on the back of a cigarette packet; no seriously, it was a proper drawing done with a ruler and everything. It must have been OK as it passed! With only one proviso. It had to be on a proper stone base, which I didn't mind too much as I enhanced the look of the thing, but it did entail taxing my bricklaying skills as well as my joinery skills to the full, which both are a little dodgy.

Undeterred by the slight lack of expertise, I set to. First I ordered a large amount of concrete for the base. The sort that comes in a large mixer on a wagon, the ones that roll around while they are getting to you. Five cubic metres doesn't sound a lot but it's more than little old me can spread out and level without it setting with me stuck in the middle in my wellies, requiring a road drill to free me. Enter my long-suffering friends.

Why do they do it? The only reason I can think of is I will always give anyone a hand if called on, but they never ask me to plod around up to their knees in wet cement for three hours doing back breaking work for a cup of tea and a biscuit at the end of it, so it must be I have true friends. So let this be dedicated to all my friends over the years who have got involved in one or more of my little projects with little notice or warning and with very little complaint, and a knowledge that they are inevitably going to end up knackered and dirty, rewarded only with hot sweet tea and bickies.

So a quick phone call and I have a team of two armed with wellies and shovels when my mixer arrived. If you are nice to the mixer man he will fix a long trough to the mixer and drive along the base while disgorging the concrete so you don't have to spread it too far. Even so it's tough work. Then with a plank, with handles at each end that I had prepared earlier and a friend each end we skimmed the plank up, down, back and forward along wet concrete smoothing the surface. With no time for a tea break in between otherwise we would have had three people to hammer out of the set concrete as it was damn quick-drying stuff. The tea and cakes at the end were very welcome, with a good laugh and jokes at the inevitable odd slosh of wet cement over our wellie tops and the splatters on our clothes and faces we had all received.

A few days later with the base set solid, it's brick laying time. After the back-breaking work of mixing a barrow of concrete I decided I needed a cement mixer. I did my usual trick of wanting something badly enough and it will turn up on your doorstep the next day, well sort of. There's usually a little twist. This twist was that I spied a rather dilapidated cement mixer in a scrap yard, and it was just about to be crushed, I was on first name terms with the scrap man so he sold me it for its scrap value, for the princely sum of five pounds. Oh and by the way it didn't have an engine. No problem. I just happened to have an electric motor with a gearbox that was about the right speed from, would you believe, the curtain opener from a cinema. With a little modification

I had a serviceable cement mixer that lasted me nearly twenty years before it was returned to the scrap yard and would you believe I got more than my money back as the price of scrap had risen.

A week later and I had the mixer in the middle of the site with two rows of blocks laid out. Another week I was up to the right height and I was ready to start the wood bit. Tidying the building site which was now the inside of the stables a nasty realisation struck me. I could not get the bloody mixer out through the door. How could I have done that? It was too heavy to lift over the wall on my own and I had to maintain a little credibility and not involve any friends as I would never live it down. So I knocked part of the wall down to get the bloody thing out. I should have known I wouldn't get away with it. As I was pushing it out of the enlarged door way a face appeared over the wall and a familiar voice said, 'Now I've seen everything, just wait till I tell everybody about this.' Fair do's I would have had to tell the tale eventually. It was too good a story to keep to myself.

The rest of the construction went without much of a hitch although tarring the roof with hot tar was a little hairy. There's still a patch of spilt tar where I came close to tarring a friend when I dropped a bucket full of the boiling stuff just inches from him. Again with a little help from my friends it has remained waterproof for many years now and kept a number of horses dry. It even has two families of swallows nesting in the roof space which I think makes it worthy of being called 'proper stables'.

I've always fancied building a log cabin! A proper one, made out of logs and all. An opportunity arose as always seems to happen with my little ambitious projects when the electricity company inspected the overhead cables which came across my land to the house. This is bit obscure at the start but bear with me. What it was, twenty years ago I planted a small wood in the front field but because of the overhead cables I couldn't plant trees under them. Christmas trees being cut down in their prime when only six feet tall, for sale at Christmas were the ideal solution. The only problem being the live Christmas tree market took a bit of a dive as imitation trees took off. They don't drop pine needles over your carpet, well not the better quality ones anyway.

So over the years I did sell a few but a lot grew too big for living rooms and started to get dangerously close to the overhead electricity wires. So when the electricity company engineer came around he shook his head and took a sharp intake of breath through his teeth and said they would all have to be cut down. Now I like trees and over the years I've surrounded the house with all different kinds, so I got a bit defensive and compared the destruction of the rain forest to his condemning my overgrown Christmas trees. I think that hit a bit of a raw nerve but he was adamant that there was no alternative as the whole lot could catch fire or electrocute someone if they touched the twenty-thousand volt overhead cables. After a bit of a consultation on his mobile to his boss he then offered me a compromise. They would still cut down the trees but they would plant a few hundred small bushy trees and rhododendrons which wouldn't grow tall enough to ever touch the overhead wires. I'm pleased I settled for that as it's let a lot more light in and the rhododendrons eventually flowered and look really great. Then wheels started turning in my little brain, the logs would be the perfect size and length to construct my dream, a log cabin.

How do you build a log cabin? The Internet is just wonderful. You type it in click and the answer is there. There's a book on how to build one, would you believe, it's taken from an original that resides in the Congressional Library in America, and with a few more clicks of the old mouse it appeared through my letterbox a few days later.

It's an amazing book full of pictures and diagrams, with instructions on chimneys, fireplaces, furniture all made from logs and even tools you will need, just as settlers in the wild west would have constructed their homes from what was available in the forest around them. One of the essential tools the book explains is an adze. It's sort of an axe with the slightly curved blade mounted sideways. This is used for tidying up the logs and cutting out the grooves at each end so they slot into each other. It just so happened I was in possession of such an item as I had picked up one at a car boot sale some years earlier to chip away at some old beams I used in my house renovations. I had become quite proficient in its use. The knack is to straddle the piece of wood you are working on with a leg either side of the log and swing the adze down between your legs. The secret to avoiding serious injury is to keep your legs as far apart as possible as it has been known for inexperienced wielders of said tool to take painful chunks out of their shins. I would like to add after extensive use of this tool I am still in possession of pristine shins.

I decided to do the job properly and build foundations with a stone base. Luckily at this stage I had worked out that in spite of my asking the guys from the electricity company to cut the logs as long as possible they had got carried away with their chain saws and cut a large proportion into short lengths. With a measure up and a quick calculator it was apparent I did not have enough long logs to build the cabin to a decent size. Not to be beaten, just a little ingenuity was required. With a little extra work I could make my log cabin eight sided, so I could use shorter logs at the ends. Even then I would struggle to find enough logs. Then I remembered I had been given three large sheets of curved glass, so with a little modification one whole side of my cabin would be glass. The book didn't have a section on glass-sided log cabins so from there on I was on my own.

With my foundations and base in place it was time for the logs, but first I had to build the fireplace and chimney. This had to be constructed from stone as it was going to be a proper working fire. When finished, without the walls it looked a bit strange just a fireplace and chimney. It reminded me of old cowboy films of log cabins in the Wild West after Indians had attacked homesteaders and set fire to the cabin, just leaving the stone chimney unburned. All that was missing were cowboys lying around with arrows sticking out of them.

Now I'm not bad at stone work especially if it's supposed to look rustic with plenty of cement and random stone so it is not tragic if the courses are a little out. My uncle who was a craftsman joiner summed it up when I showed him the finished cabin. I asked him what he thought of my handy work. His reply was that he could not have done what I had achieved. I questioned this as he was far a superior at constructing than I am. His reply was ,'I don't do rustic.'

Back to the woodwork. Once I got started with my adze chopping out the grooves in the ends of the each log and slotting the next one on top layer on layer it soon started to take shape. What I found most amazing was how stable the walls were. The walls of the cabin could not have been stronger if I had constructed them out of concrete blocks, the joints at each corner locked so well even with my inexperience in log cabin building. The extra joints in the eight sides created twice as much work than if I had longer logs but looked really good and added to the overall strength.

Doors, windows, and the roof all slotted in to my plans with a little help from my little book. The roof overhangs the walls by a couple of feet to stop the rain running down the walls as they aren't very watertight even with the cracks filled with waterproof plaster. The final bit of the jigsaw was the large sheets of glass down one wall. It was a tense moment as logs aren't very precise and glass doesn't bend. Bloody amazing they fitted! Well near enough with a little chiselling here and there. The whole effect is very weather proof. Even in winter with the fire lit it would be quite feasible to live in there.

Pride may be one of the deadly sins, but sod it I'm really proud of my log cabin. I've filled it with appropriate knick-knacks like a imitation bear skin rug in front of the fire I bought on the Internet from America, some imitation fur throws on the chairs and my piece de resistance is an animated reindeer head on the wall above the fireplace that sings cowboy songs. The cabin has electric and running water, a dash of civilization for my little house in the wood. There's a bridge leading to the cabin across a gully and waterfall. Underneath the bridge to complete the fantasy there is a troll door and I tell people to be very quiet as they cross the bridge or the troll will hear them and charge them for crossing… or he will eat them!

From the start of my renovations of the farm to the finished product (it’s never really finished, there's always some tweaking, repair, and new projects to get on with) took about twelve years and I've enjoyed almost every minute of it.

— 19 —

SURVIVING DISASTERS

I SEEM TO have had my fair share of near-do's, and disasters, well not exactly disasters actually as I've never broken any bones or been damaged too badly, probably down to luck more than anything

Take tree felling for example, a dangerous occupation if ever there was one. I do own a chain saw as it happens but actually one of my nearest-do's was when someone else was wielding theirs. How it happened was when I decided to take down a Christmas tree. Not as you would think after Christmas from the living room as that wouldn't be particularly dangerous and I certainly wouldn't use a chain saw. It was May and the Christmas tree in question was thirty foot tall. It had some sentimental value as my parents had planted it in the garden fifty years earlier after it had spent Christmas in the house with us, with candles lit. But it had to go!

It was only fifteen foot from the house and as much as it appeared healthy, it would have made a mess of the house if it came down in a storm, also it was stopping a lot of light. There were two actually planted about the same time after Christmas. And they both needed to come down, so considering one wrong saw cut and half my house would go, I called on the expert, my mate Mick. He's quite a dab hand at tree felling so I was confident I was not going to lose my precious abode.

First was the tough one. It had nowhere to go except my conservatory which I didn't need restyling. It was a ladder job and to be cut from the top down, six feet at a time. All went well and in an hour we had a stump, a large pile of logs and branches. It would have been a lot easier and far quicker to drop it in one but not without having to re-roof the conservatory. Our success on our first one gave us confidence, so the next one was coming down in one! It wasn't total insanity as there was a narrow avenue for the tree to fall, but it was tight. The plan was to tie a rope to near the top of the tree and the other end attach to Mick's truck, and when the tree was nearly sawn through at the bottom I was to drop his truck forward down a slope, thereby pulling the tree into the gap next to my house, simple!

It was foolproof (oh yeh). Hindsight is a wonderful thing and I'm afraid not over-endowed with fortune telling, most times. The truck was reversed up to the tree, the rope was tied to the top of the tree and down to the tow bar of the truck. Mick revved up his chain saw and prepared to saw through the base of the tree. I climbed into his truck and Mick attacked the tree. I glanced through the rear window at the now half sawn tree, and decided to make my move. Reaching for the handbrake to roll forward, it was instant panic 'Where in the name of God was the handbrake?' It wasn't at the side of the seat, it wasn't by the gear stick. A desperate glance through the rear window saw a thirty-foot fir tree descending majestically down onto the truck and me. Another desperate inspection of the controls revealed the missing handbrake tucked under the dashboard and a quick flick of the wrist released it. I thankfully rolled forward. I felt a small thud as the top of the tree clipped the rear of the truck, and I let out my breath and mentally checked my undies for signs of problems.

The underwear seemed to be unblemished so I slid out the truck and staggered over to Mick, who immediately congratulated me on my perfect timing. I don't know whether he was expecting a reciprocal congratulation on his chain saw skills, but he didn't get it, instead I enquired about the sense of having a handbrake hidden under the dashboard. Mick looked at me with a frown and said they were always under the dash in those trucks. Then the penny dropped and he just rolled about laughing but saw the not-so-funny side when I pointed out that he had just missed wrecking his truck or, worse still, my house. We did both have a laugh together over a well earned cup of tea.

Photography can be dangerous! Well if you go down a pothole with flash powder! I was enthusing about a photograph I had seen in a magazine of a cave taken with multi flash to my mate, Dave, and I wanted to use old fashioned flash powder instead of electronic flash just for effect. He said that he knew of an ideal cave up the dales which he and some mates had been down, he would take me down if I wanted. Oh yes please!

He was enthusiastic about the flash powder side of it to as he was my bomb and rocket making partner. So in preparation I accumulated a fair amount of flash powder (formulae withheld. Don't try this at home) of the kind Edwardian photographers used instead of flash bulbs or (nowadays) electronic flash, although in retrospect they would have been a lot safer for my adventure! The potholing gear was a little more sophisticated than the Edwardian equivalent, miner's helmet with a candle on the neb of our hats, but not by much. We had scrounged some bright yellow hard hats from a guy working on a local building site and taped a flashlight to the side. A pair of wellies was essential as Dave said there was a bit of water about (no alarm bells?).

With my flash powder in a water-tight Tupperware container borrowed from my mother's kitchen, and my camera in a plastic bag in my haversack we set off up the dales.

Now the pothole is quite a well-known cave among cavers, situated by the famous Settle viaduct. The day was a little overcast and it had been drizzling slightly all morning, a fact my mate Dave seemed a little apprehensive about, but which I could not quite understand as we were dressed for rain, and anyway we were going underground weren't we? (Still no alarm bells?)

After a little searching and a few false starts we found the entrance which was a sinkhole with a dead sheep at the bottom. Now I'm not squeamish and dead sheep are dead sheep, I've seen my fair share on the farm, but this little awkward bugger had passed away half blocking the entrance. When I say entrance we are not talking a six-foot cavern in a hill side, this was an eighteen inch hole at the bottom of a steep-sided round gully. We'd come this far so down we went. The sheep had probably been dead about, I would say, two weeks, just nicely matured and plenty of meat still on the bone, oozing maggots, with a smell that was like a cricket bat being smashed into your nose. But we were tough lads and we slithered down the hole feet first. Now a smelly, dead sheep at six feet has nothing on a stinking, dead sheep at six inches. But we were soon down and the view was stunning, and made up for the view at the entrance. It was a tall narrow passage obviously cut out by fast flowing water at some time. (yet still no alarm bells?). The passage was shaped like a big ‘S’ and was difficult to walk down standing up straight as you had to curve your body into the ‘S’ to shuffle forward. Eventually we came to a low part where the ceiling of the cave came two feet off the few inches of water that ran along the bottom of the cave. It was a bit awkward to get under and we got our knees wet, but what was waiting for us on the other side was awesome.

It wasn't massive, about the size of four living rooms, but the ceiling was covered in stalactites, (tights inevitably come down) and even our meagre torches picked out a rainbow of colours in the rock walls.

When we had finished gawking at the geology we got stuck in with our project. First I set up my camera on a tripod, checked the area the view finder was covering, and then made little piles of flash powder in the picture. The theory behind my photograph was that in the complete darkness of the cave you could open the camera shutter, and go around the piles of flash powder igniting them one at a time thereby exposing different parts of the picture with the light of the flash. Has any one picked out the flaw yet? Well don't worry, we didn't till the fourth flash before the cave filled with smoke, it was a whiteout! We alternated between hilarity and panic, although real panic came when we realised that the floor of the cave was six inches deeper in water than it was when we came in, and rising!

Blundering about in the whiteout I eventually found my camera, stuffed it in my plastic bag, then we groped about for the entrance/exit, which by the way was not illuminated with a green sign, not that we would have been able to see it if it had been. This is when ultimate panic set in. We eventually found the exit and discovered why it had been so difficult to find, it was well under water! We took one look at each other, our faces just about visible in the fog by our hat lights, and went for it. A big breath was a bit of a problem considering the quality of the smoky polluted air in the cave but we did our best and dived under the low now flooded ceiling. It seemed a lot further than when we came in, probably only six feet under water and considering I have no problem doing two lengths under water at the swimming pool, it seemed like a hundred yards.

Finally we were through but not out of trouble. The narrow passage was now a good half full of fast flowing water, which was very difficult to wade through. We only just managed by walking on the ridge of one of the 'S' bends but it wasn't easy and to make things worse and even scarier there was water pouring in from above. Then up ahead we saw the light shining through a waterfall! What! Well we now knew where the water was coming from, our exit! Actually it wasn't too difficult to climb up through the waterfall as we had the incentive of light and freedom. One problem was our old friend the deceased sheep as the water had washed its remains a little more into the exit. So even a little more intimacy was required to exit than was our entry as we had to heave the damned rotting thing out of the way.

The heavy rain was very refreshing as we walked back to the car and also explained the sudden flood down under. There was definitely a lesson to be learnt here. Never to go caving ever again was mine, and certainly not with flash powder and the real big one, no weather report!

Walking across a bog to reach an aeroplane that crashed during the war definitely sounds like a recipe for disaster and the survival part was we never found it! This was in cahoots with my mate Dave again. He was telling me about this World War Two bomber that had crashed in the war and never been salvaged as it was way up on the moors, in the middle of a big bog that was impossible to cross. Sounds like a challenge to me! Just think of interesting bits you could scrounge off it, perhaps a dial from the cockpit or even an engine. Mere details like how we would carry a two ton aeroplane engine across the moors or dismantle anything without even a screwdriver just never occurred to us in our enthusiasm, the big thing was to find it.

I reckoned I could walk over a bog no problem if I had big enough lumps of polystyrene strapped to my feet. A calculation was unnecessary as I had only two pieces of foam and these cut into two, a pair for each of us. A clothes line was ideal to tie our boots to the pontoons and I could always knot them back together before my mother missed her washing line.

My mate Dave was a bit vague about the exact location of the crash site but we set off anyway. Dave reckoned he didn't need a map as he had had it described in detail to him by a bloke who had got it from his mate who knew a man who had been there twice! So who was I to argue?

I would not be giving the location away if I said we arrived in deepest Swaledale, and set off across a rather desolate moor which Dave said was the spot described to him. It was about five miles across the moor, over a hill, and then in a dip was this bog and we would see the tail end of the plane sticking out of the bog. It sounded great to me so we marched off in eager anticipation.

The pontoons were a bit of a problem. They weren't particularly heavy just bloody cumbersome. With a little ingenuity we strapped them to our backs with the clothes line straps and we were away. We walked and we walked and we walked some more. We stopped on a grassy knoll for a sandwich that Dave's wife had had the foresight to pack and then we walked some more. Uphill and down dale we walked and not a sign of civilization never mind a plane crash. There was a worried look on Dave's face, but I didn't ask. Finally we did come across a small bog and decided to try out the pontoons anyway. Strapping them to our boots with the washing line sounds so simple, and perhaps testing them out before we set off would have been a good idea, but you have to be careful not to stifle spontaneity and a sense of adventure with too much preparation, it's how you think in your twenties!

Having finally secured them reasonably well, walking in them was another thing again. If you ever tried walking in swimming flippers you would be almost there, but you would have to add weights and treble the size to imagine just how ungainly they were to walk in. An added disability were tussocks! No, not Russian Soldiers, or an area of Scotland. These were clumps of tough grass growing in humps sticking out of the bog. Now Dave is no wimp but as he pointed out, 'You made em, you try em.' So I walked out into the bog. Now give my impromptu design due credit, I didn't sink, well not until I fell over that is! Bog mud has a flavour and smell all of its own. After Dave managed to haul me out, I was pretty disgusting. It did galvanise us into admitting that we weren't actually lost, but as for the location of the plane wreck it was possibly one of those urban myths. That is unless you know different?

There's a distinct possibility that it was fortuitous we never found the plane wreck. For on our way back we speculated on what we may have found, a few bombs, bullets or even a machine gun or two. Oh well it was not to be. Another good reason for not finding the elusive wreck is that if the bog would have been any bigger or boggier Dave, might possibly not have been able to drag me out, so all’s well that ends well. And it would have been even more frustrating to have found the plane wreck and not been able to reach it. But it would have still been rather fine to get some souvenir. So if you are ever in those parts and come across four big chunks of polystyrene, you are nowhere near a plane wreck!

Dave was a clever lad and a good friend. He built his own astronomical telescope and was friendly with Patrick Moore of the television who presented ‘The Sky at Night’ (the longest running TV show in the world at that time) but he moved away and we lost touch. Although recently I heard he was detained at Her Majesty's pleasure for he had a bit of a passion for unregistered guns. Silly lad.

I was unsure whether to put my next experience in ‘Daring Do's’ but decided it was more a survival of a very potential disaster i.e.

drowning, and not to romanticise it, but to catalogue it as one of my more excessively stupid acts. I confess I jumped the Stridd! Both ways!

If you've never visited the Stridd it's well worthwhile as a beauty spot but DON'T TRY TO JUMP ACROSS IT! Not that you probably would, 'cos it's really scary.

The Stridd is located just up from Bolton Abbey in Wharfedale. It's a narrow water-filled chasm through which , the not insubstantial river, even though not all that far from its source, runs in a turbulent cauldron of swirling, foaming, bubbling, and, , very fast running water . It's about seven foot across but twenty-five foot deep and you can imagine the force of the water. It also has undercut sides that can drag anyone in it under them with fatal consequences. The banking is wet, slippery and moss covered, again making the leap destined to failure. All in all it's not got a lot going for it as a long jump practice. It's taken tens of lives over the years to my knowledge, some of the bodies not being found for weeks as the current and undercutting holds them out of sight.

Have I convinced you of the unsuitability and darn right foolishness of a leap? It might have been nice if some of my friends at the time had convinced me not to do it. Or perhaps they tried, but I can be a tad stubborn at times.

This was in my early twenties, full of the impetuosity of youth and that is my best and only excuse. We were in a group of lads and lasses on a stroll in the country. We had walked up the river from Bolton Abbey, a very pleasant walk may I add. We finally came to the Stridd and the narrow gap which the river flows through in such a spectacular fashion. I had read and heard the stories about the Stridd so I was not naive to the dangers. It did not look beyond my capability and I did a few dry run practice jumps of equivalent distance. I've been back there many times since, and as I've got older the distance seems to have increased and I'm sure it has nothing to do with erosion.

With warnings of deaf and dumb breakfasts for a fortnight from my partner, and a definite assertion that she was not going to jump in and save me if I fell in, I jumped.

At this point I would like to say that the rest of my friends were divided on the suitability of my adventure. As true friends I'm happy to report that during the lead up to my jump, there was no money changing hands among my happy band on my chances of survival , (as far as I was aware). In retrospect this might have been due to no-one being confident enough to put money on me actually making it. On my landing safely, there was an audible gasp from my audience, and probably from me as well. I staggered forward, for staggering backward would have been a really bad idea as I had landed only a foot from the edge, and then started to breathe. I did have the presence of mind to compose my face from fear to serene confidence before I turned around to wave nonchalantly to my friends. By the look on their faces, I decided that an offer to join me would not be taken up, so I looked to rejoining my group.

It's strange. In the midst of my meticulous planning of my jump, choosing my take-off and landing sites, practising my jump, and my two minutes of meditation to concentrate my Chi, I had overlooked one rather important detail, my triumphant return!

There are two bridges over the Wharfe in the area and even wide shallow stretches where you could wade across and still not get your underwear wet. There are even some rather fine stepping-stones that cause much amusement among the intrepid and foolish but they all were miles away.

There was only one option, yes really, jump back. Now the return journey needed a lot more surveying. The outward take off point was higher than the landing point and gave me an advantage, but a return from this point would be fraught. So I went looking for a more suitable site. Meanwhile back on the other bank my partner had calmed down enough to shout across to me. 'And what are you going to do now ... oh you are not?'

I gave her a winning smile, shrugged my shoulders and carried on my search. Having found a potential site, I did a quick risk assessment. Years ahead of my time really. There was not all that much choice, the take-off point was mossy and wet and the landing site was at the same height but seemed slightly further than my excursion over to this side of the foaming, bubbling, churning, scary, Stridd.

Well I'd done it once, I could do it again! Here lies a warning for the dear and beloved partners of adventurous idiots. Don't shout 'NOOOO!' just as they are running up to jump over the Stridd. 'It's not nice and it's not helpful. Luckily I've always been a bit deaf since a nasty bout of

Meningitis as a kid and with the noise of the water, it didn't put me off too much. This time I didn't stagger forward, I fell forward as one of my feet slipped off the edge.

It was a quiet walk back to the cars, with a slight limp from skinned and bleeding shins, although some of the lads did surreptitiously pat me on the back and wink. And it wasn't deaf and dumb breakfast for a fortnight but damn near.

Well I'm still here forty odd years later with never a broken bone in my body. I'm a lot less adventurous these days and when I look back, I say to myself, did I really do that?

— 20 —

FANCY DRESS

I'M NOT PARTICULARLY into dressing up and no-one who knows me would say I was even a smart dresser, but probably due to my Thespian background if invited to a fancy dress party I try to throw myself into it and do it with style, panache and just a dash of eccentricity.

One of my more exotic costumes was for a doctors and nurses party thrown by the local flag crackers (Morris dancers) members. I would like to point out that as I've disclosed in previous chapters I can't dance and was not keen on the bells, but my better half was a member of the woman's Morris. Anyway we were invited and just to be different, I went as a witch doctor. Now this involves being black, and as much as I'm not pale I needed to be much darker for the full effect.

I asked some theatrical friends what I could black up my body with, and when I had weaned out the obvious malicious suggestions like black boot polish, soot, and blackboard paint. I settled on cork charcoal, although it was said with a whimsical look it seemed the lesser evil. For the uninitiated in the finer arts of charcoal burners, charcoal is wood burnt without air. This was on an industrial scale in medieval times to produce charcoal for iron smelting and was achieved by starting a large bonfire then covering it with earth to restrict the air getting to it, then leaving it to smoulder for a couple of days. On the scale I needed I popped half a dozen old wine corks in a treacle tin, jammed the lid on tightly, speared it with a nail to allow the gas to escape and popped it on our open fire. After about quarter of an hour, thin smoke jetted out through the hole as the cork caught fire, and then I was away.

After a couple of hours lifting the can carefully off the fire and taking great care not to drop it on my mother's best hearth rug I let it cool and prised off the lid. The black lumpy powder when cooled and crushed to a fine powder sure enough had the desired affect, although it had a slight tendency to rub off onto things you touched! Even things you didn't touch.

With the addition of a loin cloth, a chicken bone cut in half and wired so that it looked like it was through my nose, and a borrowed afro wig, I was all set.

At the party I was unique, surprise, surprise. There were a lot of boring white coats and stethoscopes and a wonderful array of sexy nurses' uniforms, not all of them on ladies, but I was the only one who'd thought of a witch doctor. After the novelty had worn off the burnt charcoal make-up became a little uncomfortable and after three hours it was unbearable. I did find a distraction though.

If I rubbed my black body up against the nurses (only the female ones may I add as some perverted males came as nurses in starched uniforms, black stockings, the works, but they were easy to spot) the effect was a bit like brass rubbing. For the uninitiated (I'm just a mine of useless information aren't I?) this is a riveting hobby on a par with train spotting, church bell ringing and stamp-collecting, in my opinion. It involves fixing paper over brass plaques, usually in churches, and rubbing a crayon over the paper so it transfers the patterns and writing onto the paper making a crude copy. The practice just beggars belief. What the hell do you do with them when you have finished, frame them and hang them on you living room wall? I digress. The upshot was when I rubbed my blacked-up body up against the bevy of nurses' fronts, the pattern of ladies' bras was imprinted on the outsides of their white blouses. This caused much merriment among the lads, but was a little less appreciated among the lady victims. I didn't quite understand just how annoyed and thirsty for revenge they had became and of course I overdid it as I have a tendency to. Eventually the discomfort outweighed the joys of bra rubbing and I had run out of victims who would let me get close enough anyway, so I asked the hostess if I could have a shower. I put her enthusiasm for me to have a shower because it meant the end to my bra rubbing. I was mistaken!

The instant I had striped off and climbed into the shower the bathroom door burst open and half a dozen Morris ladies armed with a yard brush, scrubbing brushes, a lavatory brush, small nail brush, and one enterprising lady with a tooth brush, God only knows what she intended to brush with that? Despite its small size I soon found out, and believe me it caused the most damage). I was scrubbed, rubbed, and abused, on mass. The black was washed away and then red predominated my rather now tender skin. I was eventually left alone to carefully dry off and get dressed. When I got back to the party I was greeted with a cheer from the ladies and a sympathetic looks from the lads.

On another occasion it was a James Bond theme. This was a theatre party so I knew I would have my work cut out to beat the opposition. In fact I was typecast as I'm not a snazzy dresser for Bond himself and Pussy Galore was not an option. So considering my passion for gadgets and explosives, it just had to be 'Q'.

I had the usual laser gun, a watch with a suicide Smartie hidden in it, an electrocuting pen, which when you took the cap off, it gave you a not insubstantial electric shock. However my favourite was a glasses case which when opened exploded in a ball of flame. My first victim, sorry I mean participant, in my little trick was Pussy Galore in a rather fetching cat suit. Even though she was aware of my wicked sense of humour, a reassuring smile and my favourite phrase 'trust me' soon got her into the spirit of the thing. I really genuinely do not understand why people 'trust me' but they do, it must be my charismatic personality, so she opened the case.

Just as planned the contents erupted in an explosion of relatively harmless flame. This would have been OK, for she had a strong heart and a cast iron constitution, except that she was also holding a full glass of red wine. Even more unfortunately her husband was standing behind her in a white Tuxedo dressed as one of the Bonds. Understandably she screamed, but less understandably her arms went up in the air catapulting the full glass of red vino directly over the very suave James B. I really felt that it was lucky it was her husband. There's nothing worse than spilling red wine over a stranger, don't you think? I don't think he saw it that way. Worse still, it caused such a rumpus that no-one else would open the glasses case or write anything with my electrocuting pen, not even late arrivals as they were warned at the door. Some people are just meanie spoilsports.

The next fancy dress party was a nonspecific do, so I went as a Viking! Well I had a pair of old cow horns from a car boot sale, and we had lots of old sacking about from the farm, so I set to. The first thing was to make a tunic of the sacking. Now as much as sewing is not on my list of talents I can sew the occasional button on, or a rip in my trousers when the need requires. So some old sacking sewn up with string was a doddle. I soon had a Viking tunic. Next some shoes covered in sacking and up around my legs with string binding, I was getting there. An old fur coat with the sleeves cut off made an acceptable jacket. That only left was the piece de resistance, the helmet! I scouted around for some sort of hat to stick my cow horns on and found the ideal thing, an old fashioned motor bike crash helmet in my shed.

Now you may wonder how I keep coming up with these unusual items out of my shed. Well all I can say is, you need to see my shed to understand just what's in there. They're big, all six of them!! and they are full to the gunnels, to use a nautical phrase. Although I have reduced their number to three nowadays they are still a resource valued by a number of people and organisations that contact me and ask, ‘This is a strange request but have you got a so and so?’ The reply is usually, ‘Yes, three actually.’

Well I found my biker’s crash helmet. It was one of those really old-fashioned ones, about as useful as a kitchen colander when it came to giving much protection in a crash. It was a steel shell that perched on your head and barely covered your ears. It had cork padding inside and a few webbing straps, superb for a Viking war helmet. Glue was a little inadequate for the job of fastening the horns on so I had to drill two holes each side and screw through from the inside into two bits of wood to stick the horns over. An old Celtic style brooch fastened to the front of the helmet for effect and I was set.

There were a lot of people I didn't know, a real mix of interesting people from rockers to nerds. One of the latter came up to me halfway through the evening and gave me a long lecture on the actual dress of Vikings who invaded Britain. The bottom line was they did not wear horns on their helmets and it was a myth created by Hollywood film makers with too much imagination and no research. He went on to explain Hollywood was also responsible for many myths including frog noises that go ‘ribit ribit’ in jungle scenes all over the world. In fact there is only one species of frog that goes ‘ribit, ribit’, surprise, surprise, and that lives just outside Hollywood in a swamp and nowhere else in the world. A recording was made of the little creature for a jungle film supposedly set in darkest Africa, and the same recording is probably used to this day. As interesting as this was I was fast losing the will to live and gave my excuses and moved away.

I was then approached by this scary gigantic gorilla of a rocker who not too gently lifted my ‘Hollywood’ Viking helmet off my head, inspected it, and uttered the words with malice in a gruff menacing voice, ‘You bloody vandal, that was a genuine (something or other) helmet and you've fucked it up.’ He jammed the helmet back on my head thumped the top for good measure and lurched off to the drinks table. I surreptitiously removed my helmet and left it off for the rest of the evening, just in case it caused any more controversy.

A charity fancy dress pub crawl was my next costume to be constructed, and this was a humdinger. I'd seen this guy on TV riding an ostrich, only it was his lower body in an ostrich costume and false legs dangling down the sides of the ostrich. This was very impressive but I could do one better. I had a gorilla costume that I had made for my Thespian days, and that gave me an idea. I constructed a lightweight cage with fake iron bars made from plastic water piping which I could get my upper body in, and false legs folded in front to look as if I was sat crossed legged in the cage. Next I padded out the top of the gorilla suit with chicken wire and fastened it to the cage with its arms around the cage as if it was carrying it. Now if I stuck my head and top half of my body into the cage and my legs in the bottom half of the gorilla suit, it looked for all the world as if the gorilla was carrying me sitting in the cage. You had to see it to appreciate it.

The venue for the charity pub crawl was arranged for a Friday night in Keighley, despite my misgivings about the suitability of the location and day. I can only think the organisers were a little naive as to the clientèle who frequent our little town on a Friday night. Up to a point I was proved wrong as the crowded pubs we could actually get into were very generous. I realised perhaps the unsuitability of my choice of costume as it was of a rather bulky nature and became a bit of a problem in crowded pubs. Our collection boxes were getting full and we were having a great time.

One pub we ventured into was particularly generous, even the landlord put a fiver in our box. Before we left he asked where we were going next. When we told him we were headed to the pub at the end of the street, he shook his head and explained that it was rather rough and he didn't advise it. I had heard rumours of its reputation as a 'rough hole'. So we thanked him for his advice and went outside. Gathering on the pavement we looked across the road to the pub which the landlord had warned us to avoid. Sure enough there was an overspill of rather inebriated gentlemen spewing out of the pub door onto the street, with very little access for our little band and certainly not for a gorilla carrying me in a cage.

Among our group was a rather upper-class young woman with a bit of an attitude, dressed as a chicken. When we all agreed we were giving it a miss the young lady in question said in her rather grating la-de-da voice. 'Well I'm going in. I'm not chicken!' Which was rich coming from a large yellow chicken with a bright red comb, chicken legs, and feet to match. I truly believe it wasn't a pun. She definitely had a blind spot for irony and as it turned out, for choosing to go into rough unsuitable pubs dressed as a chicken as well.

The chicken flounced off across the road and she really looked comical as it made the feathers in her tail sway exotically. When she reached the pub she barged her way in and vanished. We just stood and looked at one another, then there was uproar and we ran over to the pub. There was a lot of cheering and those on the outside were trying to push their way in. Then it happened. Yellow feathers came floating out of windows and doors. There were more cheers and the chicken staggered out of the door, unsteady on her yellow chicken legs, bedraggled, bright red comb askew, the zip at the front gaping open showing a very un-chicken like chest, and generally in bad shape. We rushed to her and asked the inevitable question, 'are you all right?' We were shocked by her answer. 'They plucked me.' OH PLUCKED! I thought you said...oh never mind. Well that's a relief, or perhaps not? The rest of the evening was fairly uneventful and we raised a considerable amount for charity. The chicken was uncharacteristically quiet for the rest of the evening and I just wonder what the reaction was when she took the plucked chicken costume back to the hire shop, or at least what was left of it.

If you have ever been to see the musical Rocky Horror Show you will know it's a dressing up job, and I do mean dressing up! It's all about transvestites, vampire transvestites actually, and the audience gets dressed up in outlandish gear as risqué and outrageous as the actors. Fishnet tights, high heels, basques, wigs, and make-up, and that's just the men! Actually the women are outshone by the men's costumes. I've been to see the show twice before and felt totally out of place going in normal clothes, so this time I decided to go for it. The tights were not much of a problem except they had to be pulled up to my chest to prevent me looking like Nora Batty. Do you women have the same problem? The high heeled shoes were a bit difficult, not finding some but wearing them. How do you ladies manage it? I was crippled after ten minutes, but I can see the attraction for you ladies, those few more inches give you a little lift if you excuse the pun. I drew the line at a basque but the rest of my costume was much in keeping with the show although I would not be seen dead in it anywhere else. The show was absolutely great and the audience was as entertaining as the actors.

One interesting phenomenon I experienced from my little dressing up session was after the show when we went for a curry, as you do in Bradford, being the curry capital of Britain. The only problem was one of our number insisted that we frequent his favourite curry house that just happened to be about three miles from the theatre (what did I just say about not being seen dead).

We were in a car so we didn't have to walk, not that I could manage three yards never mind three miles in those high heels. It was just that we came as a bit of a shock to the management and customers of the curry house as we were his only customers from the show. Actually the trek was worthwhile as the cuisine was delicious and the manager was very friendly once he had established we weren't a wild rock-band intent on wrecking his restaurant, and even had us posing with his staff for photographs.

The strange phenomenon I mentioned happened when we were waiting for a table as the restaurant was rather busy. The bar where we were waiting was jam-packed. As I was holding a conversation with my fellow Rocky Horror geared friends, I felt my bum pinched. Dressed as I was it could well have been a bloke that goosed me but to my relief and puzzlement it was a lady. Not only did I get a pinch, it was accompanied with a smile and a wink. Not only that, it happened again when a different group of ladies were behind me. I have never up to that point been pinched by a lady and not since may I add. Why did those ladies get so excited dressed as I was? Just one more reason why I will never understand women.

— 21 —

TRAVEL AND BAD FOOD GUIDE

AS I'VE SAID right from the beginning, I'm a typical Taurus the bull. I'm quite contented wandering around my own little field, with the occasional foray into the next field if there is nice juicy heifer to liaise with. Having said that I have done Europe, a dash of Asia, and as far as Oz. I confess to so far not exploring our lost colony of the USA. But I will some day as it's a cultural imperative what with Mickey Mouse, the home of Mac Donald's, and George Dubya Bush.

There is certain essentials information that I've never seen in travel guides like 'France closes on a Monday.' (Re our near starvation on landing on the Cherbourg peninsula on the dreaded Monday). Also midweek most shops are closed from twelve till well after two as the French take their leisurely glass of wine with their midday meal. (Although two to three-hour lunch breaks are becoming rarer even in

France, but still prevalent in Spain and Italy, known widely as a siesta.)

Try and avoid restaurants that have faded pictures of their meals on boards outside, although it seems to be a worrying trend. France is being submerged in crap fast food. It's chips with everything (pardon my French, I mean French fries). Considering Brittany has vast acreages of vegetables growing in the fields and their supermarkets, and markets are overflowing with an abundance earthy produce, I have yet to eat at a French restaurant that serves three veg with their meat. And as for their salad it’s to be hoped you like lettuce because that's all you'll get in the name of salad. Overall French cooking is vastly overrated, with it is a myth that French women cook healthy meals for their families. The French supermarkets are loaded with convenience food, just like ours. It always amuses me that Brit supermarkets have vegetables on display with not a hint of soil on them, unless they have a special promotion on organic potatoes, when they put a sprinkling of sterilised peat over them to make them look like they actually grew in soil.

To jump half way across the world to OZ, the food is tasty, healthy, and well prepared if not a little excessive in volume. I found it very difficult to clean my plate as they usually come piled high. I suppose it’s the rugged pioneering image although there are still a lot of rugged pioneering types about, and that goes for some of their women too. One aspect about OZ food that is quite trivial but fascinates me is that you can dunk their Ginger biscuits for in excess of thirty seconds and they don't dissolve into mush at the bottom of your tea or worse still drop all down your tee-shirt, on the way to your mouth. Whereas if you try that with Brit ginger biscuits for more than ten seconds, you have to slurp it out of the bottom of your mug with the dregs of your tea, or, worse, have to lick it off the front of your tee-shirt.

Away from Sydney there's a definite feeling of the frontier as the men get bigger and rougher and readier, as do the women, although I discovered a surprising fact that Ozzy men wear thongs! No worries ladies, thongs appear to be sandals out there in OZ. There are a lot of tattoos out here and not all of them are spelt properly, and that's only the women. Some of the Aussie women are really scary, a little bit butch and rather aggressive. Having said that, there are some very beautiful young ladies strutting about. But don't let looks fool you there's a touch of the outback spirit even in the most petite young lady. This was graphically demonstrated when I bought a bottle of juice at a shop. Being rather thirsty I thought I would have a swig as I left the store. Now I'm no wimp but could I unscrew that damned screw cap? Are OZ caps screwed on tighter than in UK? So I went back to the counter to ask the young lady serving if she had something to open the bottle. The young lady without hesitation just took the bottle from me and without even a grimace unscrewed the cap. To give her due she saw the look of horror on my face and explained that I must have loosened it. I accepted this explanation willingly to cover my embarrassment. Then damn me it happened again at another store. This time the young lady behind the counter saw me struggling, despite some effort to disguise my frustration. Reluctantly I handed the bottle back with a pathetic plea not to make it look to easy. She didn't! Or more accurately she did, with a flourish, off came the cap and I crept out of the shop, right shown up.

The life style and healthy food are certainly a positive health factor. That's not counting for the flora and fauna that appears to be darn right deadly for instance the Cassowary, that's a six-foot aggressive turkey on steroids who will kick you to death after clawing out your innards if you try to feed them (or if you don't). Frogs that you definitely don't kiss as they will not turn into princes but poison you, and as for spiders, ants, snakes, crocodiles, sharks, and jelly fish, don't even go there, and don't believe the locals, they either joke about it, exaggerate, or understate the risk, and not particularly in that order.

On your way to OZ a must is Bangkok. I'm sorry, ladies, Thai girls really are the most beautiful in the world, with personalities to match. In fact everyone is very courteous and genuinely friendly. Just a word of caution, gentlemen, there is a certain rather strikingly beautiful section of Thai society that appear to be ladies who aren't (they have dicks! Albeit well hidden) and they go under the name of 'Lady Boys.' Now that's no worry if all you intend to do is look, but for a massage or any thing else the shock has been known to kill strong men if they find out too late.

My first experience of foreign travel was the proverbial week in a Brittany farmhouse in the seventies. I was never into holidays with mates on the Costa Del whatever, although the sand, sea, and sex, did sound rather inviting. Nor Butlins, although I've heard the Redcoats used to go round the chalets at night and knock on the door of young men's rooms and ask whether they had a woman in there. If you replied 'no' they used to say, 'Hang on I'll get you one.'

The wife and I did various crossings on the Ro-Ro car ferries, that's roll on-roll off with your car, not row-row by the way. It was not all that long ago your car was craned on and off. This was a lot slower but only just, as you still seem to spend an awful lot of time queuing on the quayside.

The cars I could afford at the time were always a little unreliable, and it was always touch and go whether we would make it or not, but we always seemed to manage. Having AA or RAC membership was expensive and diminished the challenge of stripping down the engine at the side of the road in a foreign country. Having said that, a recent trip to France, in a reasonably new car with breakdown cover, ended up rather traumatic when the cylinder head gasket went, filling the road behind us with white smoke. It was towed to a rather expensive French garage where the mechanic did the classic car mechanic shake of the head with a slow intake of breath through his teeth, with the addition of a Gallic shrug for good measure, when he looked under the bonnet.

The most challenging was a trip to France in my nineteen-thirty-five Humber and my nineteen- forty-eight Triumph I've described in an earlier chapter. Surprisingly we had only a few minor problems. Relatively minor that is, if you call a brake fluid leak a minor problem.

We had to stop to top up the brake fluid reservoir with water as proper brake fluid would have been too expensive, as it took about a couple of gallons to get home.

The most physically challenging was the time we went to France on bicycles in a mini Tour De France. We weren't big on cycling, didn't own any, had not cycled for years, and then not more than a few miles, so had to borrow some old bikes from friends. Mad or what?

We took the ferry from Portsmouth to Cherbourg and cycled slowly down to St Malo only a hundred miles or so but it took us two weeks cycling for a day, then resting and sightseeing for two days. We landed in Cherbourg on a Monday with no food, naïvely expecting to buy food there. Now it's a little known fact, as I said earlier, that France closes on a Monday. Yes, the whole of France closes on a Monday, shops, restaurants, cafés, the lot. We would have starved to death if it was not for a French fries van on the beach for breakfast, dinner, and tea till France comes alive on Tuesday. Progress was slow and got slower when we took a wrong turning and ended up on a rather busy motorway. We were stopped by a police car and told to walk our bikes to the next exit as bicycles were not allowed on motorways in France. Not having the French to tell him they weren't all that legal on English ones either, we trundled off the motorway and back to side roads which weren't all that safer but we had less hassle from the police.

I do have a passion for France, so when my partner and I were offered a freebie week in the south of France at a little house up in the hills above Nice belonging to my ex's new husband (still all very amicable), we booked a flight and we were off. There are some beautiful towns on the coast down there like Antibes and Cannes. It's all a bit posh down there and further up the coast, Monte Carlo is even posher. To make the best of them all, we hired a car which we picked up at the airport. Nice airport is quite small considering, and when we were there they were constructing an additional terminal, so things were a little chaotic and had been for a few years (and still is by all accounts). The car hire was on the airport site but a little distance from the main terminal where we landed, at terminal two. Picking up the car went without a hitch and we enjoyed a wonderful week driving around the area. When it came to the flight home I decided to drop off my partner at the main terminal with the cases while I returned the car to terminal two. Having duly dropped off both baggage and partner, I proceeded to drive the short distance to the car hire drop-off. No problem, just follow the signs to terminal two then the car hire sign. In sequence it was terminal two, terminal two, terminal two, Genoa! What! I was out of the airport on a motorway speeding towards Genoa, and fast approaching a toll barrier. I had no money, no passport, and no desire to go to Genoa. But I did have an option! As it was quite early in the morning there was hardly any traffic about so I mounted the central reservation, which luckily didn't have a crash barrier, and sped back down the motorway to Nice. I had no difficulty getting back in the airport for the sign has a little aeroplane on it, but I was back to terminal one.

Trying again, I followed the signs to terminal two, terminal two, then suddenly I'm in an industrial estate, not a very friendly industrial estate may I add. There were burnt out cars, gypsy encampments, and rather scary-looking ladies waving at me. I didn't panic, just a hint of stark fear, with a few three point turns at dead ends and a determination not to give in to panic and definitely not waving back to the scary ladies. Again I was back in the airport, the bugger of it was I could see terminal two and the car drop-off point. I decided to ignore the signs this time and just point the car in the right direction. This seemed to be working until I was about to enter a one-way road the wrong way. At this point a small matter of driving down the wrong way down a one-way road pales into insignificance compared to another excursion to Genoa or to running the gauntlet of the City of the Dead industrial estate. I went for it! only forcing two other cars off the road. Driving a hired car with French number plates did not warn the French drivers that the oncoming vehicle was driven by a desperate Brit who regularly drove on the wrong ... I mean right ... left ... coming towards them, the wrong way. With only a swift wave of the fist they capitulated and pulled over and let me through. It was all worth it for I was at last at the car hire. I unceremoniously threw the car keys over the counter and scooted off to terminal one to partner, cases, and plane to home.

Meanwhile Jan was having a fit. Time was getting short for checking in. So she decided to queue without me and try to check us in. She must have had a fraught look (understandably as I had been gone a good three-quarters of an hour) for a lady behind her in the queue asked her if she was OK. Having explained my absence, the lady reassuringly told Jan that she would probably never see me again as the airport had a reputation for its ambiguous roads and signpost system. Jan had a vision of skeletons lost and abandoned at the side of the road. I personally didn't actually see any skeletons myself, although the burnt-out cars on the industrial estate from hell could possibly have contained bodies of lost Brits trying in vain to return their hire cars back to terminal two. But I was a little distracted with my own search for the elusive terminal two and thought it best not to stop and investigate.

At the point Jan was about to call the police and report me as a lost person, I turned up. I was a little surprised Jan didn't show concern about my prolonged absence. Although once she had explained the dire omen of my unlikely return by the lady in the queue I understood.

By all accounts Nice airport has a world wide reputation and I have had similar stories told me of lost souls wandering the maze of highways of Nice airport.

An incident in France that sticks in my memory is when I bought a rather fine keyring. This particular shop, which I frequent every time I visit that area, is filled with numerous tacky items. This key ring was in the jokes and rude section along with naff things like mugs with tits and knitted willy-warmers. But the keying caught my eye. It was called 'Orgasm'. Being in a flexible clear pack I pressed the red button on the fob, then moved away quickly as this very loud noise emitted from the packet of a rather passionate lady having one hell of an orgasm (faked or not it was impressive). It was a must-have buy. Waiting for the lady to finish and a gathering of rather puzzled, shocked shoppers to disperse, I picked up the packet, careful not to set it off again and headed to the till. Nonchalantly laying the package on the counter, as if I was about to purchase a keying with Nissan on it for my car, I was appalled when the young lady at the till picked up the item, waved it in the air and announced in a loud, sexy, but bored French voice, 'Price of the orgasm? Price of the orgasm?' to another young lady at the other end of the store. Her reply, in an even louder voice was, 'Five Euros' Every male shopper in the place looked over to the counter, nodded, probably thinking that the young lady on the counter was getting good value! I paid and made a swift exit.

It has been a source of great amusement as people can't resist pressing the button, I even recorded it as my ring tone on my mobile phone but that became a bit freaky when I was rung several times in crowded places, particularly the one at Morrisons at the checkout.

At the top of my hate list, perhaps excluding politicians and bankers, at least for now, is suicidal morons who drive two feet from my back bumper. I can be doing a steady seventy miles an hour down the motorway and some pillock oblivious to the danger, with no sense of imagination, coming up behind me and driving so close his headlights are out of sight below my boot. I class this in the same category as a suicidal, psychopathic, maniac holding a gun to the back of my head.

Has the brainless nutcase any idea what carnage he would cause to me and to no lesser extent to him- or herself (women are just as capable of this gross act as men) if I even took my foot of the accelerator, never mind touch the brakes?

Mind you the Brit tailgater's pale into insignificance compared to the French and marginally more so the Italians. On a recent trip driving around France I was aghast that it seems to be the norm for driving on certain motorways where the speed limit is eighty MPH to come up behind the car in front and drive for miles tailgating, despite a clear road to overtake, just for the sake of moving to the outside lane and overtaking. Why?

As far as I can remember from my highway code, which I must admit not reading since I took my test, forty-five years ago, you were recommended to drive a car's length for every ten miles an hour you were travelling from the car in front. All I can think is if perpetual tailgaters ever read the recommendation in the highway code they are regressing to their childhood when they played with Dinky toys, with cars only inches in length.

I have such a thing about it that instead of just ineffectually gesticulating to the driver tailgating me I purchased a gadget which sits in the back window of my car, and when a idiot gets too close I press a button on the dash and a sign lights up in the back window saying, ‘BACK OFF’. It's not always effective as I can only surmise the offenders can't read, which is confirmation of their lack of basic intelligence. I'm sure all of the people reading this intellectual tome are victims rather than offenders so I won't have offended anyone, will I?

A recent little episode that can only fit in this chapter by default although I was in a car only half a mile from home (luckily). I was on my way home up the hill, and, just as I reached the narrowest part, a car met me. Now with a little scraping of paintwork and loss of wing mirrors on the high walls with stones jutting out you can squeeze through but, after driving up and down there for the past fifty years, experience tells me it's just not worth the hassle.

There are passing places, and I do not hesitate to back into one if I am the nearest, but in this instance the pillock in the other car just pulled in to the side and waved me through the gap. My first attempt at sarcasm was to reciprocate and wave him through the gap down the side of my car but he shook his head and waved at me again to attempt his gap. It was obvious that we had a naive newcomer to the road so I wound down my window and pointed to the passing place twenty feet behind him and shouted for him to reverse into it. Now it dawned on me we had a driver that couldn't reverse! And more of a surprise it was a man! Sorry to all you wonderful women drivers out there, but experience does tell me that although you have numerous other attributes, for a great number of women, backing a car is not one of them. Hope that wasn't too patronising. So on with the story.

My window gestures did not achieve the appropriate response, and other cars were arriving so I climbed out of my car and walked over to the driver. He was a little reluctant to wind down his window as I think he thought I was going to drag him out of his car and deck him, the thought that had never crossed my mind.

When he did condescend to wind down his window a few inches, not enough may I add to drag him through, I explained to him my long-standing reluctance to scratch my paint work for the sake of him reversing twenty foot into a passing place, and if he had a problem reversing I would gladly do it for him. As he was about to give me a load of bull about there being plenty of room for me to get through, I realised I was wasting my time with the prat and went back to my car to wait for him to arrive at the conclusion I was more stubborn than he was. As I lifted the door handle my heart stopped, I had locked myself out of my car! SHIT!!! or has Homer Simpson would say 'Doh!!!'

A lot of things passed through my mind at that point as I glanced through the window at my car keys still in the ignition, with the engine running, and to cap it all my house keys were on the same keying, and my better half was away for the day. The option to pretend to faint did cross my mind. It seemed to work well for Victorian ladies, in tricky situations, but I was unsure if that was the best thing to do, although it may have won a little badly needed sympathy from the ten or so drivers that were now stuck in front and behind me. I decided against it as the ambulance may have had difficulty getting through.

One of my saving graces is I adhere to the philosophy that's written on the cover of The Hitchhiker's Guide to the Galaxy 'Don't Panic' and usually I don't, well not much, after the first thirty seconds of paralysis. So I turned to the waiting crowd, smiled, and in my best theatrical stage presence said, 'Sorry, sorry, ladies and gentlemen. I appear to have locked myself out of my car!' I don't usually get standing ovations for my stage performances, but I did expect a little reaction, apart from groans. Then the driver of a little sports car behind me wound down his window and asked if he could squeeze through the gap. A quick spatial assessment ascertained he would make it without deforming his aerodynamics. I waved him through then asked him if he would drop me off half a mile up the road at my house to pick up my spare keys. He readily agreed and with a another quick apology to the trapped hordes and a jovial Schwarzenegger phrase, 'I'll be back,' I climbed into the sports car and left the chaos behind.

When I got out of the sports car at my house the driver kindly asked me if I wanted a lift back down to my roadblock of a car. I declined; I didn't want to delay him any further as I was unsure how long it would take to break into my house! After a quick survey of my house I decided an upper conservatory window was the best bet to break into and repair afterwards. It was just going to be a little traumatic to climb through, as I'm just not as athletic as I used to be and a few extra pounds in the middle was going to make it a bit of a squeeze, literally!

It's really scary how easy it is to break into a house. Once I had prised the window open, splintering the frame, the climb through was horrendous, if not worse than I had anticipated. As I was half way through, the window closed on my legs removing my shoes and dropping them outside in the process. I did have the thought that I might receive a tap on the back, as I was half way into the window, from a passing vigilant policeman, enquiring of my legitimacy of my suspicious method of entering a house. Luckily that wasn't a complication I encountered.

Taking a few minutes for my abused body to recover from the climb through the window, I grabbed the spare set of keys, retrieved my shoes from under the window, and started back down the road. I'm just not in any condition to run a half mile even downhill even though the situation demanded it, so I flagged down a car that wouldn't have got through the jam my car was causing anyway. I explained the situation leaving out a lot of detail. Luckily the gentleman was of a gullible nature and believed a total stranger's ludicrous, garbled story and gave me a lift to the scene of chaos. By this time my accidental roadblock was successfully impeding about twenty cars jammed either side of my car. As I walked to my car I repeated my apologies along the line of stuck vehicles. There were quite a few people out of their cars wandering about looking in my car and over walls searching for an escaped lunatic. A bit a cheesy grin reassured them.

A little known fact is that with your keys in the ignition the little button on your key won't unlock the doors, but having locked myself out of my car once before in less traumatic circumstances (some people never learn do they?) there's a hidden keyhole in the passenger door. Just a slight problem I was parked quite close to the wall. This required a further trauma to my abused body, as I squeezed through the rather narrow gap, when the door was eventually opened. But I was in, and out of the glares of the delayed motorists. Funnily enough, I had a straight path past all the stranded cars as the road widened slightly past where I was stuck. So I made the best of my escape and zoomed off home, leaving the jam to sort itself out.

I spent the next day repairing the damaged window and making it more secure and hope I don't have to break into my own house again.

I bet you thought this chapter was going to be about visiting exotic places and eating in cordon-bleu restaurants. Get real, who do you think I am? Egon Ronay? This next little episode happened twenty miles down the A1 and afterwards all I needed to pass my lips was hot sweet tea to calm my nerves.

I have this large box trailer that's very handy for taking some of my accumulated junk to antique fairs and car boot sales, to eke out my meagre, inadequate wage. I acquired the trailer by slightly devious means, helped by the fact I was working for Auto Trader at the time photographing cars for their magazine. I was called out to photograph a trailer for a company who used it for going to exhibitions so it had only been used for a few weeks a year and I wanted it. I had had an old army generator trailer that had finally given up the ghost after lots of modification and repairs so I was desperate for a trailer of some kind at the time. They wanted a fair price for it but I was a bit skint at the time (nothing new there). Anyway I took their money for photographing the trailer, took my commission and was immediately on the phone to two of my mates to convince them they needed third shares of a superb box trailer. Because they transport a lot of their stuff about they jumped at the offer and trusted me that when I told them it was a bargain not to be missed. Now this is the devious bit. I went and made an offer on the trailer an hour before the magazine went on sale, and got it! The icing on the cake was my mates were pleased with their purchase, and it's still on the go to this day.

I digress, I was bombing down the A1 to an antique fair with my trailer full to the gunnels with junk. In retrospect perhaps a little too much junk and heavy junk at that, as I was interested to see just how much my new trailer held. There is this big antique fair at Newark that went on for three days and I had planned to sleep in the trailer, for when I had emptied all the junk out it was like a caravan with no furniture.

When I said bombing I was only doing a steady fifty when suddenly my wonderful trailer developed a mind of its own. Technically it's called fishtailing which is inadequate to describe the ever-increasing violent thrashing side to side of the trailer, then that violent motion transmitted to the car. The culmination being the trailer overtaking the car in a classic jack-knife, usually reserved for articulated trucks. Finally coming to a skidding, grinding stop I took stock of my situation. I was facing back up the three-lane carriageway! And just to exasperate the situation, I was being met head-on by three cars, one in each lane! Now one of my many attributes, well OK one of my few attributes is that I don't usually panic. As I've said before I've read the cover of the 'Hitchhiker's Guide to the Galaxy' which firmly states whatever dire circumstances befall you, 'DON'T PANIC' and it must be right as it was a very popular book.

That left me with only one option and that was to do a rapid U-turn, as a quick calculation revealed I could achieve it seconds before the wall of oncoming cars ploughed into me. I reckoned I could make the hard shoulder to recover myself, although it was unsuitable to change my underwear as that had to wait for the next motorway café. It would appear by my repetition of this phrase that I suffer from weak bowel control but I wish to stress that I was in nappies the last time I filled my underwear and it's merely an over-worked phrase and I will endeavour to find a new one the next time the need occurs.

Well I'm still here so my calculation for the U-turn proved accurate and I got some wide-eyed looks from the cars that passed me as I recovered my composure on the hard shoulder. This story has a moral, well a recommendation really. Don't overfill your trailer, and for God's sake, fit a bloody stabiliser. They're not all that expensive but they are a life-saver, and I got mine from a car boot sale.

Another bit of advice about transporting things I will pass on that may seem a little obvious which again I learnt the hard way, miraculously with no loss of life or damage to property. This concerns ladders on a roof rack. It's really important to tie them on securely, and preferably not using those elastic ties with hooks on each end. Apart from being totally inadequate to tie even the lightest of objects to your roof rack, they can make you blind. Not, may I add, by sexual self abuse. If you hook one end to your roof rack then pull, it can unhook and the hook takes your eye out. Well I didn't go blind with their use, but as I was driving down the road once with a large pair of double extension ladders insecurely strapped to my roof rack held only with the dreaded elastic ties, I took a corner perhaps a little too fast and the ladders swung around and were now sideways on my roof rack. So as I was facing down the road my wayward ladders were across the road! How I didn't wrap them around a lamp post or wipe out pedestrians or cars coming the other way God only knows. Anyway before my luck ran out I screeched to a halt, and amazingly the ladders realigned themselves with my car, so I just carried on. Only joking! I got out and secured them properly. This time at least with some strong string.

— 22 —

I COLLECT THINGS

I'VE GOT TO admit to being a bit of a collector. Nothing obsessive you understand, just a few odds and ends like car horns, medical instruments, Buddhas, bottles, faeries, horror masks, rocks, yellow flashing lights, owls by default, and things that might come in handy one day.

I think I invented the saying 'One's lonely, two's a pair, but three's a collection!' Once I get something, and you see something similar, if I get that it's a pair, and the next ones make a collection, just as easy as that!

I put it down to my birth year. Not Taurus this time although they have a tendency to acquire things. It's the Chinese version where each year is represented by animals. Me, being born in the year of the rat, I collect things as a pack rat and take it back to my nest.

Funnily enough I've been called a skip rat for my tendency to root through skips at the least opportunity. You can find some amazing things in skips I can tell you. I think one of my first forays into other people's rubbish was at an unofficial tip a couple of miles up the road. I used to visit it regularly on my bike and fill my pockets and saddle bags with all sorts of junk. One of its regular tippers was a ex-army store. The things they threw away are most likely to have set off my interest in electronics, as there were boxes of relays, components and gadgets that were very interesting to dismantle.

Apart from skips, jumble sales are ace for interesting junk, then car boot sales, the stuff some people don't want is phenomenal! Antique fairs are great too but a little on the expensive side. I've even frequented car boot sales in France when I have been travelling over there; they call them 'troc a puce' which I think means trunk sale. The dodgy ones are called 'overt' which means open but also means anything goes, so buyers beware.

Now to give some explanation for the list of my collections. First the car horns. Well you hopefully have already read about my passion for old cars so the car horns were naturally a desirable accessory. No vintage car is complete without a Klaxon horn, or two. For those unfamiliar with the subtle sound of a Klaxon horn it's the distinctive 'haaarooojaaar'. It's also the melodic noise you hear on films when the captain of a submarine shouts, 'Dive, dive, dive.'

Of course there are your naff plastic replicas that would never look acceptable gracing a vintage car not even tucked away out of sight under the bonnet. Genuine ones are rather expensive and although I've picked up a few reasonable ones at car boot sales they lacked a certain 'je ne sais quoi' (that's French you know, influenced by my long-suffering partner who's fluent in the François lingo). The mechanics were OK, with a cast iron motor housing but the horn parts were a little inadequate and tinny. There are some amazing brass vases at car boot sales and they are cheap, as brass vases seem to have gone out of fashion. Not that they appeal to even my taste, but they do make fantastic car horns. If you hacksaw the tinny horn off the base of the horn, then hacksaw the base off the brass vase, with a little careful soldering of the two together you have a rather fine brass genuine fake vintage Klaxon car horn. I used to fit these to my old cars but now I've matured, not in taste, but in the ability keep the bloody things on the road. Now I drive a boring Nissan that's warm, dry, economical, roomy, and reliable and I don't have to go around scrapyards to find spare parts. It is a little incongruous to have a Klaxon horn on a modern car and I'm not quite sure if it's legal in these times of PC and laws against being different, but I have one anyway. One advantage you can blow your horn and people look for a car like Chitty Chitty Bang Bang. It definitely turns heads when my friend John and I pass on the road as he has one in his modern car too, 'cos he's as daft as I am.

The most unusual and amazing horn I actually didn't buy was a ship's fog horn! It was at an antiques fair, I was trying to sell a load of junk, as you do, and was just having a look around at the opposition when I saw it. It stood about six feet tall starting with a large box with all the mechanics in and this mega horn rising out the top, funnelling up to a massive aperture curved at ninety degrees at the top. I had visions of blowing it on a foggy day and a mile away all the cars in the Aire Valley pulling to the side of the road thinking there was a ship coming. Sad to say I didn't buy it, times were hard and I hadn't sold enough junk to justify the hundred quid he was asking for it. In retrospect it's probably just as well as I'm sure there's some inane law against setting off a fog horn inland even if it's foggy.

Talking about antique fairs but a little off the subject I was at one once and this guy had his merchandise spread out on the grass. I must admit his was quite an interesting collection. Among the items was a large trunk with a child's skeleton in it. It was real and must have been a medical specimen at one time. As I was staring at it, the stall holder sauntered over to where I was standing. Just at that moment a wicked idea entered my head. The stall holder was trying to drum up a sale and said, ''It's a child's skeleton you know, very rare.' I gave him a piercing stare and said in my most mystical voice, 'She's not happy you know.'

He gave me a wild-eyed look and said, 'Who?' Again with my

slightly over the top Macbeth Thespian voice I replied 'The child wants to be buried in consecrated ground, she's very angry, she'll get you, you know.'

I knew he was shaken for he turned on his heels and told me to sod off. At that I moved on to the next stall before I had a giggling fit and gave the game away. Five minutes later as I came back down the other side of the aisle I noticed the trunk and skeleton had gone and was stuffed back in his van. I had a vision of this guy burying the trunk in a graveyard by moonlight one dark night soon.

You may have noticed I called the child's skeleton 'she'. Now I didn't inspect the bones to the degree of forensic analysis although I do remember from my school biology class that the sex of a skeleton may be deduced by the size of the hips and the gap at the base of the pelvis, the gap for females being larger to necessitate childbirth although this is not very pronounced in a child. I have also heard the slightly sexist theory of sexing a skeleton by the jaw bone, the female jawbone being better developed and the tendons and muscle connections larger due to generations of female excessive nattering and nagging. Of course I do not believe in this theory for a second!

One may think that to choose a female child spirit to haunt this hapless antiques dealer would appeal to his paternal sense towards a helpless young girl. Actually just the opposite. The female of the species can be very vindictive, far in excess of the amiable male. I remember a line in a film called 'Species' where some scientists had created a supposedly human being from a blueprint received from outer space. The being looked like a young girl and had escaped. The scientists had enrolled the help of some bounty hunters to recapture her. One of the bounty hunters had asked the scientists why they had made her female, and was told that they thought a female would be more passive and easier to control. The bounty hunter's reply was, 'You don't get out much do you!' I do like one-liners and wish I was quick-witted enough to spontaneously come out with them from time to time.

As I write this it suddenly occurred to me, perhaps it wasn't one of my wicked thoughts but a subconscious message from the little girl's spirit wanting to be put to rest. Spooky or what?

Another little incident at an antique fair was when I bunked off work to do a three day event with my usual collection of junk. It was a nice sunny afternoon plenty of people about but a lot of three 'P-ers' about (that's a stall holder's technical term for the public who pick up an item from your stall, put it down, and piss off.) I was just about to nod off when a camera crew appeared with the mahogany sideboard that's David Dickinson. For the vast majority who don't watch 'Dickinson's Real Deal' on the telly, he was slowly working his way down towards my stall making sarcastic comments about the goods on offer, followed closely by his entourage of camera-man, sound engineer, director, and a little bespectacled lady with a clipboard. Despite my contempt for his programme I joined the gaggle of gawpers till he was up to my stall. Perhaps I was looking for an opportunity to inform him what a pillock I thought he was, but the moment passed as he pulled a face at my junk and quickly moved on making a mumbled remark to his director something like 'this bit needs cutting'.

It was when he was three stalls down that I realised I should not be here, certainly not on TV when I was supposed to be at work or at least in bed at death's door. When I got back to work I made subtle enquiries to my boss to ascertain whether she was a fan of the 'mahogany sideboard'. I was surprised and relieved to find she had more taste than I had given her credit for, as she thought he was crap as well, and doesn't watch his programmes either.

You can say what you like. People buy my junk. I remember one antique fair where I was next to a really posh stall with a small marquee and shelves of really expensive ceramics and pottery. I'd done quite well and was just about to pack up when this posh lady from the next stall engaged me in conversation. When I say conversation she was having a rant about how badly she had done and not even covered the cost of the stand. When she asked me how I had done I was embarrassed to tell her. But she read my expression, stuck her nose in the air, glanced at my stall, and snapped ''Well, people are only buying junk nowadays', then stormed off. If junk they want it's junk they get, at least mine's cheap junk!

Another funny incident about car boots happened when I went to a psychic show. What it is if you have never been to one is this guy stands on a stage and gives messages to random people in the audience from their dead relative or friend's spirit. It sounds a bit creepy and weird but all I can say is you need to go to one, you would be amazed, or at the very least well entertained. Anyway the car boot connection. About half way through the act this psychic was trying to establish a connection to a lady in the audience, asking if she knew a person called Fred. She did, it was her uncle who had died some years ago. He was wanting to tell her how appreciative he was for how she looked after him when he was dying. After the psychic passed on some more messages he asked her if she was very religious. She replied in rather a hesitant voice that she was not, casting doubt on his previous psychic revelations. Undeterred he persevered saying he could see her setting off early every Sunday morning religiously. Suddenly her face changed from doubt, to merriment, then to embarrassment, as she explained it wasn't the church she was going to so regularly on a Sunday, but a car boot sale!

Yet another noteworthy incident at an antique fair was when my mate Phil and I went for a day out to Newark Antique Fair which is absolutely massive. Now Phil is a bit of a collector as well only his speciality is organs, and he has some awesome ones. Harmoniums to be precise. Harmoniums have reeds to make the sound as opposed to organs which make their notes with pipes, and are quite massive and usually fixed in place, where harmoniums are reasonably portable. Having said that I've helped him shift a few over the years and some are a four-man job, ending up with a hernia each if you aren't very careful. Anyway we had had a great day perusing the junk and were coming to the tail end of the stalls when Phil suddenly did a pointer stance, as hunting dogs are trained to do when they see a pheasant. Picture the lad suddenly going stock-still with a glazed look on his face and pointing with a shaking hand to what appeared to be a pile of worm-eaten firewood in front of this stall. When Phil came out of his paralysis we sauntered over to the item of Phil's interest where he explained in hallowed tones that the pile of firewood I so ineptly described, was a unique Colin Brown Voice Harmonium. The only other known one he knew of was in a museum and its value, regardless of its condition was priceless. As we were standing by the harmonium the stall holder sauntered over and informed us that it had been sold and the guy who bought it would be along any time to pick it up. Phil looked devastated but determined so we hung around and sure enough the new owner of the pile of... I mean the harmonium appeared. Phil got talking to the guy and soon established to his horror that he was going to break it up for the twirly bits on the front. Trying not to sound too enthusiastic he started to make offers and a bidding session ensued with the occasional check on our money situation. All through this the stall holder looked on helplessly as what he thought was junk doubled and trebled for what he had originally sold it for. Finally a price was agreed and we coppered up to pay the man, who then walked away before the stall holder could mention some sort of commission. As we were loading the harmonium into Phil's estate car the stall holder asked Phil how much it was really worth. Phil being a kindly soul and not wishing to piss him off even more than he already was, told him it was purely sentimental value, but I don't think he was convinced. Years later Phil showed me the harmonium that he had spent hundreds of hours lovingly restoring, and I now could see that it was something special, and stands pride of place in his museum of harmoniums.

I digress. Medical instruments, I do have a thing about medical things as I will explain in another chapter. For the time being it comes under collecting. I think my first purchase was at an antique fair, it was a midwife's bag, and it had the most amazingly gruesome instruments imaginable. The ultimate was a pair of birthing tongs with dried blood on them, unwashed presumably since they brought a new life into this world. Since that first acquisition I've bought all sorts of odd bits of macabre instruments from surgeon's knives, to that torch thing doctors look in your ear with, to an instrument for removing tonsils, and of course the inevitable stethoscope.

I've got things to administer enemas, take blood pressure, anaesthetise, and a rather fine glass cup with a rubber bulb attached to extract breast milk. I have a syringe for mass inoculation, it's spring-loaded and shaped like a gun. Makes you wonder if they changed the needle between jabs?

As I wear hearing aids, I could not resist an antique hearing aid. It fits around the neck on a white ribbon with a huge earpiece. It has a battery although I don't think there’s one still available to fit. I have contemplated on my next appointment at audiology to take it along and pretend it's been a long time since my last visit.

One piece of medical kit that got away was a mahogany box with strange looking tube-like instruments arranged inside that I spotted at a car boot sale once. I picked it up and took out the instruments trying to deduce their purpose. The stall holder watched me and eventually asked me what I thought they were. I admitted that beyond medical instruments of some kind I was stumped. He grinned and told me they were used to clear out pus from VD-infected penises! There's definitely a lack of washing facilities at car boot sales and this one was no exception. So a little stream at one end of the field had to suffice. How gross can you get? Fancy trying to sell something like that and I'm afraid by the time I had returned from my ablutions, they had been sold. 'Bugger!'

When I first met my significant other I was a little worried she would consider me a touch eccentric, or excessively weird if I showed her my medical instruments at the beginning of our relationship and before she got to know me better, that is. On asking some close friends on the subject, they advised me to wait at least six months to a year before revealing some of my more bizarre collections. They suggested that we should go out in a foursome so they could meet her. The evening seemed to go well and we all went back to my house for coffee after the meal. We were all sitting comfortable when my wonderful friends dropped the bombshell. 'Well are you going to show her your medical instruments now, while we are here, so she can leave with us if she wants?' When I recovered, I had no option but to display my slightly unusual collection. I'm pleased to say she didn't leave, and still tolerates most of my more bizarre idiosyncratic collections, and sometimes even shows mild interest. Not!

A side line from medical things is, I suppose, bottles. My preference is definitely for old medicine bottles preferably at least half full of the original contents, with the label intact, or at least legible. If it's faded and stained, it's even better. I choose only quite small bottles as space is always limited. Luckily the more interesting ones are three to four inches tall with weird contents like ‘cocaine eye-drops’. The Victorians and the Edwardians were rather partial to adding cocaine to their medicines to give them an extra oomph! Mind you even the original formula for Coca Cola is reputed to have had a sprinkling of the stuff.

There's green, red, yellow, and clear, the blue ones usually contain poisons. There are all shapes and sizes some with glass stoppers for the ones with expensive contents and cork for the cheap mass-produced ones. The most fascinating bottle I possess is possibly well over a thousand years old. It was a scent bottle left in a rubbish tip when the Romans were in residence in Britain, and it could well have adorned the dressing table of a Roman lady. It is very delicate and beautifully formed, and the acid in the rubbish tip over the millennium has etched the glass into wonderful rainbow patterns.

Buddhas! Yes, well apart being rather fascinated by the Buddhist religion, it was my parents’ fault I began to collect them. Well you see my mother had a yellow glass Buddha on the mantelpiece for as long as I could remember. When I set up house with my future wife the yellow glass Buddha came too and soon became two. As my favourite saying goes, one's lonely two's a pair, three...

There are a lot of them about, Buddhas that is. There are shops that seem to sell nothing else, and at car boot sales they're on every other stall. I try to not buy the same Buddhas each time as there are so many different ones to choose from. There's wood, stone, brass, resin and ceramic, with an infinite variety of poses. The only exception is the original yellow glass one of which I now have three identical ones that I have bought over the years, for sentimental reasons you understand. I probably have about one hundred and fifty by now, but I don't count them as that would be rather train-spottingish don't you think? My favourite Buddhas are a pair of wooden carvings with quite a bit of age about them. It's difficult to say exactly how old but the wood is so smooth they seem to have been polished for donkey's years. They have lotus flowers inlaid with fine silver wire all over. I paid about fifty quid for them which is a record for just about anything I've ever paid for a collecting item, but they were well worth it. A rather interesting item in my Buddha collection is a couple of Buddhas bonking! Well at least a male Buddha bonking a woman Buddha. I have two Buddha couples in fact in different sexual positions, both couples maintaining the traditional ethereal expressions may I add. I also have a rather traditional looking Buddha that you could get away with showing your maiden aunt as long as she doesn't look under the base as it has a carving of a rather novel sexual position which is probably about number one hundred and nine out of the one hundred and ten positions of the Kama Sutra. May I add that all the rest of my

Buddhas are quite tasteful.

Faeries! It was a natural progression from photographing them to collecting them, well at least ceramic ones, the real thing is so hard to catch, if not impossible. I'm rather choosy about my faeries, they have to be a bit raunchy, preferably scantily dressed and with attitude. I can't do with namby-pamby, wishy-washy flower fairies. They are even spelt differently. Some of my favourite faeries I have bought in France. French faeries, or fees as they are known over there are usually nude and very sexy, what more could you ask for? I also like scary faeries too, those usually have bat wings instead of butterfly wings, and look a bit Goth. Even the occasional whip and thigh length boots are quite acceptable... What?

I'm a bit of a rock hound I find them fascinating, crystals, fossils, volcanic, semi precious, and sedimentary, preferably colourful and unusual, in small chunks, (storage space economy again).

I used to keep my collection in a big box all jumbled up, getting all scratched and broken. Then I discovered print drawers. These are what printers used to file away all their type letters in alphabetical order when printing was set up by hand, long before computers made typesetters redundant. These sets of drawers in a cabinet were divided into little inch-square compartments, ideal for small rock samples. Sad git that I am, when I go on holiday or just walking in the country I always keep a lookout for interesting rocks. Or the occasional rock shop. When I come back from these excursions I come back with my pockets bulging. This sometimes gets me in trouble, with searching questions at Customs. Also there are places you are not supposed to just pick up rocks and walk away with them. I was nearly arrested by two armed police for pocketing rocks in Lanzarote from the top of their volcano. By all accounts if all visitors to their volcano took a handful of rocks, in five hundred years the volcano would have disappeared. Seeing as the damned thing is still smoking from the last time it spewed a few million tons of the stuff about a hundred years ago, I think it will be here for a while yet, armed guards or not

I suppose the most pointless and maybe the saddest is my collection of yellow flashing lights, with the occasional blue and green ones. You know the sort of thing, those whirligig lights on dust bin wagons, JCB's and blue ones on police cars, and occasionally green ones on doctors' cars. It's my dad's fault! Parents have a lot to answer for. Parents should be so careful about influencing their children. You see he wouldn't buy me a yellow flashing light when I was five for my ride-on plastic tractor. So I was deprived as a child, by the old chestnut, 'What are you going to do with it?' Well, it took me thirty years of junk shops and car boot sales to collect a couple of dozen, and think of a use for them, as I no longer had my plastic ride-on tractor. Come on it's obvious! Is it not? Well, maybe not to the uninitiated eccentrics among you. Mega Christmas tree fairylights! Yes you heard it first here. Picture this! I have a twenty-foot Christmas tree in my garden; it was planted fifty years ago after it had spent Christmas in the front room. Imagine twenty-odd yellow flashing yellow lights festooned over this tree at Christmas. Spectacular, I never actually got round to hanging them on the tree, for as I described in an earlier chapter I cut it down, as it was in danger of falling on the house. But you must admit it would have looked spectacular.

I'm rather partial to things that give off lots of scary high voltage sparks. Some of my most interesting ones are actually medical instruments, 'but not as we know it, Jim'.

The Victorians, having just got excited about electricity, decided it was medically beneficial or, at least if you could display it in spectacular fashion, enough people would think it was beneficial, and that was good enough. You could call it the placebo effect. My collection of these gadgets are basically high frequency transformer Tesla Coils that produce high voltage, with glass tubes filled with a gas that glows when you switch on the machine. I have about half a dozen of these impressive machines. 'As if one wasn't enough,' I've been told

I perhaps need to explain what a Tesla Coil is to the few people who are unaware of Mr Nickola Tesla claim to fame. Mr Tesla was an incredibly clever man with electricity who at one time worked for Edison in America. He worked on some of Edison's famous inventions and made them work. They parted company when Edison failed to pay Tesla, so he set up on his own and did quite well judging by the fact he has hundreds of patents in his name. Some are even held under wraps by the US military. It's rumoured there's plans for flying saucers, death rays and God knows what else. That's a bit freaky don't you think?

I was so impressed by his Tesla Coil that I decided to make a monster version of one of his inventions. It's six feet tall and will produce eight foot lightning sparks. I'm up against the usual incredulous reaction from most people when I explain my intention. A few exceptions are those who appreciate the thrill of dangerous high voltage sparks and are as eccentric as I am!

Usually when asked what it is, and what does it do, and the inevitable stupid question of why, I confuse the issue by explaining it's a miniature version of The Large Hadron Collider at CERN in Switzerland, and it will produce mini black holes that could well spell the annihilation of the earth, replicating the split second after the Big Bang at the beginning of the universe. Few ask questions after this statement.

The instructions I sent for came with a whole page of warnings; from high voltage, (slightly unnecessary as it's pretty obvious that eight-foot sparks are high voltage and dangerous) to poisonous ozone gas being produced, from the destruction of heart pacemakers at twenty feet to ultra violet light which gives you slightly more than a sun tan at this intensity. With a lethal list like that I doubt I will be having many volunteers to observe it at close quarters, but it should put on a good show at parties, albeit with the audience at a respectable distance. Undaunted and not having a pacemaker as I write this it's half built in true Victorian tradition, with lots of brass and copper, in an oak cabinet. If the big switch-on happens before I finish this book I will let you know.

Last but definitely not least, 'horror masks.' It's not really a collection, it's just a means to enhance my zany practical joke sense of humour. You must admit, jumping out and saying boo, is enhanced tenfold if you are wearing a horror mask. When kids come to the door trick-or-treating you have to hand out far less sweets if you go to the door in a sheet and a really scary mask. An interesting phenomenon I have observed is that when you don a horror mask and display yourself, you automatically pull a face under the mask. Strange!

The owl connection was that my mother who was a bit partial to a bit of collecting collected owls, and that's probably where I got it from. Now they never much appealed to me but I inherited the whole collection which was a not insubstantial, two hundred. They were everywhere, on shelves, hanging on the wall, and, when she ran out of space, in boxes in the loft. A little excessive don't you think? Unlike my collections that are quite reasonable if not a little eccentric.

The final item on the list was anything that might come in handy someday. This is recycling long before it became fashionable and I think it's best covered in chapter 26.

— 23 —

IT'S SHOW TIME!

I'M NOT MUCH of an extrovert. No really, it's just that I will try most things if there is a chance I can carry it off with some hope of staying alive or at least without too much embarrassment. Unaccustomed as I am to public speaking, I have done it reasonably successfully on occasions without too many gaffes.

I was asked some time ago to do a lecture at the local WI on photography. I'm predominantly a people photographer with a bias towards young ladies and consequently most of my pictures were of young ladies running through corn fields in long flowery dresses, and some even with no dresses on at all! All tasteful stuff you understand, very arty, nothing you couldn't show your granny, but I chickened out at the WI.

I'd decided a while back to mount a lot of my best pictures on large display boards for such an occasion. As three of the eight boards contained nudes, those were deselected and left at home and out of this particular lecture.

On the evening of the lecture I arrived at the village hall and unloaded my display boards and arranged them in front of a small gathering of chairs for the ladies. In the following fifteen minutes about twenty ladies arrived in twos and threes and sat down in eager anticipation. The general topic of conversation as far as I could make out was gossiping about whatever people who hadn't arrived or weren't coming at all were getting up to. Eventually I was introduced to the gathering and I begun my talk on the joys of photography, with useful hints on picture composition using the display boards as examples. As far as I could make out about my audience, they could teach me a thing or two about cooking, knitting, and darning socks, but I think f-stops, depth of field, colour balance, and exposure, would have been a bit of a over their heads, so I stuck to basics.

I must have inspired them a bit for when it came to any questions they were quite searching. Then someone asked where I got my models from. I explained they were usually friends or friends of friends or daughters of friends. There was a bit of a pause then the same person asked ''So where's the nudes?'

It would appear that my reputation had gone before, and word had done the rounds that I was a bit of a true artist that appreciated the finer points of the female anatomy, or something like that. That one threw me off balance a tad. I was under the scrutiny of twenty very conservatively dressed middle-aged blue rinse ladies without the hint of expression except that of disappointment that I had not put on a display of nude women.

I mumbled something about I didn't think it would have been appropriate. To which one lady on the front row said in rather a posh voice, 'Young man we are all ladies of the world. It takes a lot to shock us you know.' I could only apologise for underestimating ladies from the WI.

A year later when the 'Calendar Girls' from the WI just up the Dales from my home became famous for their daring calendar, I think if I had been a little more daring, word might have gotten around in the WI and I might have gained a spot of fame as their photographer. Missed opportunities eh?

'Never judge a book by its cover' is a really inappropriate saying for a really true observation of a true fact, as I'm sure publishers take a great deal of trouble to promote their books and one of the first thing must involve creating the best possible visual effect to catch the of the potential buyer. Conversely the cover could be more imaginative than its contents, then again... Anyway what saved me from total confusion with the ladies of the WI was my experience with a certain voluntary phone counselling organization. As counsellors we were supposed to accept rather near the knuckle phone calls. Not that I received all that many it was usually the women volunteers that had to bear the brunt of them. It always amazed me that the blue rinse brigade (as they were known as because of their grey hair tinted blue) would hold conversations with clients like, ‘I don't think you need to know the colour of my knickers, but tell me a little more about yourself’, without turning a hair, blue or otherwise.

I worked with some real characters and learnt a lot about people and gained confidence in dealing with difficult situations and people. We tried to deal with potential tragedies by supporting each other and, in doing so, gained good friends among our little band of volunteers. There were laughs as well. There was one young lady volunteer who I did duty with, let it be known that she was a lesbian. It was my first encounter with a self-confessed lesbian but she appeared quite normal in all other respects so I didn't give it much thought. After some weeks working with her she gave me a bit of a shock when she told me she was disappointed that I had not asked her the usual three questions she usually received when men found out she was a lesbian. After giving a little thought I admitted my naivety, and asked what were the three questions men usually ask? She said they were in this order: 1. What do you actually do with another woman? 2. Can I watch? 3. Do you fancy being converted? I may have been naive but at least I wasn't predictable, I thought about it and then spoilt my unpredictability record by uttering, 'OK how about...'. But before I got any further I got a 'No'. The same lady soon after that initiated me into other sexual deviations. No, not 1, 2 or 3 but it certainly expanded my understanding of a few things one hears in smutty jokes as a teenager. For a few months later this certain lady rang me one particular evening in a bit of a state and asked if I could come over to her flat and open a lock for her rather urgently as she had lost the key. She was aware of my mechanical skills and I assumed it was a locked drawer or cupboard, so I popped my toolbox in the car and went around to her house. She had told me to just come straight in as the door was unlocked. When I got through the door this voice from a room to my right shouted to come in. I wouldn't say I was shocked as much as taken aback. At one end of the room was a double bed with two naked occupants huddled under the sheets. One I recognised immediately as my friend the lesbian, and handcuffed to the bed head was a man! Do you laugh, sympathise, or make silly jokes to cover their embarrassment. After attempting all three, I whipped out my tool ... a small screwdriver. What? To pick the lock on the handcuffs, silly. Luckily they were rather simple ones and it took me about ten seconds. Being able to do this is not the product of a misspent youth may I add. Just to explain, I've taken a lot of locks to bits, along with a lot of other mechanical devices, and the secret of picking locks is to be able to visualise the inside.

I retired to the kitchen and put on the kettle so allowing the couple to get dressed, now unhindered by the restricting cuffs. Coffee was poured by the time they emerged. I decided to restrain myself to a discreet smirk as we drank our coffee. When we next worked together she was quite descriptive of the events leading up to their realisation that the key to the handcuffs was missing and the desperate phone call to me. I'm sorry to say her description is far too graphic for this book!

Bingo, two for the price of one, initiation into the world of bisexuals (described graphically as 'bats both ways') and bondage, into which of course I have never indulged myself.

I digress, I was once asked to do a talk on another of my passions, science experiments. A headmistress friend of mine asked if I would come to her school and entertain the children with some science experiments. It sounded like fun so I was up for it.

I got permission to borrow a few interesting items from the science lab where I worked and decided on a series of demonstrations.

On arriving at the school I was ushered into the assembly hall and I set up my demonstration. When I was ready they ushered in the kids. There was a slight misunderstanding about the actual numbers, there were hundreds! The whole school in fact! I'd done class experiments before but this was a little scary. I was only overawed for a second or two, then my Thespian, extrovert side took over and I was away. I was duly introduced to my audience by the headmistress and welcomed by enthusiastic applause and I got stuck in.

The old chemistry trick of changing water into different colours when poured from one glass jar to another is always a good start. I am always aware of the difference between teaching magic and science, so I went by the words of a science teacher I knew. He said if you are demonstrating science experiments to a class that is going to struggle with the principles and the theory just make it spectacular, and if any are inspired enough with the results they will remember years later and hopefully understand how it worked. A good, albeit extreme, example of this, was when the same teacher was demonstrating the combustibility of hydrogen. It was his usual trick to fill a fairly large balloon with a mixture of hydrogen and oxygen, connect a fuse to it, light it, and let it float to the ceiling above his desk. At this stage may I explain to my non-scientific audience that a spectacular example to illustrate this was the historic explosion of the Hindenburg airship that contained hydrogen and a little oxygen from the atmosphere.

The teacher in question on this occasion related the incident where the balloon obediently rose to the ceiling with the lighted fuse attached but the slight mistake he made was that while he and the class awaited the fuse to ignite the balloon, was to open a window as the room had become a little warm. This created a draught that sent the bomb ... sorry I mean balloon over his class and under a number of glass light-fittings.

The class watched in fascination as it drifted over their heads, but the teacher did not share their naivety and watched in dread. The balloon exploded shattering the light-fittings and showered the girls and boys with a sprinkling of fine shards of glass. The story had a happy ending as the class were so impressed they were totally unconcerned about a bit of glass in their hair and spent the rest of the lesson combing it out of each others hair while the teacher swept up the floor. I'm willing to bet that each and every one of those children will remember to this day a good twenty-five years later every detail of that experiment perhaps being inspired to become nuclear physicists. Or maybe if they were to go on ‘Who Wants to be a Millionaire’ they would be able to answer a question on the combustibility of hydrogen and oxygen.

Needless to say I passed on that particular demo for my show. So back to my little water to wine display. I started off with a glass jar full of water and just to prove it was just pure water I drank some. Bit of a mistake that. Realising my error I glanced over to the headmistress who was wide eyed and shaking her head. Quickly recovering from the withering look, I reminded my audience that of course one must never drink anything out of a science lab or anything they were unsure about. Going on quickly I poured the water into another jar, and immediately it turned bright red. Then with a flourish, poured it into another jar and it turned blue, another jar and it turned back to red and for a grand finale, it turned back to clear water. Well at least water with a sprinkling of chemicals, enough to deter me from proving it was only water again by sipping a mouthful, apart from remembering the disproving look from the headmistress. But with appropriate gasps and applause from my audience, I was a star

I won't get thrown out of the magic circle for giving the secret away, because I have never been in it. The trick is a simple bit of chemistry with a touch of sleight of hand. The water to start with sure enough is just tap water hence my lack of inhibition to drink some, but from then on tasting sessions are not recommended. The second apparently empty jar has a sprinkling of a red dye in the bottom which was invisible to the audience. Pouring the water into it again with a flourish and a bit of height instantly mixes to an impressive bright red liquid. The second jar similarly has a splash of ammonia in the bottom which turns the red to blue changing it from acid to alkali. Then a touch of household vinegar in the next jar and you are back to acid and a vivid red. With a final flourish, as a grand finale and a smidgen of bleach in the final jar you are back to clear water. Well at least we will say it's clear liquid, voilà!

Next I demonstrated how genii appear on stage. A little heap of theatrical flash powder, a battery and some fuse wire, and you have a way of remotely setting it off without losing your eyebrows. To add a little excitement I asked for a volunteer from the audience. That in itself was a bit of a mistake as I was a little swamped by volunteers, when the entire audience stood up and made for the stage. Luckily I was rescued by the watchful headmistress. Eventually one young man was brought forward and was given the honours of making the genii appear by pressing the button. In retrospect I perhaps just slightly overdid the little pile of flash powder, as I do have a tendency to. There was no danger of anyone getting burnt as we all stood well back but after the spectacular flash and the appropriate 'Ooohs' and 'Ahhhs' the smoke did cause a bit of bother, even more than I realised at the time. When all the windows had been opened, most of the smoke had dissipated, and order had been restored I was running out of time and moved quickly to my grand finale.

You may not know what a Van Der Graaf Generator is but you might recognise it from Frankenstein films. It's a pedestal with a large silver ball on the top. This stores the static electrical charge that is carried up the pedestal with a rubber belt and a motor in the base.

For this demonstration I required a volunteer. This was too dangerous for a pupil so I commandeered the headmistress's husband. We were old friends and despite knowing my reputation, he came forward without hesitation. If you are going to do something a little dangerous I find it's always best to do it to a friend!

First I got Phil to stand on a plastic bucket, thus isolating him from earth so when he put his hand on the metal globe at the top of the Van Der Graaf Generator and I switched it on he would be charged up to several thousand volts of static electricity, without it all leaking to the ground and him receiving a shock of course. This was quite spectacular as Phil's shock of curly hair stood straight out from his head. Even his clothes lifted away from his body. Now I've done this demonstration many times and it always looks impressive, but this was frightening. I can only surmise it was the smoke from genii demo I had preformed previously that had dried the air in the hall and this had the effect of allowing the static to build up to unprecedented proportions. The first Phil realised there was something wrong was when he saw my panicky look. He was just about to step off the bucket when I managed to regain the presence of mind to tell him through clenched teeth to 'Don't, for God's sake, step off the bucket!' This would have discharged him in a very spectacular and painful manner down his leg that touched the ground! If the situation wasn't so dire it would have been hilarious. Picture Phil standing on a plastic bucket, charged to God knows how many thousand volts, his hair and clothes billowing out around him, with crackling noises and a electric blue aura you needn't be psychic to see. In fact every teacher and child could see it and my mate Phil was seeing the world through it from the inside, you could say he was wide-eyed and bushy-tailed, watching me with a pleading look for instructions. I must say the audience was enthralled, but I resisted the temptation to take a bow and Phil was in no state to play up to his fan club. Having regained a little more grasp of the situation I approached the offending machine to turn it off, but was warded off by a loud hissing and a rather malignant-looking blue aura surrounding the machine. Even the plug to the extension was out of bounds as this was well within the danger zone. This is where years of dealing calmly with self-inflicted, potentially life-threatening situations comes in handy. I assured Phil there was absolutely no danger, and that I wasn't leaving him to his fate and I would be back in a flash (in retrospect this was an unfortunate phrase).

Having sauntered casually across the hall and unplugged the extension I returned to figure out how to discharge my assistant without stopping his heart with the shock. Actually it's not so much the shock, as the point that the lightning bolt enters the skin burns a small but painful pinprick. I thought it inappropriate to go into too much detail at this stage as Phil was still a little distressed being still charged up to around, I estimated, thirty thousand volts. Luckily due to the sparks and blue aura coming mainly from his hair he was slowly losing potential, allowing me to pick up the mains socket and quick as a flash (this time a rather appropriate phrase) I discharged the machine and subsequently Phil, by touching the earth pin to the metal globe. This saved my trusty assistant a painful discharge to his body.

The sudden lack of static made Phil's hair and clothes shrink back to his body causing another appropriate response from the audience as he stepped down from his bucket and staggered across the hall to the staff room making himself a cup of hot sweet tea. I was a little disappointed that he didn't take a bow which was a little unprofessional I thought and rather ungrateful for not thanking me for saving his life, or at least discharging him painlessly. But after three cups of hot sweet tea, we did have a laugh about it and we are still good friends.

My next demonstration was rather impromptu. It was a sunny Sunday afternoon with a leisurely BBQ with friends and relatives in the garden at the farm. Amongst those present was my mate, John and the conversation soon got around to some of our escapades, for the benefit of those present who were unaware of our more spectacular joint exploits. Inevitably the subject came around to things that go bang, and how quite innocuous kitchen ingredients can be explosive. We were explaining how flour mills have an unhealthy tendency to spontaneously explode. There were some gathered there who were sceptical of our assertion that fine dust as in finely ground flour is rather unstable and explodes with the tiniest spark such as in static discharge.

What John and I decided what was needed was a little demonstration to educate our audience. Some hosepipe, a treacle tin, a candle, and some flour and we were set up. There was some debate whether it should be plain rather than self-raising, but the debate was settled when I could only find plain. The ladies present insisted that we conduct our little experiment at the other end of the garden as they felt there was some danger involved, even with something as simple as flour, especially in the hands of 'you two!' Now what prompted that I wonder, obviously our reputation had gone before, completely unjustified may I add, just because at that moment word was spreading maliciously about the exploding tractor battery.

We reckoned if we placed the lit candle in the tin and blew the flour through the hosepipe into the tin through a hole made in the lid we should get results. John was poised with his lips to the pipe which had flour sprinkled down it. We all held our breath; the ladies put their fingers in their ears, a count down from me and ... nothing! The candle blew out, why hadn't we anticipated that? After three aborted attempts and a lot of raucous comments from our audience, which we accepted in the spirit they were given, we decided to up the candle power. A Calor gas torch poked through the bottom of the tin could only bring about the desired results. Three puffs later and no explosions and the audience was getting out of control with comments like 'Rubbish' and 'Pathetic' and 'Give us our money back'. This called for drastic measures; our reputation was at stake here.

On my last trip to my workshop I invested in a little insurance. I had a few fireworks left over from last year's Bonfire Night and pocketed a large banger as I collected the gas torch. With a wink to my fellow demonstrator, and with sleight of hand I popped the firework into the can, lit it with a flourish as if I was lighting the Calor torch. I jammed on the lid before the smoke from the firework fuse gave the game away. Another quick wink to my fellow conspirator who stood well back pipe in mouth and cheeks well puffed. With an appropriate loud BANG! the lid flew up in the air, the audience went 'wow' and our reputation was restored. The explosion covered John in flour which shot back up the tube he was holding, but it only added to the effect and was soon brushed off by his wife who has a rather low opinion of our little experiments, There was only one among our audience who gave us a knowing look but kept his mouth shut, that was John's son who knows us oh so well.

I'm quite partial to electric gadgets especially if they produce large amounts of high voltage sparks. The Victorians were ace at creating amazing machines then finding a use for them. They were convinced that passing a couple of thousand volts through sick people was a universal panacea for a multitude of ailments. I've acquired one of these which sat upon most doctors' desks not all that long ago and was used on their patients. Without going into too much detail it consists of a vibrating spark gap passing electric back and forward through a coil, giving a few thousand volts with very little current, so is unlikely to kill you (unless you have a heart pacemaker) but gives a mild tingling with spectacular sparks. To add to its visual effect which no doubt also enhanced its healing placebo effect was a collection of sealed glass tubes of various shapes like combs, probes and massage tools which were full of a gas that glowed as the high voltage passed through it. Some were Y shaped for massaging sore throats, comb-shaped to run through thinning hair to rejuvenate growth, tongue probes, double eye probe, ear probes, nasal probes, a urethral probe (not up mine you don't) and a rather phallic looking one which if you believed the instruction was a vaginal probe. I don't seem to get many volunteers to try some of these therapies and I'm quite sure not many doctors got a chance to administer it a second time to the same patient.

My party trick is to present this to an attentive group and ask for volunteers to touch one of the glowing probes, I didn't get all that many takers but all those that did, survived. A trick to get more audience participation was to get one of my more adventurous friends who had usually had tried it before and survived, to hold the probe in one hand and a four foot fluorescent tube in the other. Upon switching on the fluorescent tube would light up as the high frequency voltage passes harmlessly through his body from my machine. For best effect this was performed in subdued lighting but the spectacle was still visible in daylight! This could be reproduced with up to six people in a chain holding hands with the first one holding the probe and the end one holding the fluorescent tube. This always impressed my audience, but frighteningly enough a similar effect could be experienced if they wandered under some high tension power lines at night carrying a fluorescent tube, I'm not convinced these lines have no effect on the health of people living nearby.

The old headmaster at our school was a mad professor type and used to do some great science demonstrations, and was probably responsible for my fascination with such things. Years later when I worked at the same school I was clearing out his old science prep room. It appeared that he was also rather partial to high voltage experiments of his own and wrote notes of his experiments. One particular sheet of paper caught my eye as it was a warning from the education authority that experiments above a certain voltage should not be attempted as this could produce X-rays and prolonged exposure could cause cancer. Written underneath in the headmaster's copperplate handwriting was the sentence, 'What rubbish! If this were the case I would be dead years ago!' He actually died of cancer some years after this memo was written. Needless to say my machine only comes out on rare occasions. The only fatality was a rather expensive digital watch which someone was wearing during a demo and I assured the wearer that it could not possibly be my machine that had caused it. She was not convinced.

I have another similar device although slightly less spectacular but more stimulating. It's an electric shock machine but it was thought to be very therapeutic in times gone by, by stimulating the nervous system. This has just two metal electrodes which you hold in each hand while the operator slowly winds up the voltage until the volunteer pleads for you to stop, as it locks the muscles in your hands and arms and it's impossible to let go. I've had grown men on their knees with tears in their eyes. Most of them see the funny side as it's the macho thing to look tough in front of the ladies present but they do need to modify their language.

Talking about ladies present. One time I was offering the experience of electrocution to a group of friends when I was struggling for volunteers after the first one was taken away by ambulance... no only joking! Although there was a certain lack of male bravado until this rather sweet, petite young lady requested a go. I was a little reluctant as I'm not usually into torturing sweet young ladies but her boyfriend said, go for it. When she held the electrodes I turned on the power at very low strength. The effect was devastating for all she said was, 'Oh, that's nice.' That was definitely a challenge so, sweet young lady or not, I racked up the voltage to the point where grown men...yes well, the only response was, 'Oh, that's VERY nice.' At that point I switched off the machine and was preparing to put it away and get out the Scrabble board when the sweet young lady in question asked could she try it on her bare feet. This prompted some very wide-eyed looks within the group with the boyfriend leaning over to me and saying in a quiet voice, 'She's into pain.' Never to disappoint a young lady the electrodes were placed on the floor in front of her and she slipped out of her shoes and placed a bare foot onto each of them. Now a quick explanation of Michael Faraday law of electro physics is required here. Contrary to general belief electrons leave the negative electrode and make their way to the positive, not that this had much bearing on the effect I'm trying to describe, suffice to say voltage flowed up one leg across a certain sensitive area and down the other leg. That's the only explanation I can give or wish to think about as I racked the voltage up again to the shaky words of the young sweet lady 'Oooh that's very very very nice!' I turned down a discreet request from her boyfriend to borrow my machine over the weekend (name withheld).

Recently I was asked to give a talk on the Cottingley Faeries at a local book shop who were promoting a recently published book by the daughters of Frances Griffiths one of the two young girls who, ninety odd years ago, took photographs of faeries in the dell in the village of Cottingley. It got around I was an authority on them and had taken photographs of faeries and written a musical about the story. I wanted to do the job right, so I borrowed a video projector which I could connect up to my laptop so I could show some of my photograph in style. It was a bit of an echo of my WI talk only this time I didn't chicken out and showed my nude faeries. As I have explained in a previous chapter I'm not into pretty, pretty, flower faeries. Real faeries are vibrant, uninhibited by human morals and have no hang-ups about showing their beautiful bodies and above all don't feel the cold as they aren't quite in our dimension. If you think talking about other dimensions is science fiction just have a read of a very scientific and prestigious magazine called 'New Scientist'. Admittedly they don't discus faeries but they go into great depths debating the possibility of up to twelve dimensions and particles from the sun zipping in and out of at least two on their way to earth. So I reckon faeries are quite capable of existing in at least some of them. It's my theory so there!

I did postulate this theory at my lecture but I think I failed to convince them. My audience seemed more concerned about the fact that my faeries were nude and could not see the need for it. So I pointed out that great artists throughout history have been honouring the beauty of the female form by not hiding it under irrelevant frills. Again most of my audience tutted under their breath missing the subtleties of my argument, although I was congratulated by some of the more informed of my audience. So the bottom line is I believe in faeries, so there!

— 24 —

MEDICAL MATTERS

FEELING ILL ...?
Then you need to see
Nurse Leaver .. Now.

OLD AGE IS a 'reet bugger', things stop working and other bits drop off all together. It's one of the first signs of getting old when you are showing pictures around when old friends get together and the conversation goes something like 'He's dead', 'She's dead', and 'He's got dementia.' Another topic of conversation is discussing your ailments and comparing your medication with your friends', so stand by to share mine. I've had a few medical problems in my time and true to form nothing is ever straightforward.

One of my first brushes with the medical profession was in my late twenties when I started to suffer from pains in my wrists, particularly at night, making it difficult to sleep. The only relief was to hang my arms out of bed, dangling to the floor.

A trip to the doctor informed me I had trapped nerves caused by the tendons squeezing the nerves as they pass through the wrists and I would need an operation. The doctor then referred me to a specialist at the hospital. At the hospital the doctor enthusiastically strapped me into a device that sent little shocks up my arm to measure precisely where the restriction had occurred, so they could cut me open and relieve the blockage. The doctor told me I would need a small operation on both wrists and he gave me an appointment for the following month to attend Out-patients. To be quite honest I'm not fazed by the prospects of them cutting me open, well not in the minor way the doctor described and was looking forward for a week or two off work.

On the day of the op I duly arrived and was given an operating smock. Just why I had to wear a backless smock that exposed my bum with nothing underneath when I was about to have my wrists operated on was completely beyond me, I put it down to the nurses being a bit kinky. You hear all sorts of rumours about nurses and I was naive enough to believe some of them. I did contemplate putting it on with the gap at the front just to give the nurses a treat until a rather scary looking nurse stuck her head around the corner of the changing-room door and demanded to know why I wasn't ready yet.

After donning the gown the correct way round I was ushered into the operating room, being careful not to expose my bare bottom to the scary nurse as I lay on the operating table. A rather prettier looking nurse put a mask over my nose and mouth and I managed to count to seven and the next I knew I was in a side ward on a trolley. When I had recovered enough to make the decision to inspect my hands it was a bit of a shock as I no longer had hands, just a well-wrapped ball of bandages.

My initial thought was that the surgeon's scalpel had slipped and amputated my hands. A rather sick joke briefly came to mind, about a surgeon approaching a bed of a patient from whom he had just amputated a leg. 'Now sir, we have some bad news and some good news.' The patient asked the doctor what the bad news was first. The doctor replies that due to a clerical error he has amputated the wrong leg. After a brief tantrum and tears the patient enquires what the good news was, and the doctor replied that his remaining leg was getting better! And for a real bitter twist the guy in the next bed offered to buy his slippers!

My surgeon eventually arrived to inform me that all went well and the good news was I should have the bandages off in about a week, with another week where my hands would be very weak. Slowly the situation dawned on me: as much as I had still had hands for the next seven days, they were no use whatsoever.

For the next eight days I found out who my friends were! Simple things like undoing your flies never mind extracting your John Thomas from your underpants and aiming it becomes a major concern, and as much as tracksuit bottoms with no underpants are acceptable around the house, you look a right pillock down the pub in mid winter, apart from the cold giving you brass monkeys. Getting dressed in general was a major fight, buttons and zips being a major no-no. Thinking back perhaps wiping my arse was the biggy for, while my wife dressed me and held my willy for a pee, I drew the line at that, although, bless her, she did offer. I found that treble paper was OK though not totally thorough but we won't go there. Let's just say skid marks on underwear were a constant embarrassment.

One bad moment was when, becoming a little stir crazy watching daytime TV, I decided to go for a walk. It was a bitter cold day but with a bit of shuffling I managed to don an overcoat. Quite pleased with my independence I set off. It felt good doing something not affected by my temporary disability. I'm not one for sitting around doing nothing and as much as I read a lot, basically I'm a hands-on practical sort of bloke and when you ain't got hands you're buggered. It gave me food for thought about thalidomide children, not just how they managed but thrived as artists, athletes and mothers bringing up children, living practical useful lives.

When I got home I had lots of time to contemplate about the overcoming of adversity as I could not get my overcoat off. In fact I had a moment of panic when I half got it off and was then hamstrung with my arms stuck in the sleeves behind my back. Having managed to shuffle my overcoat back on I had the problem of sitting in the house and being too hot or sitting in the garden till the wife came home from work and rescued me. She was very sympathetic and stopped laughing at me after only ten minutes or so.

With some relief I went to my local doctors to have my bandages removed and my stitches out. He took one look at my hands and asked me how had I upset the surgeon at the hospital. I replied I didn't think I had. The doctor informed me I must have done something to piss him off to receive such torment, as he had never known anyone have both hands operated on at the same time, as it's so debilitating. Tell me about it!

It still took another fortnight or so before I got full strength back to my hands, the moral to this story is to be very nice to surgeons. The only thing I can think of is I may have inadvertently called him doctor as traditionally surgeons prefer to be addressed as Mr. So, take heed!

As a teenager I was always getting sore throats and my parents reckoned I wasn't thriving, as they say. So after a few trips to the doctor he decided it was tonsillitis so I got an appointment to have them out, a common operation then but frowned on now as being unnecessary, for some reason. It certainly worked for me with never a sore throat since and I thrived! The only problem was when I was admitted to the ward. It was the children's ward as it was classed as a child's complaint and not appropriate for the adult ward. It was horrendous. I'm not keen on kids at the best of times but twenty screaming, noisy, little buggers in the same room, and me being a captive audience. Great! Anyway the little gremlins were a lot quieter the next morning when they'd had their tonsils removed. They couldn't even bawl without experiencing pain, and they were quieter still when they found out that ice-cream was the order of the day, dispensed to cool down our burning sore throats. One phenomenon encountered was waking up from the operation with the world upside down. I thought this was due to the anaesthetic causing hallucinations but I eventually found out I wasn't dreaming. It was common practice to turn you upside down till the wound in your throat stops bleeding, to prevent you drowning in your own blood.

It's possible the experience in the children's ward did put me off kids for life and luckily I married a woman of similar tastes. The catch-phrase was kids are noisy, smelly, and expensive, not particularly in that order. Other people's kids were all right for about an hour then the novelty wore off and I would start losing the will to live and only recover two hours later, after they had left. I was also partial to the phrase, 'kids are fine I just couldn't eat a whole one.'

So, the decision was made to be a child free family. Rather than have pills and condoms and such like, I decided to have 'the op'. My doctor was a little dubious. I was only thirty with no kids and the vasectomy was unlikely to be reversible. If I wanted this in the future, it involved quite a difficult procedure with no guarantee of success. But undaunted I persevered and finally he agreed.

The snip, as it's affectionately known, has a light hearted, jokey, kind of feel about it, as opposed to the actual feel about it on the operating table. But I will get to that later. As I entered the out-patients ward I was directed to a room with about a dozen blokes sitting around the edge. We were all a bit reticent to admit what we were in for but eventually with a few 'what you in for ...' and 'yeh me to ...' and lots of knowing sheepish grins, we established we were all in for 'the snip'. Now I can only describe this as a set-up by the nurses, for suddenly a rather scary huge matron type nurse with an angry look on her face barged into the room and declared 'Now which of you men hasn't shaved? I hate shaving men!' No-one replied. It was unnecessary as the three unfortunate victims... I mean patients who hadn't shaved turned white and looked as if they were going to make a dash for the door and freedom. The ones who had had the foresight to have shaved, or had been forewarned by their wives who had had their trip to the maternity ward and the joys of being shaved, looked so relieved it was immediately obvious that the scary nurse marched out of the room. Without a backward glance she said in a really exasperated voice, 'Then you three better follow me.' With that the three hapless unshaven followed her out with appealing glances to the rest of us for help. It wasn't in any way with malice that we all sniggered, it was pure relief. Half an hour later they came back in with pained expressions on their faces and walking a little funny. We thought they had already had the op, but they explained it was the heavy-handed nurse's shaving that caused the discomfort, which prompted further cruel jokes. We all sobered up a little though when one of the hapless three described the scary nurse, approaching them with a cut-throat razor, demanding they drop their trousers, unceremoniously grabbing the nearest penis, roughly stretching it up in the air and using deft strokes, shaved clean the organ, balls and all.

We all winced then fell silent as the scary nurse entered the room again pointed to one of our number saying, 'You're first, follow me'

From then on our numbers slowly dwindled and we never saw them again. Finally it was my turn to be taken away to be executed... I mean operated on. I was given one of those backless gowns to change into and led into the operating theatre. I was expecting to be wheeled in on a trolley but no such luxury here. As I walked into the operating room, I looked down to the floor as it had bits of bloody tubing scattered about, cut from the previous victims. Were these placed there on purpose or was the surgeon a bit of a butter fingers? If they were there on purpose to remind us of the seriousness of our decision to become sterile it was a little late as the scary nurse ushered me forward with little chance of escape. On the other hand if the little bloody tubes, carelessly cut and discarded from the previous fellow-vasectomised victim's balls were the result of a ham-fisted surgeon it didn't bare thinking about. The thought was taken from me as I was helped up on to the table and told to lie down.

The surgeon turned out to be one of these types that wanted to explain his modus operandi in excruciating detail which was only two points up from one who was ham-fisted, for as he started to describe what he was about to do to me, I was starting to change my mind about the whole affair.

He started by holding the syringe up in the air and squeezed the plunger slightly so a stream of liquid squirted out, catching the light beautifully. He then held forth in a rather bombastic voice saying, 'Now I am about to anaesthetise the local area by injection. The secret is to press the plunger as the needle is inserted thereby anaesthetising the area and minimising the pain of the needle.' It didn't work! We are talking about inserting a needle into my balls here. The male readers will undoubtedly understand my distress, but for the ladies reading this, men's balls are rather delicate and sensitive to any form of violence i.e. knocks, over enthusiastic squeezes and definitely needles cause severe pain and distress. From what I hear of women's complaints of childbirth, it's on a par or even worse to have ones nuts knocked. (Complain about that one if you like, ladies. I have my pain, you have yours). The pain was excruciating and getting worse, so quick as a flash the only thing to do was hyperventilate. It didn't relive the pain but it was something to show I was in pain without actually screaming and showing myself up.

My distressed state prompted the doctor to get one of the nurses to hold my hand and talk to me, to take my mind off the pain. Not the scary one much to my relief and she was quite pretty. Under different circumstances this might have been quite pleasant but she tried to take my mind off the pain by asking how many children I had which got rather a sharp reply of, 'None. I can't stand the little buggers, that's why

I'm here.'

Luckily by this time the anaesthetic was having some effect, and as the pain decreased I started taking more notice of my surroundings. Over the operating table was a large light with an even larger reflector. Looking up into this reflector, there was my reflection laid out on the table, legs ungainly spread akimbo with this surgeon guy in a mask taking a knife to my genitals, which gave me the feeling that I had died and was having an out of body experience, and was seeing myself as my spirit would see my body as it left for the after life. Luckily reason returned in time to prevent me from screaming, jumping up from the table and running out of the room. It must have been something in the anaesthetic! So I just shut my eyes.

By the time I had recovered some of my composure I opened my eyes and glanced up to my reflection in the light reflector again to see a fascinating sight of the surgeon hunched over my genitals sewing away as if he was a master seamstress.

The next thing I knew I was being helped off the table by the scary nurse, over the bits of bloody tubing on the floor of which some were now mine, to the door. I did feel like pointing out to someone I did not expect to have to walk after major surgery but the scary nurse was going a little too fast and I certainly was not going to risk telling her. I was ushered into a cubicle with a bed. Florence Nightingale (not) then handed me a jock strap, with the oh so true words as far as I was concerned, 'Put this on, you don't want me to put it on for you do you?'

As I lay there with the anaesthetic slowly wearing off it did cross my mind that I may have got the surgeon's prefix wrong again, calling him doctor instead of sir, considering the pain he put me through. But perhaps the procedure is inherently painful and he really did try his best to minimise the pain.

My next problem was getting home. I had made arrangements with the wife to come to the hospital for me when I phoned, and as I was now dismissed by Florence I shuffled my way carefully to the public phone box giving a decent impersonation of a walk like a cross between John Wayne and Charlie Chaplin. I explained that I was alive and well to wifey, that although a little tender I was feeling brave and would walk out of the hospital up to the main road if she could come for me.

With a brave face in adversity, suffering severe pain and displaying a large helping of macho bravado to compensate for having the equivalent of having my balls cut off, I set off out of the hospital for the main road and my lift home. On reaching the road there was no sign of my transport, so feeling better for some fresh air I carried on in the direction of home.

Two miles further on and getting a little worse for wear I staggered into my home to find my dear wife on the phone desperately trying to find someone to pick me up as our car would not start. (It being a 1948 vintage as I've described in a earlier chapter and was a little temperamental to start).

Two weeks later and stitches removed by a very confident, gentle nurse who only hurt me to the point of a near faint, I was ready for my first test. Not quite what you may think. This involved a bottle, a porno mag, and a trip to the hospital lab to have the sample scrutinised for anything live and swimming.

The results were due that week and in the meantime I was attending a social event when an acquaintance who worked at the lab where I had taken my sample approached me and across a crowded room said in loud voice, 'Your test was negative, you are OK for it now.' and winked rather suggestively. Perhaps a little unprofessional of her and I did contemplate reporting her but it only confirmed what I thought of her anyway so I didn't bother. I had made no secret of my op anyway as it was always good for a laugh. I've got to say in the end it was all worth it, I was just a little disappointed I was not issued with a certificate as I would have been a good chat up line. But, heigh-ho, I was married anyway.

I received lots of get well cards. One of them I remember which I found rather appropriate was a card with a plumber on the front standing outside his workshop and the sign over the door read 'Joe's Pipe and Tool Works'. I did think it would get a laugh at parties offering to show my operation, but I got little response, except from my mother-in-law. I am not sure if she was serious or just winding me up, but I declined anyway.

I do feel I have a medical bent and I do believe I was some sort of doctor in a previous life. Even if it was a witch doctor! I'm good at removing spells (the wood splinter type may I add), putting plasters on cuts and cutting my partner's toe nails. (Hey come on! Now that's almost medical although it's called podiatry nowadays and you can get a degree in it). If you doubt my credentials so far may I explain that I have been a school nurse. The story goes that I worked in a school as a technician, and the proper school nurse retired. She was affectionately known as Granny Aspirin because that was her universal panacea. I had it on good authority that she inserted aspirins between a child's toes, secured with tape, to cure athletes' foot. I have no idea whether it cured it or not but it made the child walk funny for days till he had a bath and they dissolved.

The school decided that a first-aider would be adequate for the school's health and safety requirements so I was volunteered to go on the course. I was rather looking forward to wearing the black stockings and the starched uniform, but I was told it was not part of the job (shame!).

Apart from bandaging sprains, sticking plasters on minor cuts and pulling out the occasional splinters from woodwork students, I spent long hours taking pupils to the local accident and emergency and sitting in the waiting area. I remember one time I had taken a young man to the hospital for a possible broken wrist. We seemed to have been there for hours, and I was in danger of missing my lunch. I suggested to the young man, only joking, that if he pretended to faint he would be seen by the doctor much quicker. Either he also was worried about his lunch or he thought I was serious, but I just managed to pull him back to his seat before he hit the floor. He was game, but my conscience over-ruled hunger.

I had quite a few funny incidents, I remember on one occasion a young lady came to me with a very red, inflamed, sore, watering eye. I assumed that she had got some dust in it and was preparing to wash it out with saline solution, but when I asked what she thought had happened; she said in a mumbled voice that it was 'condom lubricant'. I said, 'Pardon?' 'Condom lubricant,' was the exasperated reply. I was just about to ask a third time when the penny dropped. She didn't seem all that embarrassed so I had to ask the inevitable question. 'How did you manage to get condom lubricant in your eye at school?'

With some relief on my part and slight indignation on hers, she explained that the class had been practising putting condoms on carrots in Humanities sex lessons. Not much surprises me nowadays, but funnily enough it caused some consternation at the local A & E, especially after going through the 'condom lubricant' routine. After the doctor asked for the third time, I stepped in and rescued the young lady by giving the perplexed doctor the full explanation. He just raised his eyebrows shook his head and then went away to phone the toxicology unit in London to find out how to treat the young lady's, by now, streaming eye

While on the subject of condoms and school I heard this rather amusing story from one of the teachers at the school where I worked. She asked one of the sixth form girls if she would baby sit for her. The girl was quite enthusiastic but asked if it was OK if she brought her boyfriend along. The teacher was a little unsure about them being left on their own in the house together, but she said, 'Fine as you are both over sixteen,' and with a vague, 'You will take care.' To this the girl replied with total frankness. 'It's all right, Miss, we take precautions.' Relieved but inquisitive by the girl's assurance and frankness the teacher pushed on and asked, 'You can afford contraception on your pocket money?' The girl replied in reassuring tones, 'Yes, Miss, we use cling film.' It poses the question do the couple take their own cling film on baby sitting jaunts, or does it conjure up the scene of the frantic search through the kitchen drawers and only coming up with 'Baco' foil. This, may I add, was many years prior to the informed lessons of condoms on carrots in Humanities lessons. I did relate this story to some friends and got the rather surprising response 'We had to use crisp packets when we were teenagers.' It's sometimes best not to have a vivid imagination! (Salted or unsalted ... no, don't go there.).

Another time when I related this story to a group of friends, I was informed that a popular contraceptive in the sixties when birth control was still difficult to come by (no pun intended) a popular method was a Coca Cola douche, complete with a ready made delivery system 'shake and shoot applicator' in the shape of the classic Coca Cola bottle. Its arch rival drink was also popular I believe.

Medicine has certainly moved on in my lifetime. Heart transplants, lung transplants, even face transplants, and the medical profession no longer scatters asbestos dust on burns as I described in chapter three. One of the amusing changes to me is when nurses and doctors stick needles in you for one reason or another. The phrase 'just a little prick' was always uttered just before the needle went in, and was a standard phrase. Nurses must have run the full gambit of licentious replies from their male patents from, 'I've never had any complaints so far' to 'It's not! Look'. Now we get a rather inaccurate 'just a little scratch.' What can you joke about to relieve the pain with a phrase like that? I suppose it might be for the best in this politically correct world.

As I said, old age is a 'reet bugger' when all of a sudden things stop working, and bits keep dropping off. Just lately I feel like the bionic man, although not quite as robust as Steve Austin, the 'Six Million Dollar Man.' You will remember the one. 'We have the technology to rebuild him.' Well more like NHS freebies. I've had glasses for a fair while but now I need to wear them all the time. For long distance, for close up and everything in between (the potato knife I suppose didn't help much, but heigh-ho.)

Then there's my hearing aids. OK, it was forty years ago when I had a bout of meningitis which damaged my hearing, but it's relatively recently that I can hear nowt unless I have the damned things plugged in and switched on. Although there is an up side to that, I can be very selective about who and what I listen to. A surreptitious hand to the ear can switch them off and leave me in peace, oblivious to noisy kids and twittering women, with only the minimum of concentration to nod when you receive a inquiring look that deserves an opinion.

In defence of the NHS, they have now given me digital hearing aids that are miles better than the old analogue ones they used to hand out. They did take some convincing I was deserving of the new type as there was a waiting list and priority were young children just learning to speak. (which is fair enough) but the other priority were people who were dying so they could talk to their relatives before they went. (What can I say to that?)

I told them I was feeling a bit depressed lately and I was thinking about going to elocution lessons at night school as my broad Yorkshire accent was holding my career back as a news presenter. I thought my wicked sense of humour had blown it until I got an appointment to have them fitted. So when they turned out to be so much better I was very appreciative.

It was fascinating (well to me anyway) how they programmed them in to my personal hearing loss, with frequency compensation and automatic volume control. (Not quite six million dollar stuff but rather impressive).

The real pits was when a double crown at the front that I had nursed for donkey's years fell out, in Australia of all places. My dentist at home had warned me for years it was a problem, but I had resisted further invasive dentistry on it. It was when in OZ that the dentist there described my roots as a 'Disaster' (pronounced in an Aussie accent) as he temporarily glued it back in. Then back in Blighty I decided to have it seen to.

I was devastated at the solution to my gappy grin was 'dentures'. I was just as devastated at the cost. My apprehension was justified, wearing dentures is horrendous! I was never eloquent at the best of times, but with these falsies filling half my mouth I'm unintelligible!

The little leaflet you get with them explains how you will suffer excessive saliva. Just to be awkward, I suffered a dry mouth and I can only think I'm allergic to the plastic the dentures are made of, making my whole mouth swollen and sore. My dentist explained this was very rare, little compensation for my discomfort. Anyway after my dentist gave up on me I stopped wearing them, but after frightening children and ladies when I smiled at them I decided to persevere. Not suffering the dry, sore mouth but to modify the offending dentures. This involved sawing off a good two thirds of the plate that the two teeth are set in. The logic behind this was to reduce the amount of plastic that was making me allergic and allow me to speak proper, like 'whot I always do.

Well it worked, I no longer scare small children, and women find me attractive again, and I'm eloquent, well I think so!

My modification does take a large dollop of Fixodent to prevent it dropping out onto my plate at posh dinner parties, or actually under most circumstances I can think of in polite company! I have tried other alternatives to secure my denture like Araldite (not actually tried as I decided it was a little permanent, probably toxic, and if the smell is anything to go by really bad tasting). Another alternative I actually tried, albeit by accident was pile cream! You know how it is first thing in the morning brain not in gear, eyes half closed, hand-eye coordination a good hour off being capable of distinguishing any thing smaller than a box of corn flakes. The big question is, what the hell was that cream doing in my bathroom cupboard anyway. It's not one of my medical problems so where did it come from? Let this be a lesson to us all, check your bathroom cabinet for redundant medications even if you don't have dentures because I don't particularly recommend haemorrhoid cream to brush your teeth with.

With my extensive collection of medical instruments I have often considered starting a career as a doctor or even a surgeon, but with my recent successes modifying my dentures I am now considering taking up dentistry.

So I'm now bionic heaven knows what's going to fall off next. Just to send me peacefully into old age I have developed diabetes. This offers wonderful prospects of toes, legs, or God knows what falling off, with cataracts to prevent me from noticing what's missing. Both my parents were diabetic so it didn't come as too much of a shock. Just another loose thread in life's rich tapestry.

From the bit I've read and the vague explanation I have received from doctors, diabetes has various causes. Apart from the hereditary connection, it could be my immune system attacking my pancreas, poor thing. You would think it had enough to get on with, with all the nasty germs and viruses there are about! Of course there's the old inevitable chestnut that it's because I've always had two spoonfuls of sugar in my tea for most of my life. Needless to say I don't partake of the deadly stuff now, well not in tea anyway. I was told that after a few weeks, tea with sugar would be undrinkable. It was one of the few times a doctor was right about anything (sorry about my slur on the medical profession, they do a good job really. I just think they don't know everything, some just think they do!).

One of the strangest explanations is that my cells no longer like the flavour of the insulin my poor pancreas turns out and it is then under pressure to produce more and more till the poor overworked thing packs in altogether. So I pump insulin from the pancreas of dead pigs into my spare tyre next to my navel, twice a day. I just wonder how many bacon sandwiches have to be consumed for me to be supplied with insulin from slaughtered pigs. A bit of an anomaly really as I avoid pork. This stems from when my dad kept pigs, I found them at least as intelligent as dogs, and, as much as their hygiene isn't up to much, I found them charming animals. The main problem for me is not unsurprising. Bacon to me smells of pigs.

Well as I finish this chapter nothing else has stopped working or fallen off so we live in hope.

WOW! I've just recently had a heart attack 'That'll learn mi' not to think I'm invulnerable. Boy was that painful! I was rushed into the local hospital and wired up to all sorts of gadgets and tubes. They said I had only a mild one. God knows what a bad one would be like. Having thought about it, it wouldn't be as bad, because you would be dead. The doctors said I needed to be taken to Leeds as they could fit me up with a stent. But a lot of people were having heart attacks at the time so there weren't any beds available so I would have to stay where I was for the time being. Now as much as the nurses were wonderful and the food wasn't too bad, I was still tethered to the bed by tubes and wires so it was necessary to pee into a bottle and do the other into a paper top hat on a chair at the side of the bed. This naturally involves developing a bit of a technique as the top hat isn't very deep, so the secret is to lift yourself up as you... Too much information! One up side of being tethered to the bed was my first blanket bath by a pretty young nurse, although it's not all it's built up to be it takes a lot of restraint, the detail of which I'm not prepared to go into in this book.

I lost count of the number of times they stuck pads with wire on me and ripped them off, I'm not suggesting there was any sadism involved but I think I should have shown more pain as it seemed as if they were seeing if they could make me wince. I know this much, if I'm ever rushed into hospital again with an heart attack I'm going to shave my chest first!

Eventually after about a week and a half of waiting to be shipped to the other hospital with the facilities to do the op, I got really fed up waiting for a bed to become available so luckily I had another angina attack. This seemed to prompt me into being taken to Leeds in an ambulance with the lights and sirens blaring. I am a little prone to motion sickness; boats, small planes and coaches, if I read a book in a car, that sort of thing. I can now add ambulances being driven rather fast with siren and lights flashing to the list. I've been pretty ill on a ferry to France in a storm but that pales into insignificance to that ambulance ride. I told the attendant nurse I was going to be sick and was handed the inevitable top hat, then I pleaded for the ambulance to stop, then passed out! I came to in a lay-by but as soon as I showed signs of life they set off again. 'Death where is your sting?' Eventually I was deposited in the hospital but was so ill they couldn't take me straight to the operating theatre and I took three days to 'stabilise' so the lights and siren were a waste of time. The morning of the op I was dressed in the traditional backless gown with the rather fetching addition of pink paper knickers and wheeled into the operating theatre. Wow! Was that place impressive. Star Ship Enterprise had nothing on it. There was this enormous machine in the centre of a large room with TV screens and, what I presume was an X-ray gadget on the end of a moveable arm, hovering over a table which they laid me on. I was then wired up with sticky pads and a drip in each arm, and told to relax! Yeh right! At that moment my beating heart appeared on one of the TV screens, sound and all.

The next procedure was to have an artery opened up in my wrist to insert the wire to push the stent up into the restricted artery in my heart. I'd been warned about this by a sadistic friend who went into great detail about the alternative. Sure enough after a lot of digging about in my wrist the surgeon declared he couldn't make a big enough hole in my wrist artery and would have to go up to my heart from my GROIN!

A nurse immediately ripped my pink paper knickers and the surgeon started digging about in my groin, after he had anaesthetised the area I'm glad to say. The TV screen now looked really impressive as you could see the wire snaking its way up to my heart. At this point all the technicians, nurses and the surgeon seemed to lose interest and I was left lying there, I thought it was an inconvenient time to have a tea break and a little mean not to offer me a cuppa. Luckily or perhaps not I still had my hearing aids in and heard a technician on the phone to what I can only imagine was the manufacturer of the vast impressive machine which was showing the surgeon where to stick his stent! The conversation went something like this. 'Well, it's all locked up ... well we need someone out straightaway, we have someone on the table now ... you say it's crashed ... reboot it ... how? ... just switch it off and on again ... OK' I did manage to attract a nurse as she passed and I offered, half joking to see if I could fix the machine as I was pretty good with computers and mechanics but the offer was declined. A few minutes later there was a sound like 'Star Trek Enterprise' coming to a full stop in space, and then a sound like it going in to warp drive and all the technicians returned to their posts. A nurse came to me wielding a hypodermic and explained that this injection would stress my heart to see if the stent was working OK. I was just about to explain I was stressed enough when the drug or what ever it was took effect. 'Oh my God' I thought. The heart attack was bad but that was worse. But I survived! So the stent must have worked. Next I was wheeled back to the ward and the nurse, putting the bell push in my hand, told me to keep an eye on the wound and if it started to bleed to ring the bell.. Now as much as I'm a fair way from obese and I haven't quite lost sight of my genitals it was a bit of a strain to keep checking my groin. But sure enough after about an hour, there was definitely a warm wet feeling down below and a hint of red on the sheets. After a quick check to make sure I hadn't lost bladder control with the trauma, I pushed the bell. When the nurse finally came after some delay, I hadn't bled to death so she whipped back the covers exposing my bleeding groin. She explained in a very professional manner that she was just about to apply a little pressure to my groin and I would not believe how many men she had to do this to in her ten years of nursing. It was not erotic, believe me, it wasn't even pleasant, it was bloody painful! We got around to discussing the weather and even politics in the ten minutes she applied the pressure to my by now very abused and sore groin. An Elastoplast was then applied to the spot and I was given a cup of very welcome hot sweet tea, I didn't even complain that I didn't take sugar as I was diabetic. It was very welcome.

And that was that. The next morning I was told to get up as the bed was required for the next heart attack, and to arrange my own transport home. They handed me a carrier bag full of medicines I was supposed to take. I've got to say apart from dropping some of the drugs that I appeared to be intolerant to, on my GP recommendation, (just my little hobby horse about side effects of drugs) I've never felt so good, well at least for the previous eighteen months. In retrospect I was going downhill leading up to the attack. The only fly in the ointment is that the cardiac rehabilitation nurse insisted that for the next six weeks. I do a twice-a-week gym session at the hospital. She was so enthusiastic and pretty with such a winning smile I couldn't refuse. The last time I was anywhere near a gym was at school and I hated it!

It's so reminiscent of those over-enthusiastic muscled gym mistresses telling her pupils to 'find a space and pretend to be a tree blowing in the wind.' Oh well we all have our crosses to bear and I'm almost sure it's doing me good.

Here are just a few medical remedies from the past you may not like to try. Just to put this in perspective this isn't from some old history book from the dark ages, this is from my youth, well not actually from my youth as my parents were quite modern in as much as they believed in doctors. . On occasions, my dad would rub horse liniment on my bruises or even, if I got an infected cut on my hand, would squirt some bright purple stuff on the wound that was used for sheep foot rot. It used to sting like hell but would soon clear up the infection. This was OK as these things were proper medical stuff, albeit for animals. Not like some of my school friends who confided in me some of the quack remedies they were subjected to. About the worst was butter on a burn. For a cough try this one. A large table spoon brimming with soot and Vaseline, the Vaseline being melted on the gas stove and the soot added by scraping the spoon on the coal fire back. I've been informed one spoonful was sufficient to instantly prevent any further coughing at least in the presence of the administrator of the remedy, to prevent any further dose. Ear wax was regally removed by pouring a tablespoonful of Hydrogen Peroxide in to the ear. Yes, that's the rather powerful oxidizing chemical for bleaching hair. The effect I've been informed is a spectacular fizzing, popping and gurgling sound for some time, then the dissolved wax just runs out on to your pillow at night. Still sounds a bit dodgy to me. And last but not least my friend confided in me his mother regularly gave him a soap enema just to keep him regular and free from worms! He did not go into to much detail of the method or at what age this procedure was maintained till.

— 25 —

A WICKED SENSE OF HUMOUR? NO!

I HAVE BEEN accused of possessing a bizarre, obtuse, and sometimes a damn-well-not-funny sense of humour, the latter usually by victims with no sense of humour of their own. To set the scene so you may judge, one example was when I took a chain saw to work for the workshop technician to sharpen for me. He reckoned he was a dab hand at it so he got the job. I had already taken the chain off and as I was passing the office I noticed two secretaries having a tea break.

The film 'Chain Saw Massacre' suddenly sprung uninvited into my head, so I fired up the chain saw. Now I'm assuming we are all aware of the mischievous imp perched on our shoulders, who whispers naughty thoughts in our ear, no? Well I am, and mostly, but not always, I ignore it, or at least I do if I realise the consequences in time.

As the chain saw burst into life and revved up I made my grand entrance into the office shouting, 'Here's Johnny.' In retrospect the phrase 'Here's Johnny' might have been a little lost on my audience as I may have mixed up my films or for the fact my shout was barely audible over the noise of the chain saw, even though I have a rather loud voice. Also, my audience was not the horror film watching type. Last but not least, the trauma of my entrance may well have been a little distracting, and of course there was the little thing of hot tea everywhere. Now what could be wrong with a little practical joke like that? Back tracking, I would point out the chain saw had it's chain removed so even if I had inadvertently touched one of the sectaries on the neck with the blade no damage would have been done, well at least not physically.

The office was the butt of quite a few of my little pranks over the years. Even sad events weren't exempt on the grounds they needed a little light humour. This particular time, one of my work mates had died after a short illness. As he did not have any relatives I took it upon myself to arrange the funeral. All went well and we all gave him a good send off, and after the cremation we all went to the pub.

Some weeks later I received a phone call from the funeral parlour that someone needed to come and collect the ashes. I collected his ashes after work one evening and took them into work the following morning so we could decide what to do with them. Passing the office on my way into work there was no-one about. With a little hint of mischief I placed the urn containing the ashes on a filing cabinet in the office, and went about my work.

I must confess I then forgot all about John's remains for about a week or so, until one morning I was invited for coffee into the office. As the conversation waned one of the secretaries asked me if I knew what the container was on the filing cabinet, because no-one seemed to know whose or what it was. My nonchalant reply was, 'It's John.' Pause ... 'It's what?' 'No not what, it's who, or was' Pause ... 'You mean it's ... Oh my God get it ... I mean ... get him out of here.' Result! People can be really strange about dead people, even their ashes that are completely harmless, as he had left them long ago and even if he was hanging about John was such a friendly soul.

I explained that I thought it would be nice if we all decided where we scattered John's ashes, and did he ever mention it to anyone, implying that it was the sort of thing he would have mentioned while he was well. Some people are so easy to wind up it's almost a disappointment. After a bit of a lecture on being more respectful of the deceased and of the gravity of the situation, it was decided that John's favourite spot was on the moors overlooking the Aire Valley. So I was despatched forthwith to do the deed.

It was a fine, sunny, spring afternoon albeit a little breezy on the moors with a fine panoramic view of the Aire Valley, and with a little farewell and a cautious sprinkling of John's ashes into the wind, I avoided taking any particles of John back with me as I set off back to work. Driving back I had an idea for one last laugh with John that he would have enjoyed, for as I entered the office I was dusting off my hair and clothes while fishing about with my tongue as if I had something on it. I looked at the secretaries as they watched me with a questioning look and said, ‘By it wer fare windy up theer.’ Then I counted up to eleven under my breath before the penny dropped and there was an uproar of disgust! Some women can be so delightfully sensitive.

You may guess this was pre PC-gone-mad days, even so looking back I was lucky to get away with some of my little jokes. There was the time when some mad scientist from America, where all the best mad scientists come from, sent letters containing Anthrax powder to a few politicians who he believed needed getting rid of. In a lot of ways I can empathise with the man, I can think of a few I would like to remove myself, but I think I will just not vote for them in the next election!

What I did to the rather naive-at-times secretary was to leave a little pile of flour on her desk first thing in the morning so she would find it when she arrived.. Luckily I hung around to watch the fun as she took one look at the powder and started to phone the police. OK, so anthrax is rather nasty stuff, but I was amazed she made the connection to the mad American scientist and confused as to why she would think he would want to eliminate her. Anyway after making her a cup of hot sweet tea she finally agreed not to phone the anti-terrorist squad and eventually forgave me.

I try not to pick on the old and the vulnerable with my little jests so when I visited my parents one day I was concerned when they informed me they were packing a picnic to go and visit a secret up to now, undiscovered village up the Dales. They had heard on the local news channel, about a little village way up in the Dales called Lambs Dale. It had been cut off from the rest of the world for hundreds of years and all the people there lived like peasants, with no electricity, cars, or communications like radios or phones, and was not on any maps. My parents were so enthusiastic about visiting this place and were just about to set off when I asked them today's date.

'It's the first of April,' my mum replied. 'Didn't you know?' I replied, 'Yes, didn't you? Does the date have any significance to you?' A cloud started to appear across her face as she snapped at me that it can't be an April fool as it was on the BBC. They don't do that sort of thing. I had to leave at that point but two days later I asked if they had had a good time in Lambs Dale. The subject was quickly changed and never mentioned again.

The BBC certainly do get involved in April Fool's Day. Even my hero Sir David Attenborough got in on the act and caught me out. If I ever meet him I will have to give him a piece of my mind for playing jokes on the old and vulnerable ... Well at least not to do it on TV where vulnerable people can be caught out. There I was sat watching the TV as they were interviewing Sir David about some of the wonderful wildlife programmes he has turned out over the years and the exotic places he had been to. He was asked what was one of the most memorable; he mentioned the programme on gorillas, and filming birds of paradise that had never been filmed before. Then he said that the most intriguing was filming flying penguins in the Antarctic. He then went on to describe this phenomenon while they showed a very convincing video of the penguins indeed flying.

I was convinced and impressed. The penguins, with their little flippers, flapped and glided around icebergs and over snowy plains, with such speed and grace. I have to confess it wasn't until I was laid in bed the next morning that I realised. I sat bolt upright and exclaimed, 'You pillock, sodding penguins can't fly!' You just can't believe what you see on TV nowadays! And Sir David at that!

I was once asked to make up a game to raise money for charity. I constructed a wicked version of the old wire game where you have to try and pass a small ring along a suspended wiggly wire without touching and setting off an alarm. Well mine certainly sets off an alarm. When the ring touches the wire, it's a rather loud Klaxon horn from a fire alarm, which has been known to make strong men dive for cover.

That's OK but I needed something a touch more original. I did contemplate a hefty electric shock triggered when the ring made contact with the wire, but decided against it considering the potentially very young and very old that may want to have a go, or come to think of it, anyone with a weak heart. I could not risk being sued for any deaths. Now I always find water is always good for a laugh especially someone else getting a good soaking. With a little ingenuity and an old car windscreen washer pump, and the little jet which squirts the water on the windscreen I had the perfect water surprise. Just to add a touch of grossness, which I always try to achieve, the jet was mounted inside the mouth of one of those ugly rubber goblin-type toys. Did I mention I once collected them?

It went down great, women giggled, children screamed, and then brought their grandparents to try it, (without telling them of course that they were going to get a soaking), and young men threatened me with violence. It was a show stopper, and made a lot of money for charity. There was always the smart kid who spends his life playing computer games and has developed a steady hand who is just about to complete the game without a soaking, when a surreptitious kick of the table the machine in perched on ensures the smart arse gets a wetting. It was always advisable to sort out a couple of hefty minders as protection and to discourage any vengeance attacks.

The wire game raised good money for charity over the years, with only one hiccup. I loaned my wet wire game to my partner to take to her work, for a charity fundraising event. It was set up in the works canteen, staff came in their tea break to be entertained and get wet, and of course paid for the privilege. All went well with lots of laughs and quite a few screen-wash top ups, until a rather over-enthusiastic lady turned up with a new hairdo. Now if you are quick and make an early side step and you end up with just a minor splash. But if you are concentrating on your dexterity with the loop, getting wet seems to go unnoticed. (Just goes to show not all women can multi-task). This lady had to be tapped on the shoulder and it had to be explained she was getting a little wet. 'What do you mean wet? Oh my God, my hair, it's ruined.' It didn't help the situation when her fellow workers rolled about laughing. She stormed out of the canteen and complained to management. My wet wire game was removed on, you've guessed it, 'Health and Safety' grounds! I did get a bit of a laugh out of it though as my partner's sister worked in the same department as the lady with the wet hairdo. She came in ranting and raving about that 'stupid woman and her machine' not knowing the connection. Needless to say my partner's sister kept quite.

In my early years the extent of my party tricks was that I could mimic the laugh of the little Indian in the cartoon Deputy Dawg and the woodpecker in the Woody Woodpecker song but that became a little dated, as I'm sure only a very limited few of you readers would remember them. So I moved on to bigger and better party entertainment.

One of my little party tricks which always goes down well which involves water and inevitably people getting wet, is the so-called Oxford and Cambridge boat race. The secret is to make people think that it's a competition then in the heat of competitiveness people lose all common sense not realising I am about to drench them. I am giving this secret away as I have tried this on all my friends that I have no friends left ... foolish enough ... that haven't been baptised!

It's a 'humdinger'. It has all the ingredients of a perfect party game, competitiveness, anticipation, the unexpected, and everybody gets wet. This is one you really should try at home preferably among friends. I've performed it at posh events and people still speak to me afterwards. I've done it where it's a miracle I don't get beaten up afterwards, and to friends that I really should be kinder to. So do try it at your next party, it's sure to win you lots of invites to lots of other parties. So here is the secret.. How it goes is this. You get a large tea tray. Place it on a sturdy coffee table and fill it to with a quarter of an inch of water. Depending how many victims ... sorry players, each gets a matchstick perched on the edge of the tray in front of them as they kneel around the table, level with the tray. You then explain the rules of the game whereby each player has to blow their match across the tray. Just to add a little competitiveness you position the players all around the tray so that they are going to be blowing against each other. If you are really lucky and have eight people stupid ... I mean willing enough, kneeling around the edge of the lake. You would be amazed how many people take this seriously and require you to make up volumes of imagined rules. After everyone is happy with the rules, you explain that you are going to say 'Ready, Set, GO' and they have to start blowing. So big breaths, get close to the tray and 'Ready, Set GO!' BUT before they release their first puff, you bring the palm of your hand flat down into the centre of the water, preferably with an excessive amount of enthusiasm. Picture if you will the scene of absolute shock and confusion as the victims (there I've said it without apology) stagger from the now almost empty tray, wet, bedraggled and looking for revenge. Some just kneel there stunned, some go hysterical, but most have a good laugh about it, well eventually, well perhaps with the exception of women with expensive hairdos, I do have trouble with women with expensive hairdos, but I always say you can't please all the people all the time. A quick removal of the tray is essential as there is always one who takes it on themselves to empty what's left in the tray over your head, as if the perpetrator isn't wet enough, but a quick dispensing of dry towels usually gets people to see the funny side of their soaking. I would like to point out that I do sustain a few splashes myself, as one can imagine, slapping one's hand hard into water, but admittedly the victims receive the brunt of the ensuing Tsunami with a few drops even reaching innocent bystanders.

Why do they still trust me? Needless to say I don't get repeat mugs ... I mean participants for this game. It inexplicably seems to stick in people's memory.

My collection of horror masks not only come in handy to scare kids trick-or-treating off the doorstep on Halloween, they are also good for a laugh in all kinds of situations. We had guests for the weekend one time and I was showing them around the house, when I happened to take them into my workshop. The lady showed an interesting reaction to my horror mask collection hanging up there. As we entered she took one look at the masks and ran out screaming, instantly the little imp on my shoulder winked at me.

Just before bedtime I slipped into the guest room and placed one of my favourite masks over the lit bedside lamp. I was rather pleased with the effect as the eye sockets glowed a rather appealing yellow with the rest of the face just a subtle green, I left it to be discovered.

I was a little disappointed when the husband went to bed first, and a little confused when there was no reaction. I assumed that he had removed the scary mask from the lamp before his wife spied it. After a few minutes the wife went to bed then seconds later there was a scream and the lady came rushing out of the bedroom. As much as I got a telling off for frightening her, her husband really got his ear bent. Apparently the husband had just climbed into bed and lay there reading a book by the light of the demon’s glowing and fiery eyes. She just didn't believe he hadn't seen the mask (I find it a little inconceivable too). She believed he had been in cahoots with me to scare the life out of her. Result! They are both still friends by the way.

Another time I discovered a gratuitous use for my horror masks was when our neighbours warned me they were throwing a party for a group of friends, and to be prepared for a bit of noise and music. I wasn't too worried as the couple weren't exactly revellers. In fact we didn't ever hear them from one month to the next.

As the evening wore on I went out into the garden. There was not a whisper. Deciding that this was just not good enough, I thought their party needed a little extra zing. The zing consisted of a rather weird alien mask which I secured on the end of a long pole. The pole was necessary as next door is one of those upside down houses with the living room upstairs where I assumed was where all the action, if any, was going on. With my alien on a stick I stood under their living room and slowly raised the mask up to the window. No reaction! Down it came and up again hoping the movement would catch someone's eye. Still no bloody reaction! In desperation I gently taped it against the glass. Still no sodding reaction! I gave up, pulled the mask off the pole, and went in and made myself a cup of tea.

Some weeks later I asked my neighbour how his party had gone. 'OK,' was his reply, 'a little quiet.' Too bloody true I've heard a bunch OAP have a more lively party, so I asked him if he had any uninvited guests like ET perhaps. Reaction! 'You pillock, I should have known it was you!'

Apparently he had just caught a glimpse of this alien face disappearing out of sight below the window frame for the last time. He had run to the window to look out and just missed me. He had run outside and called everyone out to search for the ET, and I had been unaware of all the fun as I sat inside drinking tea. Still, it got a laugh in the end.

Quietly my dad also had a wicked sense of humour too and that could well be where I got it from. When the farm became unprofitable, not even just to feed us, my dad went out and got a job driving a dustbin lorry for the council. This not only gave my parents an income but gave my dad opportunity to collect things which I also, surprise, surprise, have inherited. When I inherited the farm it took me literally years to empty the barn and sheds to start renovations, but that's another story. You would be amazed what people throw away. In times of cash flow problems I would wear clothes my father had picked out of dustbins. Shock horror! It’s not as bad as it sounds. He only got cloths out of better class dustbins, and only clothes which the thoughtful owner had washed, placed them in poly bags, and laid them carefully on top of the rubbish, obviously feeling a little guilty about throwing good clothes away. My dad was happy he was recycling before it became fashionable, although my mum was a little perturbed and said I shouldn't wear the trousers as I could catch AIDS from them. I declined listing the possible ways to catch the disease. I have never been a snazzy dresser although for the time when my father was on the bins you could say I was slightly better dressed.

He worked with a gang of right comics, some of who were invited back to the farm and I became friendly with. One particular character was heavily into dealing in antiques which he salvaged mostly out of people’s dustbins. One day as my father was sitting in the driving seat of the dustbin wagon waiting for the men to finish loading a set of bins when his door opened and this particular guy thrust a rather fine barometer under my dad's seat. He asked my dad to look after it and he would pick it up after work. For whatever reason he didn't collect it, so my dad took it home. Next day he asked my father if he had seen it, and for a joke, my father said he had left it in the wagon. The guy walked away mumbling something about, 'bloody night security probably nicked it' then turned to my dad and asked, 'Are you sure you haven't seen it?' Since then whenever he saw my dad he asked the same question, so it became a bit of a game, that my father thought was hilarious. Now he asks me, now my father's been dead for some twenty years, and I still keep up my dad's game. Just recently the guy turned up on my doorstep and we had a right laugh about old times he had on the bins with my dad. Just as he was leaving and was standing on the doorstep he turned to me and asked the old question,. 'You haven't seen an old barometer your dad got off me have you?' I didn't inform him that he should have, as he was sat under the very barometer drinking tea (if he reads this book I promise on my dad's grave to give it him back).

A final little twist to the story as I write this was that a mate of mine who knew this guy and was doing some work for him, was telling how he was now selling things on Ebay and doing quite well. I told my mate the next time he saw him, to give him a wind-up that he should tell him I am also selling stuff on Ebay and I had just sold an antique barometer, that my dad got out of the dustbins years ago, for four hundred pounds! I live in anticipation of a knock on my door.

My sense of humour is fed on things like You've Been Framed and daft stuff on You Tube. You know the kind of thing, fat ladies climbing out of boats and falling in the water and people doing dangerous stunts with no training, no thought of safety and no imagination what could go wrong. I wonder why I find that fascinating?

Another source of amusement is people using words that have a different meaning to what they believe they are trying to say. I know someone who called their dog Dyke because it sounded butch. It was quite a while ago not long after Harold Robbins downgraded the word from a ditch to a butch lesbian woman. After bandying the name around to friends stroking the dog and asking its name and reading a Robbins' novel, she changed its name to the Latin, Dykus Brittanicus Rex, only partly to show she took Latin at school, but it was still a problem to call it back in the park.

Then there was the couple who called their cat 'Chlamydia' because it sounded rather sweet, in total ignorance that it's bacteria with a rather unsavoury potential to infect most animals including humans and is a sexually transmitted disease. They got some very strange looks from neighbours hanging out the door late at night shouting the cat in. I can't remember what the cat's name was changed to. Not that it matters much with cats as they don't usually answer to names, not like dogs.

I once worked with a very nice lady whom I thought of as quite worldly wise, but you never can tell. We all have blank spots in our education of life. The problem started when she started calling people things like 'you daft dildo' or even worse 'you big dildo'. No-one seemed too keen to explain its popular meaning, so I took on the task. Don't women look cute when they blush? The blushes increased when she started to relate the number of people who she suspected she had said it to.

Another pretty young lady I worked with once came back from her lunch break and asked a group of colleagues stood around, 'What does this gesture mean?' The gesture I can only describe as a rather suggestive upward movement of the right arm while holding the crux of the arm with the left. To be quite honest I'm not sure how the gesture relates to its implication of 'I would very much like to have passionate sex with you' but I was well aware of its meaning. The group was a little stunned until someone dared to ask why the young lady needed to know this. We did not know how to deal with the answer she gave. 'Well I was walking down the road and this wagon driver hung out his window and did the gesture to me, so I did it back!' I chickened out on telling her how happy she had made the wagon driver and left it to one of our less imaginative colleagues.

It can happen to best of us, literacy being no protection. It even caught out the poet Robert Browning in 1841 when he used the word 'twat' in one of his poems. Apparently he had come across the word which meant the same then as it does now, but somehow misunderstood the meaning and thought it was a nun's headgear. Thankfully he went to his grave in blissful ignorance, as no-one dare tell him its meaning.

— 26 —

A SKIP RAT SCROUNGER

AS I'VE EXPLAINED before I'm a skip rat scrounger and proud of it! After all, recycling is all the fashion nowadays and I've been doing it for donkeys years.

It's not only skips I occasionally root through for interesting things that are bound to come in handy some time even if I can't find a immediate use for it there's always a car boot or antique fair to pass it on to some one who might make use of it. I look at it like this, things that are made to last and of quality, you don't own as much you just look after them for a while and then pass them on as they will probably be around longer than you are.

I do get invitations into interesting places to, Take for instance the time my friend John was invited to remove some old projection equipment from a local cinema that had closed down and was going to be changed into a carpet warehouse. One of the problems was that there was no electric connected, so we were working a little bit in the dark as we could only get there after work, so even if the place had windows it was pitch dark. No worries as I just happened to have bought very cheaply at a car boot sale a pair of miners' helmets complete with electric light on top. Just why I bought a pair of miners' helmets after my experience down the pothole from hell God only knows, but I did, and knew they would 'come in useful sometime.'

John had been given keys for the place so we let ourselves in, donned our helmets and went up into the projection box. What an amazing sight met us! The little room looked just like someone had shown the last film, switched off the electric, walked out the door and never come back. The equipment was early twenties antique, practically designed and built to last with a beauty all its own, well if you like that sort of thing. It was the kind of thing John and I would display on our sideboard as a work of art. That is if only our respective wives would allow it.

There were two large projectors, a bank of amplifiers, and two large rectifier valves half filled with mercury to power the projector arc lights. The bank of amplifiers for the sound was stacked in one corner, all valves dials, and Bakelite knobs, you could believe Marconi himself had a hand in making. They still worked when we tried it out later which was irrelevant in its way as it had an intrinsic beauty all its own.

Without further loss of saliva, drooling over the equipment, we set to dismantling it to take away. John wanted the projectors and I had my eye on the rectifiers. They were large glass exotically shaped bulbs, half full of silvery shining mercury. While John was unbolting the projectors from the floor I carefully detached the rectifiers. One slip and we would be up to our knees in liquid mercury, which is rather undesirable. At a rather crucial moment in my extrication of the glass rectifiers there was a loud banging coming up the steps, leading from the projection box down to a loading bay door on to the roadside, where I had parked my car nearby to load our booty.

I assumed that it was the local yobs messing about with my car so I rushed down the stairs, kicked the push bar on the door violently, swinging the doors wide, and shouting bugger off you vandals, expecting to give the little buggers a shock.

Well I certainly gave someone a shock, but unfortunately it wasn't the local yobs it was the local bobby, and the door had knocked his helmet off into the bargain. He had seen the flash of our torches through a little window and had come to investigate, thinking we were burglars. He was just about to drag me off the loading bay and cuff me, when

John, hearing the commotion, came to my rescue. Luckily John knew the bobby and as we had a legitimate reason for being there, we were saved from an impromptu visit to the cop shop. After three more nightly sessions we had stripped out all the goodies. I still have the mercury and have yet to find a safe use for it but I'm sure it will come in handy one of these days. John however did very well from his antique projectors as he eventually donated them to a museum where the connection eventually got him a job.

The next cinema we dismantled was even better. The theatre group where I was a member had been offered some cinema seats for our theatre as the present ones were getting a little tatty. The cinema was about to be pulled down so we had free rein to liberate anything that looked interesting. Once I had helped to get the seats back to the theatre I got down to a little scrounging of my own. There were a number of curtain opener motors that I came away with and at least one came in handy for my cement mixer as I described in an earlier chapter.

I got a parrot ladder; well that's what I was told it was called. This is a plank of wood with foot holes cut out along its length. This was fastened to the wall leading to a loft area and took a fair bit of effort to get out but worth it in the end as it did come in useful. I described in an earlier chapter, it now adorns my barn living room leading up to my minstrels' gallery (doesn't everybody have a minstrels' gallery in their living room?).

The best useless item I scrounged out of the cinema was a six-foot square speaker from behind the screen. It took a hell of a job to get it out of the place, and did I ever find a use for it? No I didn't, and it's about the only time the question 'and what are you going to do with that?' was justifiable.

My greatest downfall came when I tried to explore a back room looking for goodies. It was nearly full to the ceiling with boxes, not stacked, just thrown in. I opened boxes as I went, struggling across the mountainous pile, as I had my eye on a large cabinet way to the back. Some of the boxes I was climbing over were empty; some were half full with paper cups. Some had leaflets from past films, and some contained bingo tickets, as the last few years of the cinema's life it had been a bingo hall. Even I could not think of a use for this stuff, making me even more determined to press on to the back of the room to my ultimate goal.

Then bingo! No, not more bingo cards, but the large chest with a lock and hasp on the lid. What could be so valuable locked up and abandoned when the cinema closed? Clearing a few boxes piled on the chest, I pulled out a screwdriver which I had been using to take up seats, and prised off the lock. With eager anticipation I lifted the lid, with bated breath, luckily as I really did not want to breathe in what leapt out of the cabinet but still made me choke. No, wrong again, it wasn't the monster from the pit that was last shown at the cinema; it was eighteen-months old rotting ice-creams which had been abandoned and the fridge was turned off. Shhhhhiiiiiit the green, putrid, mess half-filled the chest freezer, with a stench that was almost alive enveloped me. Screaming and retching at the same time I fell backwards into the pile of boxes, the confined dark space only adding to my panic. On tumbling out of the room, my face rather green, but thankfully not due to the rotting ice-cream monster giving me a lick, just a little nauseous, I was surrounded by my fellow seat shifters who said they thought I was being murdered. I was still retching so was unable to explain until someone poured me a cup of hot sweet tea from a flask, and we all had a laugh about it.

I've not been back to a cinema since, well at least not one with eighteen-month old ice-cream in a turned off fridge, but I did go scrounging in an abandoned wood yard. How it came about was when a teacher at work was telling about a wood yard that had closed down in the village where he lived and had just been abandoned. It had become a free for all with the locals going there at night and scrounging the wood that had been left. When I showed some interest he said he was going that night with some neighbours and would I like to come. Never one to turn down a good scrounge, even one being a little dodgy, I arranged to meet him at his house that evening.

I must admit to a little apprehension as I'm not in the habit of breaking the law but this seemed a bit of a grey area, so I turned up after dark and was immediately reassured when I was introduced to the local vicar who fancied himself as a bit of a carpenter (now who was the other religious type who was a carpenter?) and was part of our raiding party ... no, not quite the word I was looking for ... oh never mind, so we set off for the wood yard. I think previous raiding parties had got the best bits but I picked up some nice pieces of chipboard that would eventually come in handy and loaded them into my car. When I went back in to tell him I had got what I wanted and was off, he took me to one side and with a wicked grin told me to watch the action. Bear in mind my mate's next action was perpetrated against a group of friends and a vicar, who were on the next floor innocently, well furtively, breaking the law. He had obviously come prepared as he pulled a whistle out of his pocket and blew it full belt, then yelling, 'Police, this is the police, you three take the back stairs. You, you, and you follow me.' Well his three mates were in a bit of a state when we went upstairs but nothing compared to the vicar whom we had difficulty locating initially, until we discovered him cowering in a cupboard on the verge of tears. I suppose he had more to lose than the rest of us as divine retribution tops a night in the local lock-up and a caution. We virtually had to carry the poor sod out of the wood yard and take him back to my mate's house, feeding him numerous cups of hot sweet tea until he was in any state to return to his wife at the vicarage. He did recover and took his service on the following Sunday by all accounts. I just wonder what his next sermon was about.

— 27 —

MY HEROES AND PEOPLE WHO INTEREST ME

... AND A FEW THAT DON'T

Photograph © Sheila Dibnah by kind permission

ONE OF MY heroes I admire is Stephen Hawking who is an amazing cosmologist, astrophysicist and mathematician, the guy in a wheel chair with a terrible wasting disease and can only speak through a computer controlled by eye movements. Regardless of this terrible disability he has written books and presented science programmes. What a mind trapped in a useless body. I saw a TV programme about him once where he was taken up in a special plane that goes very high then plummets to earth, so giving the effect of being weightless for the passengers. It must have felt good to be free of his wheel chair even for the thirty seconds it lasted. Quite a brave bloke

Another is Richard Dawkins who is a biologist and geneticist who also has written some incredible, very readable books and who defends science and in particular evolution, against an alarming tide of religious fundamentalists who in my opinion have some quite strange and potentially dangerous ideas and who would like to advance their lunatic ideas in our schools.

Another has to be the late Fred Dibnah who was a steeplejack by profession, but his love and knowledge of Victorian machinery plus his Lancashire straight talking and wit made him a TV presenter of distinction. With his collection of steam engines and old machinery, to me he was a national treasure, especially demolishing factory chimneys in a rather unconventional way. That to me was just the bee's knees.

I would very much have liked to meet Fred. The nearest I did get to actually meeting him was when I was driving through Bolton one morning and who should be steaming towards me in his impressive steam roller but the man himself. He had a full head of steam and I was in a hurry but I did manage to blow my Klaxon horn at him and he replied with his steam whistle.

I do have a bit of a thing for scary women. Nothing sexual you understand, just a fascination with modern versions of Boadicea and Joan of Arc types, just so long as their tattoos are spelled right that is. The most famous of course is Margaret Thatcher, the Iron Lady as she was affectionately known. Now power and ruthlessness is really scary, especially in the hands of a woman. Her male cabinet just paled into insignificance, and I imagine were just flunkies and go-fors. I imagine if they had opinions they kept them to themselves. The story I like most, allegedly true, but could just have easily been a Spitting Image clip was that Margaret was sitting in a restaurant with her cabinet, when the waiter who was taking her order for the main meal asked, 'What about the vegetables?' Her reply was short and to the point. 'Oh they will just have what I'm having!' True, myth or Spitting Image, regardless I just love witty spontaneous answers, and I could just imagine her saying it.

My next scary lady has got to be Seven of Nine, What, you don't know who Seven of Nine is? Don't say you never watch Stare Trek Voyager. She's the woman who was rescued from the Borg and made human again (well almost) after her assimilation into the collective, do you remember now? She has an hour glass figure and attitude. Rumour has it when she first appeared in the series she had to wear a fibre glass corset under her uniform to enhance her figure. The corset was so uncomfortable that she asked the director that if she could do exercises to get her figure to the same proportions as the corset, could she dispense with the thing. He agreed and she did!

Another of my scary heroes is the sometimes funny but mostly scary

Joanna Lumley. Just one glance of those big accusing eyes could turn you to stone. I saw her on the news after she had a private meeting with the minister who was dealing with the restriction on entry into the UK for retired Ghurkha soldiers. When they came out, the press gathered around. Joanna immediately took control and announced that the meeting had been a victory for the Ghurkhas and they would all be granted UK citizenship. The poor hapless MP hesitated to confirm that this was true but after a stony look from the very scary Joanna he stammered they had reached an amicable decision. Not to be fobbed off with a typical politician's vague answer she pushed him further, in front of the press, to confirm that the retired Ghurkhas would get citizenship, and with another penetrating stare from our Joanna, which would have turned Lot never mind just his family to a pillar of salt, the beleaguered MP stumbled through the required confirmation that our loyal Ghurkhas would be given UK citizenship. One gets the distinct feeling that he would have rescinded on his agreement with Joanna if she had not set him up in front of the press. Spot on Joanna! Even though I find you a bit scary, you are an OK lady but really truly scary to the poor hapless MP who I suspected needed a cup of hot sweet tea or even a stiff whiskey with a long think about his explanation to the PM after his impromptu press conference.

Princess Anne has had a mention before but I believe she deserves a quick mention in the scary section. I'm sure she would never use her riding crop in temper on her horses but I wouldn't put it past her to take a swipe at any one who was a little disrespectful or crossed her.

Kirsty Allsop, You know that scary lady on 'Location, Location, Location.' who poor Phil Spencer has to rein in before she devours the difficult couples who show any reluctance in purchasing houses she chooses to offer them. Having said that I think she is great, she says it as it is, and calls a spade a spade. If she does say things about people who aren't there at the time she at least says it in front of the cameras so there is no doubt they will eventually find out what she thinks of them. So keep on saying it as it is, Kirsty.

The dreaded WHY question. At the risk of being sexist I'm afraid it's a question women seem to be the main culprits of asking. Any statement made, followed by the question WHY is just so infuriating. For instance: 'I've just crashed the car.' 'WHY?' 'Did you know our Galaxy contains two hundred billion stars?' 'WHY?' 'Oops I've dropped a cup.' 'WHY?'. 'It looks like snow.' 'WHY?' 'God created the heavens and the earth in six days and rested on the seventh.' 'WHY?' I'm all for an enquiring mind, but one must always remember the saying. 'A fool can ask a question that a wise man cannot answer.' A certain lady I know is an aficionado at the 'WHY' question, but she will remain anonymous, as come to think of it, as she also fits into the category of scary women.

As I write this it has suddenly dawned on me where my fascination/ MILD obsession comes from. It's my mother's fault! Of course she was definitely a scary lady and my first encounter with one at that. She had a reputation as a very forceful lady and would tackle anyone or anything head on with no prisoners taken. That's definitely not an Oedipus complex or any thing, is it? I've never had a relationship with any scary ladies so I think I'm OK.

I do have two friends who fit well into the Boadicea/Joan of arc category, and may well be proud to be named, but just in case they don't appreciate the compliment they will remain anonymous as I prefer my balls dangling just were they are, thank you!

Far less dangerous fantasies about ladies on TV could be described as slightly strange. I did have a bit of a thing about Felicity Kendal at one time which is not too bad but I also had a pash for Doris Schwartz. Who the hell is Doris Schwartz you may ask? Ten points if you remember the TV series ‘Fame’. One of the students was a wannabe comedian by the name of Doris Schwartz. I wonder how many remember her or even the series for that matter. I sometimes have difficulty remembering what I had for breakfast by lunch time the same day, yet I can remember an obscure woman in an American series forty odd years ago. It's an age thing! A bit more up to date but no less obscure for some people is a lady called Kari Byron. Ring any bells? Well if you’re not a fan of ‘Mythbusters’ on Discovery Channel she will be lost to you. But let me tell you she's well worth a viewing! She can weld, shoot, set off rockets and use explosives to blow things up, and she is absolutely gorgeous, all that and a smile that makes you weak at the knees and with a bubbly personality. Anyway that's enough of my fantasies, real or imaginary.

I’ve started to watch ‘Grumpy Old Men’ on TV. Not only because it’s entertaining, it's empathy with what they talk about. For those of you who don't watch it, the programme is a collection of ageing pop stars, comedians, and just well known celebrities, sitting in their homes telling it how it is. From what pisses them off about the world, to the vagaries of middle- to old-age.

I've been called a grumpy old man from time to time, for quite a long time actually, and I have even been given a tee-shirt displaying a pair of grumpy old men from the Muppet Show, which may I add, I wear with pride. So this chapter is dedicated to my grumpiness and I hope that it may create a little empathy in the reader.

At the top of my list, perhaps are suicidal morons who drive two feet from my back bumper. I can be doing a steady seventy miles an hour down the motorway and some pillock obviously to the danger, with no sense of imagination, coming up behind me and driving so close his headlights are out of sight below my boot. I class this in the same category as a suicidal, psychopathic, maniac holding a gun to the back of my head. Has the brainless nutcase any idea what carnage he would cause to me and to no lesser extent to him- or herself (women are just as capable of this gross act as men) if I even took my foot of the accelerator never mind touch the brakes.

Mind you the Brit tailgater's pale into insignificance compared to the French and marginally more so the Italians. On a recent trip driving around France I was aghast that it seems to be the norm for driving on certain motorways where the speed limit is eighty MPH to come up behind the car in front and drive for miles tailgating despite a clear road to overtake, just for the sake of moving the outside lane and overtaking. Why!

As far as I can remember from my highway code, which I must admit not reading since I took my test, forty five years ago you were recommended to drive a cars length from the car in front for every ten miles an hour you were travelling, all I can think is if perpetual tailgater's ever read the recommendation in the highway code they are regressing to their child hood when they played with Dinky toys, with cars only inches long.

I have such a thing about it that instead of just ineffectually gesticulating to the driver tailgating me I purchased a gadget which sits in the back window of my car, and when a idiot gets too close I press a button on the dash and a sign lights up in the back window saying 'BACK OFF'. It's not always affective as I can only surmise the offenders can't read, which is confirmation of their lack of basic intelligence. I'm sure all of the people reading this intellectual tome are victims rather than offenders so I won't have offended anyone, will I?

A law recently passed in France was to ban the burka as worn by Muslim women. A very impressive controversial law, as laws restricting religious beliefs always evoke fanatical unrest. Could it happen in Britain? There's talk of it and I must admit I personally would approve. I find it the ultimate sexual discrimination that women have to be the ones to cover up to stop man's supposed lustful intention, as is stated in their Koran. I also find it very sinister to see them walking down the street, although not as sinister as hoodies!

How about this for a positive suggestion, all you feckless politicians. Ban the burka in Britain but also ban the hoodie at the same time. It's not religious, just a way of avoiding being recognised on cctv when people are up to no good, or at the very least, a symptom of their inadequacy that needs addressing anyway. We live in hope that it would not be deemed a violation of their dreaded 'human rights' and can be even considered.

One last grump, 'doggy bags' not the ones restaurants used to give you the food you didn't eat at the time so you could pretend take it home for the dog but instead warmed it up for your supper, but so called 'pooper scoopers.' Now I'm all in favour of dog owners cleaning up after their pooches in fact it's a must, but when I'm out walking I am appalled by little black bags of dog turds dumped at the side of the path. What are they thinking about? They would be far more ecological to leave it where the dog did, or at least kick it into the undergrowth where it would rot down in a week or two. But to leave it wrapped in a plastic bag that, regardless of whether or not it is biodegradable, will take at least five years to rot down. My words to the mindless prat dog owners is, 'Take your shit home with you.'

– 28 –

LOOKING BACK

(NOSTALGIA JUST ISN'T WHAT I USED TO BE)

AND LAST BUT not least (unless something comes to mind before I sign off) things just aren't what they used to be when I was a kid. It's far too easy to look back over the past fifty odd years of my life and say the world has gone mad. We have so many luxuries compared to sixty years ago, still to say we have never had it so good doesn't ring true ether.

Take for instance expectations of young people today. Not that it's bad to have expectations, it's just that they think that they should instantly have everything their parents have like a nice house, all new furniture, TV, stereo, computer, car parked in the drive. They usually fail to realise that it has taken a lifetime of hard work to achieve these.

Now when we first set up home we were lucky to have a bare minimum of furniture, all second hand and begged, borrowed, and while not particularly stolen but definitely liberated out of a skip without going into to much detail as to who owned it. We would take years to make our little house liveable in. Today it's the expectation to have all new set-up before the wedding day, usually paid for by the bank of daddy. My bank of daddy was bankrupt and was not capable of financing me

My first wage in nineteen sixty five as an apprentice TV engineer was astounding two pound ten shillings. Mind you, you could go out on a Friday night to the pictures, get fish and chips in town and the last bus home and still have some change left over from a quid, or so we used to say looking back, before inflation. My mother always insisted that decimalisation in nineteen seventy one was just a governmental con to cover up inflation. She stuck out for years still quoting the price of items in old money as she was very good at maths and could convert decimal money back into pounds, shillings and pence in seconds.

As a group of friends we would aspire to earning the magic wage of twenty pounds a week, the astronomical figure at the time of one thousand pounds a year. I personally was about the last in our little clique to reach that fabulous sum and well into my twenties. Mind by that time the dreaded inflation had taken a bite out of the grand fantasy of wealth. You need to bear in mind that the cost of my first house in 1970 was twelve hundred pounds, a little two-bedroomed terrace, but today would be a hundred and twelve thousand.

I strongly believe I am of the generation who can say that with conviction. Apart from cars, computers and the demise of Communism, in my lifetime I feel the world has changed in a rather sinister way. I'm under no illusion looking back when I was young there was violence, crime, and the world was not a safe place for the unwary. Maybe there was a naivety that insulated people from the real world. I was certainly naïve in the early seventies in my twenties. I did some voluntary counselling in Bradford, and part of my job was to answer the phone overnight once a month. The centre was in a rather run-down area and the duty involved going there late at night. I remember getting an interview from the police during the Yorkshire Ripper enquiry as my car had been parked overnight outside the centre, unfortunately a stone's throw from an area renowned for ladies of the night, and was the haunt of the Ripper himself. These two tough looking coppers turned up on my doorstep and grilled me on why my car had been parked overnight in a red light district, and where I was on various dates stretching back two years to establish an alibi. I thought I had managed to convince them I was innocent, but as they left one ugly looking plod stepped in-between my wife and me and asked her if she thought I might be the Ripper. For if I was, I would be whipped down to the station and she would never have to see me again. I am glad to say she didn't hesitate or at least not long enough to have me taken away, so the two plods left and I breathed a sigh of relief.

Another of my duties was once a month was ‘flying squad’ which sounds rather adventurous and exciting until you get a phone call at two in the morning to go out to a distressed person. This particular time the phone call was at one in the morning and still slightly unwelcome but I'd volunteered so I was resigned to go.

The centre wanted me to go to a house where a man was distressed and had threatened to shoot himself. A little apprehensively I agreed to go and asked who I had to pick up to go with me, as we were only allowed to go out in two's. I was regretfully informed that they could not get anyone else to go out with me so was I OK to go on my own? My reply was a little reticent considering the hazards of going out at one in the morning to a house in the middle of Bradford to someone with a gun! Even in two’s! But on my own? Naive, foolhardy, dedicated, or what? But I went!

Turning up at the house I knocked, called through the letter box, and tried to peer through the curtains. There was no reply so I trundled off to a phone box to ring the centre. This was a time long before mobile phones, not even the ones the size of a house brick, so eventually finding a red, pay phone box, I enquired what was happening to the caller. They told me the phone to the caller's house was still connected but he had stopped talking and it sounded like he had passed out.

Taking the initiative I told them to send the police to the house and I would meet them there. After about half an hour standing outside the house a lone bobby turned up on foot, looking a lot younger than me and considering I was early twenties he looked just out of school. After I had explained the situation, he asked me what I wanted him to do. Imagine a bobby nowadays asking me what to do. But taking pity on the young man, I told him he had better break in as the man in the house may be dying. He said he couldn't possibly do that, but with my most authoritative persuasive manner he eventually took out his truncheon, smashed the glass in the door window, reached through and undid the latch. Unfortunately he tore his sleeve on the glass; the poor sod was going to cop it for two things at least now when he got back to the station, unless his mummy was a dab hand with a needle and thread.

The young man was now completely out of his depth and asked what he was to do next.

Again it's all down to confidence so I told him to go into the house and see if the man needed an ambulance. OK I was being a bit of a bastard but he was getting paid to get shot, I was strictly voluntary, but I did follow him in as the poor lad's bottom lip was trembling by this time. Wimp! For God's sake, the man was only reputed to have a gun, it hadn't been confirmed! After all that, the guy didn't have a gun and was drunk, out cold on the sofa and the only thing he was clutching was an empty bottle of whiskey and the phone, still connected to the centre. While the young bobby was having a look round I took the phone and told the centre what had happened and that I would deal with it from now on. Again the bobby asked me what he should do next, so I told him he could leave and I would be OK now. 'Well I'm not sure about that, what about the door?' replied the young bobby. Quick as a flash I told him he needed to go back to the station to report what had happened. He sort of agreed and hesitantly made his way out of the door and I never heard any more from him about his involvement although I would have very much liked to have been a fly on the wall as he explained his encounter to his Sergeant back at the police station.

Now fast forward forty years to the present time imagining the same phone call. My reply to a request to go out in the middle of the night to counsel a man with a gun would go something like this. Ring, ring. ''Hello, yes, no we don't do that any more, no way! you must be joking!, get real! I don't think so, no definitely not, NO!' The situation today would involve twenty heavily armed men in bullet proof body armour, from the armed response team, surrounding the house. The door would be soon off its hinges and the drunken man hauled out in cuffs.

You may think I am exaggerating, so let me give you an example that was related to me just recently. A friend's teenage son at college was pretending to be Dirty Harry with his mates with a toy replica pistol (you know what teenagers are like!) A lecturer saw him and reported the incident to the police. When he got home there was half a dozen of our intrepid armed response team waiting for him, who after a little pep talk about their methods of dealing with anyone with guns. i.e. shooting to kill and ascertaining afterwards whether the gun was a toy or real. They left, leaving her son shaking and as white as the paper this is printed on. Needless to say he doesn't play with guns, not even toy guns, any more!

I'm not knocking the police they do sterling work under very difficult circumstances. Well some of them do sterling work. Sometimes. Not that I have personal experience of their sometimes sterling work. But I'm sure they must.

So yes times have changed in my uneventful lifetime, and dare I say, without being too much of a grumpy old man, 'not always for the best!'

Looking back over my life, would I change anything if it was possible? No, I don't think I would Maybe a few un-achieved ambitions that needed a little less dreaming and a lot more work.

The first was to be a millionaire. This probably was inspired by the taste for Mammon that my first wage, as meagre as it was, brought. But that one was lost in the mundane fight for a life with a house, holidays, a car and all the other thing that need instant resources rather than setting up a business.

The next was to fly not like a bird but piloting an aeroplane. This was thwarted in a number of ways. Definitely finance was the biggy, and I would have needed to realise the first ambition to pay for the plane and pilot's licence. My little sortie with my microlight didn't deter me, it just made me realise how improbable it was that I would ever be able to do it properly. There was of course the little problem of the potato knife in the eye as a toddler, that left me a little lacking in twenty-twenty vision which is a requirement for flying I've been told.

The third ambition to make love to a thousand women was definitely a thwarted ambition and went clean out the window.

Were we happier fifty years ago compared to kids today? I think we probably were, it was definitely a simpler time. We were naive compared to the kids today who are so-called streetwise with their mobile phones and designer clothes and iPods plugged into their ears. They grow up far too fast and miss out on the joys of innocence. Am I viewing my past with rose-coloured glasses? Isn't that's what nostalgia's about?

It's too easy to look back over my life with rose coloured glasses but being an optimist it works backwards into the past as well as looking at the future in a optimistic way. I am sure that times have got harder, especially for kids today. I don't think I would like to live my life over again as the world is today, but no doubt with my usual bull in a china shop attitude, I would manage with perhaps a little more PC and health and safety approach to certain things.

Kids today are so arrogant, moody and rebellious. Now when I was a kid growing up in the fifties, we were ... oh well perhaps we were just as rebellious. In fact come to think about it, our generation could well have started the trend. Drugs, sex and rock and roll! We were rebels with a cause!

There is a terrible Chinese curse that goes 'May you live in interesting times.' Well I've certainly lived in interesting times one way or another. It's been tough at times certainly interesting, but not particular a curse. Whether I would have preferred a quieter life in boring times- definitely not! It's a bit like saying I don't want to go to heaven as I wouldn't know anybody there.

Well ladies, gentlemen, boys and girls, that's it! Or at least some of it, there is more, some I might tell, sometime, and some things it may be best to keep quiet about.

Hope you have got as far as this page. Thank you for persevering and have found it at least mildly entertaining. Don't forget it might be advisable not to try at least some of this at home.

THE END

Lightning Source UK Ltd.
Milton Keynes UK
UKOW031328030713

213162UK00002B/9/P

9 781908 098924